# TALK TO ME

Design and
the Communication
between People
and Objects

Paola Antonelli

## HELLO WORLD

MoMA

Published in conjunction with the exhibition Talk to Me: Design and the Communication between People and Objects, organized by Paola Antonelli, Senior Curator, and Kate Carmody, Curatorial Assistant, in the Department of Architecture and Design, at The Museum of Modern Art, New York, July 24–November 7, 2011
www.moma.org/talktome

Huundai Card    GE Partner

The exhibition is made possible by Hyundai Card Company.

Additional support is provided by the Lily Auchincloss Foundation, Inc. and The Junior Associates of The Museum of Modern Art.

Produced by the Department of Publications, The Museum of Modern Art, New York

Edited by Emily Hall

Publication and typeface design by A2/SW/HK

Production by Marc Sapir, with Tiffany Hu

Printed and bound by Main Choice International Development Ltd.

This book was typeset in Cubitt Fax.

The paper is 140 gsm Hi-Q Titan.

Alexandra Midal's essay was translated from the French by Jeanine Herman.

Library of Congress Control Number: 2011927239
ISBN: 978-0-87070-796-4

Published by The Museum of Modern Art, 11 West 53 Street, New York, New York 10019-5497
www.moma.org

Distributed in the United States and Canada by D.A.P./Distributed Art Publishers, Inc., 155 Sixth Avenue, 2nd Floor, New York, New York 10013
www.artbook.com

Distributed outside the United States and Canada by Thames & Hudson Ltd., 181A High Holborn, London WC1V 7QX
www.thamesandhudson.com

Covers and page 2: A2/SW/HK; page 19: Mike Thompson. Wifi Dowsing Rod. 2007 (see page 20); page 57: Zach Lieberman, James Powderly, Evan Roth, Chris Sugrue, TEMPT1, and Theo Watson. EyeWriter. 2009 (see page 59); page 75: Jason Rohrer. Passage. 2008 (see page 76); page 99: Andy London and Carolyn London of London Squared. The Lost Tribes of New York City. 2009 (see page 100); page 133: Chris Woebken and Kenichi Okada, Design Interactions Department, Royal College of Art. Animal Superpowers: Ant. 2008 (see page 134); page 175: Chris Woebken and Natalie Jeremijenko, Environmental Health Clinic, Steinhardt School of Culture, Education, and Human Development, New York University. Bat Billboard. 2008 (see page 176)

Printed in China

# Contents

Hyundai Card is delighted to be a part of The Museum of Modern Art's exhibition <u>Talk to Me</u>, an inspiring exploration of the reciprocal communication between people and objects. Works in this exhibition exceed ordinary expectations in a fresh approach to design that is directly in line with the philosophy of Hyundai Card, Korea's leading issuer of credit cards.

At Hyundai Card, we introduce an element of style into financial services. Our credit cards are not merely a payment tool: we scour the world for distinguished artists and designers to create premium, distinctive credit cards that provide access to rich cultural experiences. Through a focus on design and service, Hyundai Card establishes a strong emotional connection between our customers and our credit cards.

The backdrop for the Museum's insightful exhibition is a shift in how design is perceived, creating not only commercial products but also cultural icons that go well beyond their original purposes. This exhibition offers a unique platform for conversations between people and objects, highlighting the groundbreaking ways that objects help us interact with complex systems and networks.

As the sponsor of this exceptional exhibition, we hope to promote the importance of great design that incorporates innovative form, function, and meaning. We welcome you to experience the diverse dialogues that emerge when design objects talk to you.

# Foreword

Glenn D. Lowry, Director
The Museum of Modern Art, New York

Talk to Me: Design and the Communication
between People and Objects continues
The Museum of Modern Art's exploration into
the new territories mapped out by design and
art. In particular it focuses on a shift from the
centrality of function to that of meaning, a shift
that has been brought about by cultural movements over the last hundred years and by
the digital revolution at the turn of the century.
From this perspective, all objects contain information that goes well beyond immediate use
or appearance, moving the task of the designer
into new realms and demanding new skills.

MoMA has always played a major
role in repositioning design. The Museum has
expanded design's representation—in shows and
the collection, in our historical and contemporary
programs—and with recent exhibitions such as
Safe: Design Takes on Risk (2005) and Design
and the Elastic Mind (2008), we have acknowl-
edged that in addition to objects its reach
includes visualization, communication, information, future scenarios and projections, scientific
inquiry, and the design of interfaces. We have
celebrated design's rich relationship not only
with art but also with sociology, politics, technology, and science, and we have reframed these
relationships in a museum context. We have
followed design as it has migrated into the digital
and networked age and mutated to adapt to
the new conditions, establishing new criteria
to appreciate them with exhibitions that placed
them under scrutiny for the first time.

Talk to Me is a snapshot in time,
recording the diversity and open-endedness
of contemporary design. Just in the past
few years, communication has exploded into
new fields, providing us with responsive objects,
ubiquitous data and information, and newly
instinctive interfaces. Design itself has become
a way of communicating, with the open-source
movement and constant connectivity changing
how ideas are conceived and products made.
Interdisciplinary collaboration and a larger
creative network are now inherent to the
design process.

This exhibition includes almost two
hundred objects and concepts, from electronic
pets to virtual worlds, from mobile-device
applications to systems designed for navigating
entire cities, all instigating a dialogue between
object and user—some in order to clarify, others
in order to help, and others still posing questions.

Organized by Paola Antonelli, Senior
Curator, with Kate Carmody, Curatorial
Assistant, Department of Architecture and
Design, this exhibition reaffirms the Museum's
commitment to contemporary design practice,
as well as its ongoing reflection on the future
of design.

We are very grateful to the Hyundai Card
Company, the Lily Auchincloss Foundation, and
The Junior Associates of The Museum of Modern
Art for helping to bring this vital new design
movement into focus.

# Talk to Me

Paola Antonelli

Whether openly and actively or in subtle, subliminal ways, things talk to us. They do not all speak aloud: some communicate in text, diagrams, and other graphic interfaces; others empathetically and almost telepathically, just keeping us company and storing our memories; still others in sensual ways, with warmth, scent, texture. Objects populate our homes and our lives; buildings and places have identities and characters; cars and airplanes speak and listen; virtual worlds beckon us; London's Tower Bridge and artist Marina Abramović's chair even send tweets.[1]

That objects—everything that humans build, at all scales (fig. 1), from the spoon to the city, the state, the web, buildings, communities, systems, and artificial realities— have meaning is nothing new.[2] It has been true for eons, since long before late-twentieth-century design prophets such as Donald Norman, after decades of functionalist preaching, had an epiphany and declared the era of "emotional design" to be upon us.[3] The bond between people and things has always been filled with powerful and unspoken sentiments going well beyond functional expectations and including attachment, love, possessiveness, jealousy, pride, curiosity, anger, even friendship and partnership—think of the bond between a chef and his knives. Philoso-phy has studied humans' relationships with objects throughout history and from multiple angles, but the relatively young field of design has taken to it slowly. After all, design's first preoc-cupation following the technological and aesthetic earthquake of the industrial revolution was to bring visual discipline and intellectual rigor to the cacophony of formal experiments ushered in by the new manufacturing capabilities. This was often achieved by suffocating objects' excessive expressiveness and irrational side, qualities equated by some with decoration, as in Adolf Loos's well-known 1908 essay "Ornament and Crime."[4]

The push toward formal reduction and functionalism did not deter the great modern architects from imbuing minimal shapes with maximum pathos. But in the hands of mainstream practitioners and instructors, twentieth-century clichés such as "form follows function," the modernist motto originally uttered in slightly different form by Louis H. Sullivan, and "design is problem solving" (about which more later) have been responsible for a great deal of soulless and lobotomized design and architecture.[5] While a belief in sentient and self-reflective buildings was kept alive by architects such as Erich Mendelsohn and Frederick Kiesler, philosopher-architect Rudolf Steiner, and even psychologist Carl Jung, design, still lacking a cohesive theoreti-cal backbone, did not even acknowledge the need for a position on the matter.[6]

Finally, in the 1960s, the course of design changed in that era's confluence of political and

← Fig. 1
iGEM 2004 UT Austin/UCSF
Team. Hello World bacterial
photograph. 2005. Photograph
by Aaron A. Chevalier.
For more about Hello World,
see page 159.

Fig. 2
Camille Bozzini of Dentsu
London and Timo Arnall
and Jack Schulze of BERG.
Suwappu. 2011. Polyurethane
and custom software, 3 ×
1 3/8 × 1 3/8" (7.6 × 3.6
× 3.6 cm)

Suwappu is a group of eight
characters, four of which
have already been released,
whose lower and upper halves
can be swapped. Image-
recognition software allows
them to live and perform in
an augmented-reality world,
making them among the first
of a new type of entertainment
environment and experience.

social turmoil, technological breakthroughs, and cultural shifts. In the minds of visionary architects and designers, buildings and cities began to breathe, walk, plug in, and talk, as did objects. The 1960s were also an important decade for the digital revolution: the foundations were laid for what we today call interface and interaction design, and the seeds were planted for several groundbreaking innovations of the 1980s. It was also in those years that semiotics and structuralism, especially the work of Roland Barthes and Michel Foucault, achieved worldwide prominence, contributing to the formation of a new theory of design. All these forces joined to make the communication between people and objects a mandatory element of the design process.

In contrast to the twentieth-century triumph of semiotics, which looked down on communication as nothing but a mechanical transmission of coded meaning, the twenty-first century has begun as one of pancommunication—everything and everybody conveying content and meaning in all possible combinations, from one-on-one to everything-on-everybody. We now expect objects to communicate, a cultural shift made evident when we see children searching for buttons or sensors on a new object, even when the object has no batteries or plug. Talk to Me: Design and the Communi-cation between People and Objects thrives on this important late-twentieth-century development in the culture of design, which can be described as a shift from the centrality of function to that of meaning, and on the twenty-first-century focus on the need to communicate in order to exist (fig. 2). From this new perspective, all objects occupy a unique position in material culture, and all of them contain information beyond their immediate use or appearance. It is not enough for designers today to balance form and function, and it is

Fig. 3
Sun Haipeng. Super Baozi vs.
Sushi Man. 2009. Video (color,
sound), 1:30 min.

Super Baozi is a steamed-bun
martial arts superhero that
loves to reenact scenes from
Bruce Lee movies. It is one
of the most recent additions
to the army of animated
objects, from sponges to
potatoes, that have captured
the popular imagination.

also not enough simply to ascribe meaning.
Design now must imagine all its previous tasks
in a dynamic, animated context, as Khoi Vinh
points out in his essay on page 128. Things
may communicate with people, but designers
write the initial script that lets us develop
and improvise the dialogue.

/////////////////////////////////////////

Rules of Engagement

In our relationship with objects, as in any
relationship, indifference is the worst offense
and laziness the worst sin. Endowed with
more and more complex behaviors, objects from
refrigerators to mobile phones to income tax
websites have become particularly touchy and
moody (fig. 3); our relationship with computers
sometimes approaches codependence. Objects
have become as complex and demanding interloc-
utors as people, as Jamer Hunt laments in his
essay on page 48, so it seems logical to apply
the rules of human communication to them, too.
In checking the five axioms of human communication, developed by psychologist and philosopher
Paul Watzlawick, against our experience of
communication with objects and systems,
we find some interesting insights and parallels,
in particular in his first, third, and fifth axioms.[7]

8

The first axiom tells us, "One cannot
not communicate." Any kind of gesture, behavior,
and attitude can and will be interpreted as
communication. In e-mail, for example, responding immediately to a message creates a particular
subtext, as does not responding at all; a congrat-
ulatory message sent "reply all" can be interpreted as displaying presence and authority
or else insecurity, and an ill-advised response
by a person who received only a blind copy
reveals . . . something else.

The third axiom says, "The nature of
a relationship is dependent on the punctuation
of the partners' communication procedures."
Communication, Watzlawick posits, is cyclical,
with each partner believing that he or she is
simply responding to the other; some of the most
common problems of the digital era arise from
the cycle of amplification and reaction that
marks our text exchanges, something that serial
e-mail gaffers and awkward users will be familiar
with. The problem is acute enough to require
the invention of ToneCheck, developed by Lymbix,
an emotional spell-check for e-mail messages
that alerts the writer to excessive displays
of anger, sadness, or insensitivity.[8]

The fifth axiom, "Inter-human communication procedures are either symmetric or

complementary, depending on whether the relationship of the partners is based on differences or parity," reminds us that the relationship between people and objects is not always complementary in the expected proportions, and hardly ever symmetrical. Power imbalance has worried generations of thinkers who have predicted a somber world in which machines are more intelligent and therefore more powerful than human beings. This event, known as "the Singularity," was first mentioned by computer scientist and writer Vernor Vinge in a speech in 1993. "Within thirty years, we will have the technological means to create superhuman intelligence," he said. "Shortly after, the human era will be ended."[9] Author and futurist Ray Kurzweil reiterated the omen in 2005, saying that it would take place by 2045; writer Adam Gopnik has argued that the Singularity happened a long time ago, when we first delegated some of our important skills to machines.[10] Whichever timeline we believe— if we believe it at all—the test proposed by computer scientist Alan Turing to determine a machine's ability to demonstrate human intelligence, including empathy, the serendipitous powers of distraction and humor, and creativity, has yet to be passed.[11] In 2011 a computer called Watson beat the two sturdiest human champions of the television quiz show Jeopardy!, but designers cannot count on CPUs—whether as mighty as Watson's or as nimble as an iPad's—to know how to behave like real people.

Under these complex circumstances, new branches of design practice have emerged that combine old-fashioned attention to form, function, and meaning with focus on the exchange of content and affect between user and used. Communication design focuses on delivering messages, and it encompasses most graphic design, signage, and communicative objects of all kinds, from printed materials to three-dimensional and digital projects. Interface and interaction design, which is sometimes brought under the more generic and functionalist rubric of user-experience design, delineates the behavior of products and systems, as well as the experience that people will have with them. Information or visualization design includes the maps, diagrams, and visualization tools that filter and make sense of the enormous amount of information that is more widely available than ever before. Critical design is one of the most promising and far-reaching new areas of study, using conceptual scenarios built around hypothetical objects to comment on the social, political, and cultural consequences of new technologies and behaviors. Its disciples are experts in "What if?"

/ / / / / / / / / / / / / / / / / / / / / / / / / / / / / / / / / / / /

Predigital, Digital, and Postdigital Affairs

In 1907 Guido Gozzano, an Italian poet, wrote "L'amica di nonna Speranza" (Grandma Speranza's friend), an unassuming and touching poem that described in loving detail dozens of "good things of awful taste" from his grandmother's apartment.[12] Empty candy boxes, a cuckoo clock, a stuffed parrot: the scene is at the same time sad, dusty, and alive with the sound of intimacy. It is just one of many literary examples of the close relationship between people, objects, and places. Rob Walker's Significant Objects project reminds us of Gozzano's nostalgic inventory.[13] Walker has launched a number of projects devoted to things, buildings, cities, and their personal biographies, whether real or imagined, including "Consumed", his weekly column devoted to our relationships with brands, which ran in the New York Times Magazine from 2004 to 2011. For Significant Objects he handpicked objects from thrift stores and other treasure troves and paired them with great writers—including Nicholson Baker and Jonathan Lethem— who endowed them with stories.

The postdigital design movement is an extreme expression of this romantic attachment to physical things. It is made up of technologically savvy designers and artists who prefer the innocence of old-fashioned objects, such as the London-based Newspaper Club: sexy geeks who declare themselves to be "about ink on newsprint" and will help anybody publish a newspaper. [14] In 2010 James Bridle, one of the club's founders, published a compendium of Wikipedia entries on the Iraq War, collected between December 2004 and November 2009, in twelve classically bound, encyclopedia-style volumes, because "physical objects are useful props in debates like this: immediately illustrative, and useful to hang an argument and peoples' attention on."[15]

This project makes a crucial point: in an era when so many mediums and channels are available, the key to effective and elegant communication is choosing the right one, the right interpreter. The most recent technology, in other words, may not be the most appropriate. Transmedia storytelling, a technique for telling stories on multiple platforms—such as a combination of television, Internet, and mobile text—is not a novelty anymore, and a few years have gone by since the first college application submitted on video made news. Our fever about virtual and augmented reality has subsided, as Kevin Slavin points out in his essay on page 164.

Sometimes the best way to say it is still with flowers.

In 2009, in "The Demise of 'Form Follows Function,'" Alice Rawsthorn wrote that "the appearance of most digital products bears no relation to what they do"; often—and especially after the first coming of the iPod, in 2001—these products are handsome, minimal boxes that perform a large number of functions.[16] Since machines have become more or less standardized in shape, and since materials, finishes, and colors do not provide enough distinction, designers have had to resort to an old human trick: a face. We expect our smart objects to communicate their complexity as well as their instructions in a clear and engaging way through their interface. Interfaces not only provide thresholds onto explanation and response, instruction and information, but also personalities. The term is commonly used to indicate the point of contact and communication between a machine and a human being; lately it has expanded to include communication with and access to wider systems and infrastructures such as cities, public services, territorial and metaphysical networks, and virtual worlds. The term has come to be identified with the digital era, but interfaces existed long before the digital revolution, for example in every clock and watch face and in the dashboards designed by masters such as Henry Dreyfuss and Rodolfo Bonetto.

In the computer world the term is shorthand for GUI (graphical user interface), HMI (human-computer interface), or HCI (human-computer interaction) and represents one of the most important and active areas of contemporary design, technology, and cognitive science. Its history arcs from its mechanical ancestors, well described by Alexandra Midal in her essay on page 92, to its graphic breakthrough in the late twentieth century, using a pointing device and icons that relied on analogies to the objects normally found in an office (desk with files and folders, trash bin, calculator, alarm clock), to the most recent gestural interfaces.[17] Some well-known milestones in the development of interfaces are the stuff of legend: Doug Engelbart's invention of the mouse and hypertext and his use of networked computers for collective activity in the second half of the 1960s; Alan Kay, Larry Tesler, and Dan Ingalls's first GUI, developed at Xerox PARC and used in the Star computer in 1981; Jef Raskin and Steve Jobs's commercial GUI, which appeared in the Lisa (1983) and Macintosh (1984) computers; and Marc Andreessen's 1993 Mosaic, the GUI that made the World Wide Web really available to the wide world. Interfaces represent a new dimension of our existence, a space in which we all spend a considerable amount of our time on earth. Even those who call themselves Luddites and profess virginal innocence from the temptations of networked technology are at least guilty of interacting with ATMs or ticket-vending machines. ATMs, among the most universal of interfaces (fig. 4), are represented in Talk to Me by two examples, a functional unit designed by Barclays, the bank that originally introduced the ATM in 1967 (page 45), and a new system developed by IDEO for the Spanish bank BBVA (page 44).

To help the public feel comfortable with advanced technology, designers often rely on the strategy of incorporating instinctive traits and appealing to our instinctive reactions, such as in computer interfaces in which items are moved around by hands and fingers or by being blown on or even shaken. These new technologies have already found widespread commercial application and have made their way into culture: Jeff Han's multitouch screens, which debuted in 2006, were used by CNN anchors to cover the US presidential elections in 2008, and John Underkoffler's gestural interface, called g-speak, which he has been working on since 1996, was made famous by the movie Minority Report (2002).[18] Other examples include the multitouch screens of Apple's iPhone (2007) and iPad (2010), and the gestural interfaces used in Guitar Hero (2005), Nintendo Wii (2006), and Microsoft Kinect (2010). With ever more-sophisticated movement- and voice-recognition software, objects are being transformed from tools into companions, and buildings from enclosed shelters into open environments.

The hardware supporting the interface—whether it is the physical shape of a computer or the chassis of a car, a robot, an ATM, or a self-service check-in kiosk—is equally significant. In choosing a sympathetic body for a mechanical mind, designers, engineers, and scientists are ever wary of the theory of the uncanny valley (page 168, fig. 8), which posits that people cannot feel empathy for machines that look almost like real humans.[19] The diagram that gives the theory its name shows these awkward examples in a dip that looks like a valley: on its left are playful, cartoonish, fictional creatures, such as AIBO, Tamagotchi (page 170, fig. 10), and stuffed animals, and on the right are healthy, real human beings. One of the most famous examples from the valley is the Japanese Repliee Q1Expo, introduced at the 2005 Aichi Expo, which was modeled after a young Japanese woman but seemed more like a Madame Tussauds wax figure come

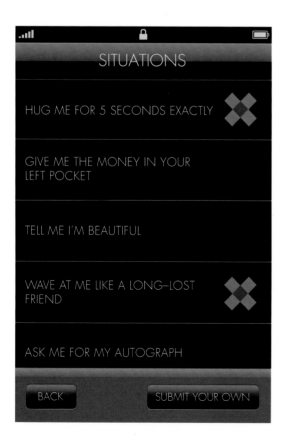

Fig. 6
Antoine Bardou-Jacquet
and Ludovic Houplain of H5.
The Child. 1999. Video (color,
sound), 3:06 min.

A couple rushes to the
hospital—the wife is about
to have a baby—in a taxi that
travels through a New York
in which everything is spelled
out in text, to the sounds
of Alex Gopher's "The Child."

Fig. 7
Chaos Computer Club.
Blinkenlights. 2001.
Photograph by Dorit Guenter

to life. The theory also applies to voices: the warnings delivered in an airplane cockpit are recorded in a human voice to effectively alert the pilots with real human urgency that they can trust; the (usually female) voice is affectionately known as Bitching Betty. Voice operation is one of the elements of interaction that is being the most thoroughly studied, from in-vehicle communication systems for cars, with their obvious safety advantages, to dictation software. Every talking object becomes an entity, immediately taking on a more important role. When there's a voice, there's a conversation.

But voice and human- or petlike appearance are not necessary for a powerful interaction to take place. Some objects express themselves subtly and intensely using abstract interfaces, such as the breathing light on Apple's white iBook G4 (2004) (unfortunately abandoned in later models because it lacked bedside manner, keeping the owner awake while the computer slept). Apple's mastery of metaphors, in both hardware and software, is one element of the company's effective interaction design. The iPad calls up a nearly atavistic memory of the acts of writing and drawing on a tablet, which is offered as a counterbalance to overwhelmingly key-based technology—just what we need; Apple was similarly shrewd

back in 1984 with the Macintosh 128K, whose domesticated presence (like a little dog sitting patiently on its master's desk) and expressive interface built on analogies and metaphors (smiling computer, trash bin, folders, question mark, little bomb) were just what we needed to comfortably integrate technology into the home.

////////////////////////////////////

Interfaces for the People

Interfaces, whether on smartphones or facades, whether composed of pixels, LEDs, or neon tubes, are laid on the surfaces of objects, spaces, and buildings but provide them with communicative depth and dynamism. Portable devices such as wristbands, sensors, and implants use interfaces that let individuals monitor themselves and be monitored by others at a distance, a very helpful way for elderly people to keep their doctors and family up-to-date on their well-being. Some websites are interfaces publicizing knowledge at different scales and with different consequences, from digital water coolers where employees rate their employers to the world-destabilizing force of WikiLeaks. Any device that receives and sends texts can call on flash mobs to commit acts of civil disobedience, but the same interfaces can be used for acts of civil responsibility, such as activating a tsunami-alert service or mapping emergency areas. Interfaces can amplify or reduce communication to human scale, whether, for example, bringing the government to the individual or the individual to the government.

We can now design the face we wish to present to the world. Where in the past we relied on family name, academic pedigree, business cards, looks, and accomplishments to augment our naked social selves, today we have the additional option of offering our riches to the world with blogs, personal websites, Flickr streams, Facebook and other social networks, and avatars. With these interfaces we think we can control the way we are perceived by the world (although things do not always work out as planned; reports are increasing of job applicants being rejected because their personal pages revealed information that didn't match the wholesome image they brought to their job interviews). By contrast, some interfaces disrupt this facade, encouraging people to let go of control and reach out to others in serendipitous ways. An app called Situationist, inspired by the Situationist International (a group of European artists and political agitators in the 1950s and '60s), connects willing participants, alerting them to each other's proximity using geotags, and

Fig. 8
Wesley Grubbs and Mladen
Balog of Pitch Interactive.
Invisible City: What a Hundred
Million Calls to 311 Reveal about
New York. 2010. Processing
software. Published in Wired
magazine, November 2010

delivers instructions for situations both intimate and friendly, and political and subversive (fig. 5).[20]

When interfaces allow users access to networks and systems, users can connect, acquire, and exchange information. At the local level, interfaces can help people share car rides and homegrown vegetables, provide support for the elderly, and find company. At the global level, people can hook their energy-monitoring systems into a local grid and contribute to data-aggregation projects that raise awareness of energy-consumption. A well-designed network or system can be a potent way to deliver an important message, such as sex columnist and activist Dan Savage's It Gets Better Project, prompted by a rash of suicides by gay teenagers in 2010. The project began modestly, with a video of Savage and his partner posted to YouTube, and quickly gathered steam to include video testimonials by hundreds of people, including celebrities and politicians such as President Barack Obama, encouraging lesbian, gay, bisexual, and transgender teenagers to see past the oppressive atmosphere of intolerance and hatred that they live in—that is, to tap into an international network of hope and acceptance.[21]

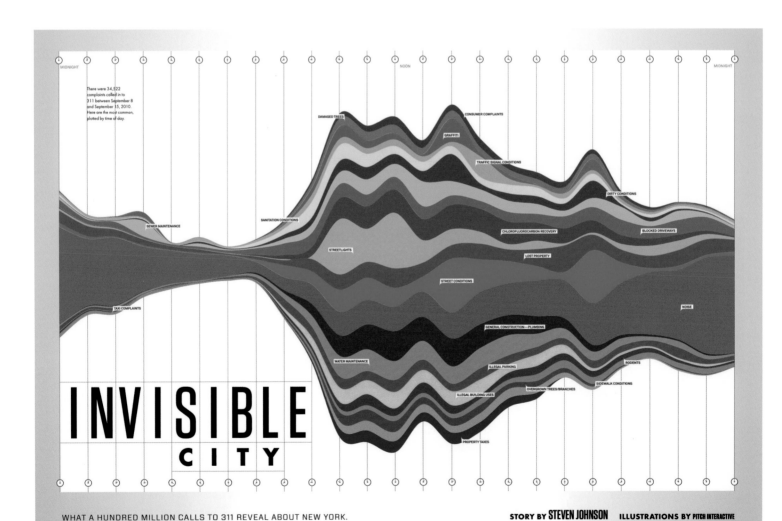

WHAT A HUNDRED MILLION CALLS TO 311 REVEAL ABOUT NEW YORK.

STORY BY STEVEN JOHNSON    ILLUSTRATIONS BY PITCH INTERACTIVE

Fig. 9
Marguerite Humeau, Design
Interactions Department,
Royal College of Art. Lucy from
Back, Herebelow, Formidable
(the rebirth of prehistoric
creatures). 2010–ongoing.
Metal, plastic tube, and air
compressor, 45 5/16 ×
19 11/16 × 59" (115.1 × 50
× 149.9 cm)

A great deal of communicative experimentation takes place in cities, which, because of their density, are the perfect testing ground (fig. 6). City (1988), William H. Whyte's great observation of the physical interactions among people, cars, buildings, and a city's other animate and inanimate inhabitants, would benefit from an update to include the additional layer of exchange now provided by digital technology.[22] New buildings talk in ways no one could have imagined in the analog years. In "Living Skins: Architecture as Interface" (2006), critic Peter Hall cited the Blinkenlights project (2001, fig. 7) as a pioneer in massive-scale urban communication: members of the Chaos Computer Club installed 144 bright lights in the front windows of the top eight floors of Haus des Lehrers, a building on Berlin's Alexanderplatz, transforming the facade into a giant computer screen. Using mobile phones, passersby could play Pong or send images to be rendered on the very low-res, very big, very dramatic screen.[23]

The city talks to citizens, and citizens certainly talk back. Several municipalities, New York among them, have set up services to enable people to communicate with the local government via phone and web. In New York that system is called 311, after its phone number. Pitch Interactive, a visualization design company, created an analysis of 34,522 complaint calls to 311 (2010, fig. 8)—a colorful depiction of the pet peeves of New Yorkers. Several countries have set up nationwide systems; in March 2010 Gordon Brown, then the United Kingdom's prime minister, announced a plan to endow every citizen with his or her own web page, in order to give them improved access to government benefits, information, and services.[24]

Design has a whole new set of clichés to deal with; postdigital design, in its embrace of the analog, expresses a fatigue not only with the medium but also with the forms of digital technology, and the apparent rejection of aesthetics expressed by hackers is an aesthetic ideology in itself. This accusation has also been leveled at Google, whose antistyle has been channeled and crystallized in many contemporary interfaces and has set a template for the DIY physical-design movement. Technological progress always brings formal innovation, which starts as creative flair but may soon degrade into routine. Thus the groundbreaking elegance of Braun, since the 1950s, or Apple, since the 1990s, can become mannered if this approach is not reinvented every time, an easy formal recipe for displaying zeitgeist sensitivity.

Talk to Me is an opportunity to anchor design's new dimension and highlight innovative interfaces that can inform designers in the future. Whether they use the skin and shell of objects as an interface or animate them from within, designers are using the whole world to communicate and are set on a path that is transforming it into an information parkour and enriching our lives with emotion, motion, direction, depth, and freedom. Now that the technological means are widely available, designers have become sophisticated enough to modulate them with a sensitive touch. They have matured past the first moments of irrepressible and immoderate enthusiasm for the new medium and have learned to wear technology, instead of letting technology wear them. It can be difficult to keep perspective on the magnitude and scope of all the interactions we engage in or witness or hear about; design is flowing into politics, philosophy, science, and religion in ways both ancient and new. The predigital Arecibo message was one such metaphysical venture, a string of digits launched in 1974 from the Arecibo radio telescope in Puerto Rico and transmitted via FM radio waves to a star cluster twenty-five thousand light-years away—a shout out into the void, a soaring attempt to talk to creatures whose essence we can't even imagine.

Design and design-related experiments are propelling us further and further into the unknown. Interfaces have been proposed that help us communicate with God; a Taoist prayer hall went electronic;[25] an app has been created for Catholic confession; the young designer Marguerite Humeau has been resuscitating long-extinct prehistoric creatures by resuscitating their voice boxes (fig. 9); and designers Jon Ardern and Anab Jain, with their evocative multidimensional camera (page 163), have attempted to embody Hugh Everett's many-worlds theory in an object that adds to the cinematic tradition of The Matrix (1999), Lost (2004–10), Fringe (2008-ongoing), and Source Code (2011), to name just a few.[26]

It might seem that design has abandoned its tested, grounded, functionalist territory to venture into an ambiguous universe where its essence is confused and a crisis of identity arises—is the 5th Dimensional Camera art or scientific modeling? Is Humeau's work creative paleontology? Are Sputniko!'s devices (pages 177 and 182) contributing to interpretive anthropology? Is Pachube (page 41) mere coding and infrastructure engineering? Not at all. I claim them, with their powerful visions and their focus on knowledge and awareness, as design, and I praise their radical functionalism. Ambiguity and ambivalence—the ability to inhabit different environments and frames of mind at the same time—have become central to our cultural development. They are qualities that embody the openness and flexibility necessary for embracing diversity, and they are critical to the questioning and imagining that are the preferred methods of inquiry. Communication is at the nexus of all these necessary human features: the most crucial function for design today.

Notes

1.    The Tower Bridge can be followed at @towerbridge, and Marina Abramović's chair at @marinaschair. The latter is the chair the artist used in The Artist Is Present, a performance at The Museum of Modern Art, New York, over the course of the exhibition Marina Abramović: The Artist Is Present, March 14–May 31, 2010, in which Abramović sat when the Museum was open, and viewers were invited to sit silently, one at a time, in front of her.

2.    "Dal cucchiaio alla città" (From the spoon to the city) is a slogan coined by Italian architect and critic Ernesto Nathan Rogers to describe the Milanese architectural and design process, which at the time encompassed all scales—and still does, unfortunately to a lesser extent. There is some disagreement about when Rogers said this; Deyan Sudjic notes that Rogers wrote something very much like it in a 1952 editorial for Domus. Sudjic, The Language of Things: Understanding the World of Desirable Objects (New York: W. W. Norton, 2009), p. 34.

3.    Donald Norman's Emotional Design (New York: Basic Books, 2005) proposed the not-so-groundbreaking thesis that emotions play a big part in the way we relate to objects.

4.    Adolf Loos, "Ornament und Verbrechen," 1908, published in English as "Ornament and Crime," in Ornament and Crime: Selected Essays, trans. Michael Mitchell (Riverside, Calif.: Ariadne Press, 1998), pp. 167. In it he wrote, "The evolution of culture is synonymous with the removal of ornamentation from objects of everyday use."

5.    "Form ever follows function." Louis H. Sullivan, "The Tall Office Building Artistically Considered," Lippincott's Monthly Magazine 57 (March 1896): 403–9; republished in Sullivan, Kindergarten Chats and Other Writings (New York: Dover, 1979).

6.    Carl Jung dedicated thirty years of his life to building a house in Küsnacht, on the lake of Zurich. He equated the building of a house with the building of self, as he explained in Erinnerungen, Träume, Gedanken, ed. Aniela Jaffé (Düsseldorf: Walter Verlag, 1971); published in English as Memories, Dreams, Reflections, trans. Richard and Clara Winston, reprint ed. (New York: Vintage Books, 1989), p. 225.

7.    Paul Watzlawick, Janet Beavin Bavelas, and Don D. Jackson, "Some Tentative Axioms of Communication," in Pragmatics of Human Communication: A Study of Interactional Patterns, Pathologies, and Paradoxes (New York: W. W. Norton, 1967), pp. 48–71.

8.    ToneCheck was listed in the New York Times's 2010 Year in Ideas, www.nytimes.com/interactive/2010/12/19/magazine/ideas2010.html#Emotional_Spell-Check.

9.    Vernor Vinge, "The Coming Technological Singularity: How to Survive in the Post-Human Era," presented at the VISION 21 Symposium, Westlake, Ohio, March 30–31, 1993, www.aleph.se/Trans/Global/Singularity/sing.html. For those readers who have caught echoes of earlier literature, Vinge clearly refers to Isaac Asimov and his laws in this speech.

10.    Ray Kurzweil, The Singularity Is Near: When Humans Transcend Biology (New York: Viking, 2005); Adam Gopnik, "Get Smart," The New Yorker, April 4, 2011, pp. 70–74.

11.    Alan Turing first described the test in "Computing Machinery and Intelligence," Mind: A Quarterly Review of Psychology and Philosophy 59, no. 236 (October 1950): 433–60, mind.oxfordjournals.org/content/LIX/236/433.full.pdf+html.

12.    Guido Gozzano, "L'amica di nonna Speranza," in La via del rifugio (Turin: Renzo Streglio, 1907). Author's trans.

13.    Significant Objects, significantobjects.com/about. The project is currently on hiatus and will reappear in book form in 2011, published by Fantagraphics Books. In one of the project's phases I provided about ten objects for writers. I consider Rob Walker to be a Talk to Me soul mate; in a blog post, the curatorial team dubbed him the Object Whisperer. wp.moma.org/talk_to_me/2010/09/the-object-whisperer-an-interview-with-rob-walker.

14.    Newspaper Club, www.newspaper-club.co.uk/about.

15.    "On Wikipedia, Cultural Patrimony, and Historiography," The Blog of James Bridle, booktwo.org/notebook/wikipedia-historiography.

16.    Alice Rawsthorn, "The Demise of 'Form Follows Function,'" New York Times, May 30, 2009, www.nytimes.com/2009/06/01/arts/01iht-DESIGN1.html.

17.    Jean-Baptiste Labrune, Jamie Zigelbaum, and Hiroshi Ishii, "From PreHistoric Interfaces to NearFuture Interactions," www.slideshare.net/jb.labrune/user-interface-history-to-near-future. This slide show is concise and incisive but, as the authors are all part of the MIT Media Lab, rather MIT-centric.

18.    Until recently, commercial screens could sense only a single finger at a time.

19.    See "Crossing the Uncanny Valley," The Economist, November 18, 2010, www.economist.com/node/17519716. Masahiro Mori first published his theory in "The Uncanny Valley," trans. Karl F. MacDorman and Takashi Minato, Energy 7, no. 4 (1970): 33–35.

20.    Guy Debord, La Société du spectacle (Paris: Buchet-Chastel, 1967); published in English as The Society of the Spectacle, trans. Donald Nicholson-Smith, reprint ed. (New York: Zone Books, 2008).

21.    It Gets Better Project, www.itgets-better.org.

22.    William H. Whyte, City: Rediscovering the Center (New York: Doubleday, 1988).

23.    Peter Hall, "Living Skins: Architecture as Interface," Adobe Design Center Think Tank, n.d., www.adobe.com/designcenter/thinktank/livingskins.

24.    "Every Citizen to Have Personal Webpage," Telegraph, March 20, 2010, www.telegraph.co.uk/technology/news/7484600/Every-citizen-to-have-personal-webpage.html.

25.    "Taoism Goes High Tech," Wall Street Journal (blog), February 14, 2011, blogs.wsj.com/hong-kong/2011/02/14/taoism-goes-high-tech.

26.    The many-worlds theory, one of quantum theory's most cinematic offshoots, postulates that what is happening in this universe becomes, in other universes, a branch from which other events and other branches sprout.

Give an object to a child, and she will look for an on/off switch or a button. Put her in front of a television set, and she will touch the screen, trying to expand the image with her fingers as if handling an iPad. Give her a computer of any kind, and she will know how to make it sing. She was born into an era of intelligent, or at least responsive, objects. But even those who have lived long enough to remember the thrill of the mechanical typewriter have become adjusted to our interactive world.

Teddy bears, medicine bottles, radios, MP3 players, and entire homes give feedback on their status (on, off, sleeping, online, off-line), on how much they are consuming, on how they are feeling, on what is happening nearby and far away, on whether or not we have accomplished the tasks they set for us. They do so by winking, lighting up, blinking, changing color, displaying urgent messages in text and diagrams, sometimes even speaking out loud.

In the following pages we explore objects, interfaces, and systems that are not just communicative and interactive but also have personalities. Some are conceptual—such as Kacie Kinzer's Tweenbots (page 23), which demonstrate New Yorkers' irrepressible impulse to help anything or anyone that seems to be lost, even if it is a cardboard robot carrying a little flag—and others functional and functioning, such as the interfaces for the ATM at Barclays (page 45) or the MetroCard Vending Machine (page 46).

At home, in the office, or on the road, we are surrounded by specialized companions and expressive pets. Some live in our multifunctional devices, like Yann Le Coroller's Talking Carl (page 31) in our smartphones, while others are autonomous, demanding to be seen and heard from their own bodies (pages 34–35). By integrating old-fashioned objects such as books and cuckoo clock boxes with mobile applications, designers have created a comfortable hybrid of old and new, of physical and digital (pages 32–33).

Most of the objects in this book are trying to find the design language that will best embody the new balance between technology and people. From sensors embedded into our home appliances (and sending information to a wider global network) to tableware that is scarred by age (page 27) or convulsed by the tension of familial disputes (page 29), the expressive range of objects is as limitless as imagination, and no object is ever the same as another.

P. A.

The texts in this chapter were written by Kate Carmody.

OBJE
CTS

19

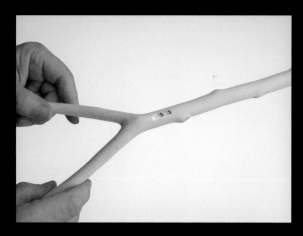

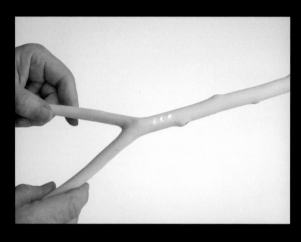

Mike Thompson (British, born 1981)

///////////////////////////////

Wifi Dowsing Rod. 2007

///////////////////////////////

Wood and electronics, approx. 18 7/8
× 6 1/8 × 5/8" (48 × 15.5 × 1.5 cm)

The Wifi Dowsing Rod provides comfort
to people who may be overwhelmed
by current technologies. Mike Thompson
has adapted the familiar form of a divining
rod—believed in the past to be able to
locate underground sources of water—
into a tool that seeks out and indicates
the strength of the unseen wireless
signals that are all around us. Thus
a tool of the past is evoked in fulfilling
the needs of the present.

Timo Arnall (British, born 1976) and
Einar Sneve Martinussen (Norwegian,
born 1982)
Oslo School of Architecture and
Design (Norway, est. 1961)
Jack Schulze (British, born 1976)
of BERG (UK, est. 2005)

////////////////////////////

Immaterials: Ghost in the Field. 2009

////////////////////////////

Digital video (color, sound), 4:08 min.

The designers of the Touch project—
which explores near-field communication
(NFC), or close-range wireless connections between devices—set out to
make the immaterial visible, specifically
one such technology, radio-frequency
identification (RFID), currently used
for financial transactions, transportation,
and tracking anything from live animals
to library books. "Many aspects of RFID
interaction are fundamentally invisible,"
explains Timo Arnall. "As users we
experience two objects communicating
through the 'magic' of radio waves."
Using an RFID tag (a label containing
a microchip and an antenna) equipped
with an LED probe that lights up
whenever it senses an RFID reader,
the designers recorded the interaction
between reader and tag over time and
created a map of the space in which
they engaged. Jack Schulze notes that
alongside the new materials used in
contemporary design products, "service
layers, video, animation, subscription
models, customization, interface,
software, behaviors, places, radio,
data, APIs (application programming
interfaces) and connectivity are
amongst the immaterials."

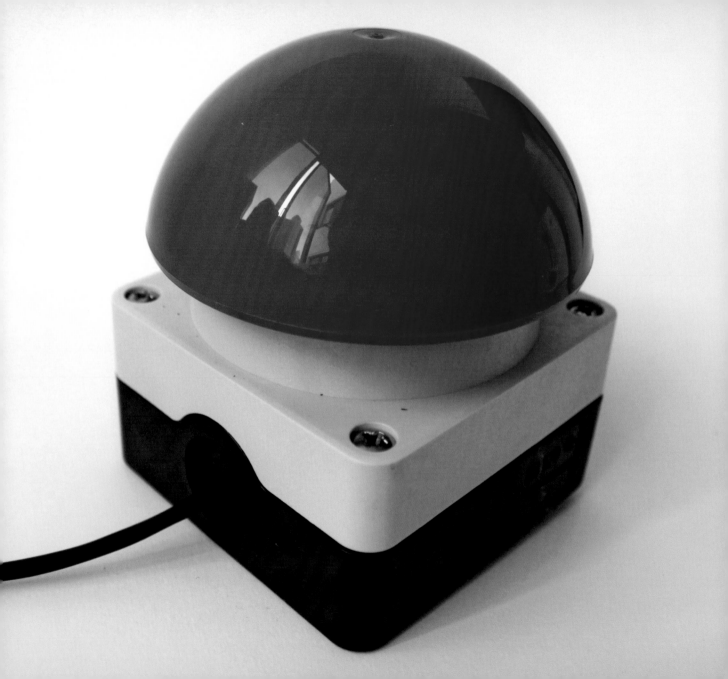

Kacie Kinzer (American, born 1983)
Interactive Telecommunications
Program (est. 1979)
Tisch School of the Arts (est. 1965)
New York University (USA, est. 1831)

/////////////////////////////

Tweenbots. 2009

/////////////////////////////

Cardboard, paper, ink, batteries, motor,
and wheels, 36 × 8 1/2 × 14" (91.4 ×
21.6 × 35.6 cm)

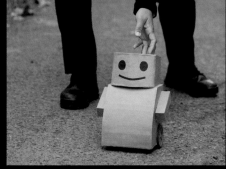

Tweenbots are small, constantly moving robots that depend on the kindness of strangers to get where they are going. Interaction designer Kacie Kinzer sent Sam, the best traveled of the Tweenbots, on many missions in New York City's Washington Square Park, armed only with a flag that asked passersby to point him toward a particular destination. She fully expected that Sam—made of a battery-operated motor and cardboard—would be crushed, lost, or thrown away, but surprisingly (or unsurprisingly, depending on how helpful you believe New Yorkers to be) he always arrived safely at his destination. "Every time the robot got caught under a park bench, ground futilely against a curb, or became trapped in a pothole," Kinzer observed, "some passerby would always rescue it and send it toward its goal." Her secret surveillance (via a video camera hidden in her purse) showed that people would interact directly with the robot and were also willing to engage other strangers in a discussion of its predica-ment. If the Tweenbot's destination seemed too dangerous, people sometimes ignored the instructions on the flag: "One man turned the robot back in the direction from which it had just come, saying out loud to the Tweenbot, 'You can't go that way, it's toward the road.'" The Tweenbots demonstrate that a clever situation staged by a designer can set a dialogue in motion between people and objects.

Paul Kirps (Luxembourgian, born 1969)

/////////////////////////////

autoreverse. 2004–05

/////////////////////////////

Digital video (color, sound), 10:54 min.

In autoreverse, five stop-motion
sequences depict electric and electronic
appliances deconstructing and then
rebuilding themselves, accompanied
by what designer Paul Kirps calls
"electro-techno-mechanic" sounds
that emphasize the objects' surreal
and redundant functions. To make
these videos, Kirps searched for items
of traditional household and office
equipment, many of them now obsolete.
The designer pays homage to objects
lost in the name of progress.

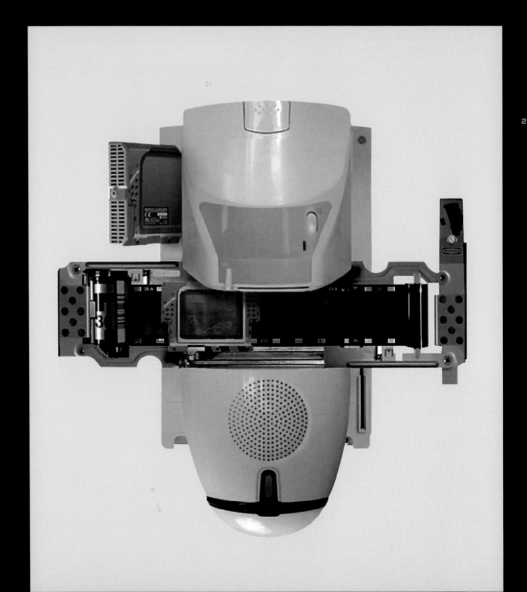

James Chambers (British, born 1983)
Design Interactions Department
(est. 1989)
Royal College of Art (UK, est. 1837)

////////////////////////////

Floppy Legs Portable Hard Drive (top)
and Gesundheit Radio (bottom) from the
Attenborough Design Group project. 2010

////////////////////////////

Various materials, hard drive: 3 7/8 ×
5 7/8 × 9 13/16" (9.9 × 14.9 × 24.8 cm);
radio: 4 11/16 × 11 3/8 × 3 1/8"
(11.9 × 28.9 × 7.8 cm)

For his final project in the Design
Interactions program, James Chambers
concocted a group of products under
the guise of the Attenborough Design
Group (ADG), named for revered British
naturalist David Attenborough. The ADG
is made up of imaginary researchers
who explore what would happen
if electronic objects displayed animal
behaviors in response to common
problems. The Gesundheit Radio, for
example, sneezes periodically through
nostrils on its front to free itself of
the dirt that may damage its electronic
insides, and the Floppy Legs Portable
Hard Drive can sense a spill—a tipped-
over coffee cup on a desk, for example—
and raise itself on four legs above the
desk's surface to avoid being ruined.
These objects operate on instinct,
programmed to act in the interest of
self-preservation, essentially allowing
them to survive longer than their
competitors and bringing the language
of natural selection into the realm
of product design.

James Chambers (British, born 1983)
Design Interactions Department
(est. 1989)
Royal College of Art (UK, est. 1837)

/////////////////////////////

Strangle Poise Lamp from the Red Goods
collection. 2010

/////////////////////////////

Various materials, 70 7/8 × 9 13/16

In response to research connecting
exposure to violence in the media with
the urge to commit violent acts, James
Chambers designed a line of speculative
products that allow users to act out
aggressive inclinations by hurting objects
designed for the purpose. The Strangle
Poise Lamp (a clever play on Anglepoise,
the classic British desk lamp designed
by George Carwardine in the 1930s) is
turned off by being strangled, a safer
way, according to the designer, to "live
out the fantasy" that begins with

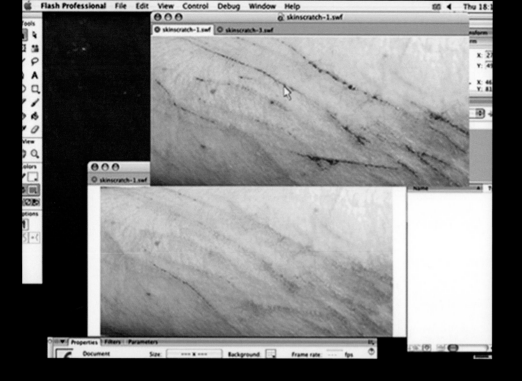

Revital Cohen (Israeli, born 1981)
Design Interactions Department
(est. 1989)
Royal College of Art (UK, est. 1837)

////////////////////////////

Me Against the Machine. 2006

////////////////////////////

Flash software

While a student in the Design
Interactions program, Revital Cohen
noticed the way that many computer
interfaces try to be as user-friendly
as possible. But are we really so friendly?
Do we really need to be? Cohen notes
that it is easy to feel out of control in
a world increasingly ruled by computers;
with her interface, users can injure
their computers with mouse clicks until
the screen bruises or bleeds, taking
out their frustrations on the computer
until they feel in control again.

Simon Heijdens (Dutch, born 1978)

////////////////////////////

Broken White dinnerware. 2004

////////////////////////////

Ceramic, flat plate: 13/16" (2 cm) deep,
11 13/16" (30 cm) diam.; deep plate: 2"
(5 cm) deep, 7 7/8" (20cm) diam.; bowl:
3 1/2" (9 cm) deep, 5 1/2" (14 cm) diam.

The plates and bowls of the Broken
White series are born pristine, white,
and evenly glazed. As they are used,
cracks and wrinkles develop in a
decorative organic pattern. The dishes
betray their age and become more
beautiful with passing time. Broken
White was commissioned by the
Dutch design producer Droog Design
for an exhibition in Lille, France, in 2004,
the year the city was celebrated as
a European Capital of Culture.

Geoffrey Mann (British, born 1980)

/////////////////////////////

Cross-fire from the Natural Occurrence
series. 2010

/////////////////////////////

Digital video (color, sound), 1:55 min.;
utensils: sterling silver, fork: 1 3/16
× 9 1/8 × 1 5/8" (3 × 23 × 4 cm);
spoon: 1 5/8 × 9 1/8 × 2 13/16" (4 × 23
× 7 cm); knife: 13/16 × 9 3/8 × 1 5/8"
(2 × 24 × 4 cm); plate: porcelain, 10 3/16
× 11 × 3 1/2" (26 × 28 × 9 cm); teapot:
porcelain, 8 11/16 × 11 13/16 × 9 1/8"
(22 × 30 × 23 cm); wineglass: glass,
9 1/8 × 5 1/8 × 5 1/8" (23 × 13 × 13 cm)

Cross-fire, directed by Geoffrey Mann
and produced by Chris Labrooy, takes
an audio excerpt from Sam Mendes's
1999 film American Beauty—a heated
argument between Lester and Carolyn
Burnham (Kevin Spacey and Annette
Bening)—and animates it, so that the
tension that tears across the room
appears to be felt literally by the objects
on the dining room table. There are no
human bodies in the animation, only the
voices of the characters and the music
of Bobby Darin in the background; the
fight's relentless sound waves are
absorbed and transferred across the
table through the silverware, glasses,
and dishes. With this film Mann explores
the effect of the sound of speech on
familiar objects—in this case with forms
increasingly warping as the fight esca-
lates. Cross-fire was commissioned
by Past, Present & Future Craft Practice
(PPFCP), a research project based at
Duncan of Jordanstone College of Art
and Design, University of Dundee,
Scotland.

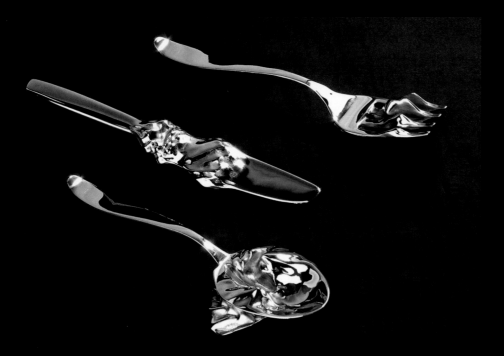

Crispin Jones (British, born 1974)

////////////////////////////////

Tengu. 2007

////////////////////////////////

ABS and electronics, 2 13/16 × 1 11/16 × 5/8" (7 × 4.3 × 1.5 cm)
Manufactured by Mr Jones Design Ltd., UK

Tengu, an interactive toy named after Heavenly Dog, a mischievous supernatural creature from Japanese folklore, plugs into a computer's USB port and reacts to sounds with its eyes and mouth, as if singing along to music or speaking when he hears someone speak. He requires no care from his owner—like the famous pet rocks of the 1970s—but he reacts when attention is paid to him.

Eva Rucki (German, born 1976),
Conny Freyer (German, born 1976),
and Sebastien Noel (French, born 1977)
of Troika (UK, est. 2003)

////////////////////////////////

TV Predator. 2003–07

////////////////////////////////

Picture frame and electronics, 15 13/16 × 20 1/2" (40 × 52 cm)

The interaction designers of Troika speculate that as electronic intelligence is built into more and more household products, behaviors may unfold that mimic human emotions and foibles. Competitiveness between these smart objects, for instance, may make them even more darkly human, turning them toward emotions such as greed, jealousy, and revenge. In TV Predator an envious picture frame that feels neglected by its owner will harass nearby televisions, forcing them to malfunction: turning them on and off at random, changing channels, or muting or disrupting the colors and contrast.

Yann Le Coroller (French, born 1969)

////////////////////////////////

Talking Carl. 2010

////////////////////////////////

3ds Max, V-Ray, and Xcode software

Carl is a box-shaped creature that responds to sound and touch. Playful and mischievous, he will repeat anything you say in a funny and high-pitched voice, with a big mouth that takes over his whole body. He laughs if he is tickled on the belly, shouts when he is poked in the eye, and growls when pinched, his uvula trembling. He is one of the most successful Android, iPad, and iPhone apps. Carl behaves in a manner similar to other app characters, such as Talking Tom Cat, but his simplified form is not intended to mimic any human or animal from real life, making him easy to love.

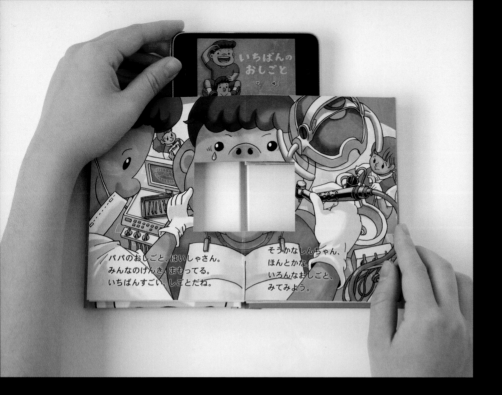

Yuki Kishi (Japanese, born 1977) and
Saori Watanabe (Japanese, born 1969)
of Dentsu Inc. (Japan, est. 1901)
Shinya Kishiro (Japanese, born 1970)
of Robot Communications Inc. (Japan,
est. 1986)

///////////////////////////

PhoneBook. 2009

///////////////////////////

Laser-printed paper, urethane, and
Xcode, Flash, and Photoshop software,
9 1/2 × 6 1/4 × 1 3/8" (24 × 16 × 3.5 cm)
Manufactured by Kodansha Ltd., Japan

Designers at Mobile Art Lab, a research
center that focuses on mobile-phone
content (part of Dentsu, a large Japanese
advertising agency), launched the
PhoneBook project with the aim of
finding new ways to connect parents
and children using the iPhone. This
hybrid of digital and analog technology—
a mobile application specifically designed
to interact with a story read in a physical
book (the version shown here is Work,
Work!)—has potential for all sorts of
interactions in the future, from educational tools to commercial products.

a Gaggero (Italian, born 1980)
Adrian Westaway (British and
nch, born Singapore 1982)
itamins Design (UK, est. 2008)
h Samsung Design Europe (UK,
1999) and the Helen Hamlyn Centre
Design (est. 1999), Royal College
rt (UK, est. 1837)

///////////////////////////////

of the Box. 2009

///////////////////////////////

r, 9 1/8 × 6 11/16 × 2"
× 17 × 5 cm)

of the Box is an easy-to-understand
ile-phone-instruction manual specifi-
y aimed at senior citizens. Designers
a Gaggero and Adrian Westaway
ked with the Helen Hamlyn Centre
Design, an interdisciplinary design-
earch unit devoted to projects aimed
mproving people's lives, especially the
rly and disabled. The outcome was
mobile-phone packaging that doubles
n instruction manual based on familiar
digital communication. Seniors often
learning new technologies frustrat-
especially, the designers explain,
they apply analogue modes of learning
he digital experience—looking in the
for help that is not there." Here,
box is also a bound book that contains
phone. The new owner leafs through
pages of the book, gradually encoun-
g both assembly instructions and
corresponding hardware parts, which
ntegrated within the bound book.
e the user is comfortable with the
kings of the phone, the package
be stored on a bookshelf.

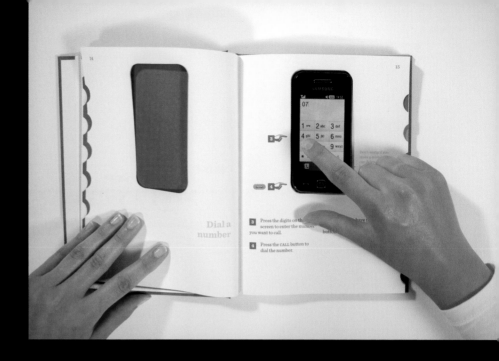

---

Tom Hulbert (British, born 1977)
and Durrell Bishop (British, born 1963)
of Luckybite (UK, est. 2005)

//////////////////////////////////

BirdBox. 2009

//////////////////////////////////

Paper, wood, and iProcessing and Xcode
software, 6 5/16 × 3 15/16 × 3 9/16"
(16 × 10 × 9 cm)

BirdBox is a combination of a die-cut
paper birdhouse and an iPhone app
for an alarm clock that awakens users
with the chirps of virtual birds nesting
inside the phone. Like a digital cuckoo
clock, the birdhouse that contains the
phone at night gives the new technology
an old shape.

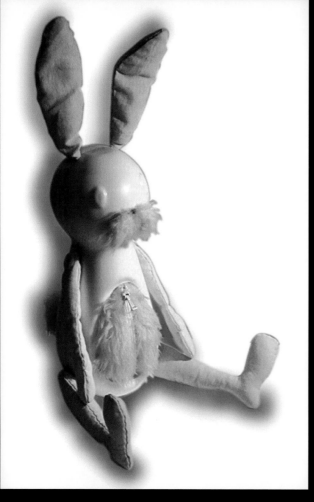

Michiko Nitta (Japanese, born 1978)
Product Design (est. 1938)
Central School of Art and Design
(UK, est. 1896), now Central Saint Martins
(UK, est. 1989)

////////////////////////////

Mr. Smilit. 2003

////////////////////////////

Polycarbonate, fake fur, fabric, and
electronics, 11 13/16 × 7 1/8 × 5 7/8"
(30 × 18 × 15 cm)

Digital pets are part of a growing group
of functional objects with zoomorphic
qualities, often as endearing as stuffed
animals, that are meant to entertain
us, keep us company, inform us about
the weather, manage our household
appliances, even spy for us, like the
infamous nanny cams hidden in teddy
bears. The possible applications of a
digital bunny, communicative penguin,
or self-satisfied chubby little martian
are endless. Mr. Smilit, designed by
Michiko Nitta with contributions from
her mother, Yumi, and her sister, Yoko,
is a toy that reacts to the noise of a
child's cry with a cry of its own, which
may cause the child to stop crying
and care for the doll.

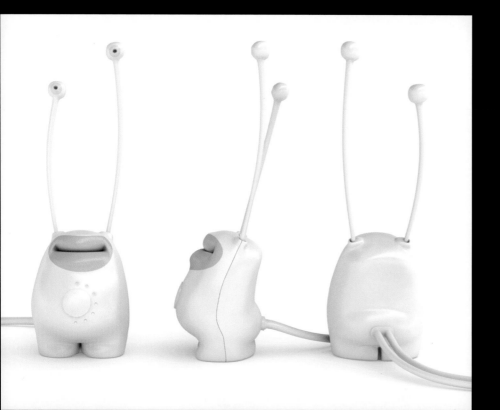

Kamil Jerzykowski (Polish, born 1981)
and Magdalena Kałek (Polish, born 1981)
of Ah&Oh Studio (Poland, est. 2008)

///////////////////////////

BugPlug. 2009

///////////////////////////

BugPlug's designers call it a "household
friend" that will help cut its owner's
energy usage. All of a user's electronics
are plugged into a single hub that is
in turn connected to BugPlug, which
monitors the status of the devices and
controls the flow of electrical current
to them. The BugPlug's antennae conta
motion sensors, so that when it detec
human presence, all of the devices are
automatically turned on. A timer on its
stomach can be programmed to turn
off the appliances at preset times.

Onkar Kular (British, born 1974)

////////////////////////////

Hari & Parker. 2007

////////////////////////////

Various materials, Hari: 9 13/16 × 3 3/16 × 1 5/8" (25 × 8 × 4 cm); Parker: 6 1/8 × 5 3/16 × 1 5/8" (15.5 × 13.2 × 4 cm)

Onkar Kular conceived the characters Hari and Parker for <u>The Science of Spying</u>, a 2007 exhibition at the Science Museum, London. He imagined an alternate reality in which children are recruited to spy for the government, tutored and helped along by Hari (a rabbit) and Parker (a bear), and he then concocted a whole line of children's products—from candy and music to books and wallpaper—featuring the characters. Hari has a microphone and intercepting text-messaging ears, and Parker's nose hides a camera, while his paw is a fingerprint scanner. The toys aid children in "[committing] subtle acts of domestic surveillance," explains the designer.

Golan Levin (American, born 1972),
Lawrence Hayhurst (American,
born 1950), Steven Benders (American,
born 1986), and Fannie White
(American, born 1943)
Carnegie Mellon School of Art (est. 1905)
Carnegie Mellon University
(USA, est. 1900)

/ / / / / / / / / / / / / / / / / / / / / / / / / / / / /

Double-Taker (Snout). 2008

/ / / / / / / / / / / / / / / / / / / / / / / / / / / / /

Windows PC running custom software,
stereo-depth camera, 6-axis robot
arm, and vinyl, 9' 10 1/8" × 59 1/8"
× 59 1/8" (300 × 150 × 150 cm)

With a body similar to a large worm
or elephant trunk, Double-Taker (Snout)
is surprisingly emotional for a creature
made of a robotic arm and a single,
giant googly eye. Snout was placed above
the entrance to the Pittsburgh Center
for the Arts in 2008, where it silently
tracked the actions of museum visitors
as they came in and out. A computer
program used information from a stereo
camera and vision algorithms to detect
the visitors' behavior and then directed
these signals to influence the movements
of the arm. The result was a mechanical
cyclops that seemed bashful yet curious
and interested as it caught glimpses
of passersby and followed them with
its eye. By endowing the robotic creature
with realistic observational behaviors,
the designers achieved a suggestion
of intelligent awareness.

Nicolas Myers (French, born 1978)
Design Interactions Department
(est. 1989)
Royal College of Art (UK, est. 1837)

///////////////////////////

Transgenic Bestiary. 2009

///////////////////////////

Installation with computer, video
projection, illustrated tiles, and Flash,
Java, and Reactivision software, overall:
39 3/8" × 8' 2 3/8" × 35 3/8"
(100 × 250 × 90 cm)

In Transgenic Bestiary, players
create virtual hybrid creatures using
a database of sequenced animal DNA.
The game's ostensible goal is to create
a potentially viable animal, but what
players learn as they progress is that
the mixed species have to be closely
related taxonomically, or else the animal
will not survive. Designer Nicolas Myers
says his concept is quite plausible,
noting that the game uses largely
existent technologies and concepts.

eevan Kalanithi (American, born 1978)
nd David Merrill (American, born 1978)
MIT Media Lab (est. 1985)
Massachusetts Institute of Technology
USA, est. 1861)

///////////////////////////////

ifteo Cubes. 2011

///////////////////////////////

code, ABS, polycarbonate, LCD
creens, electronics, and motion and
roximity sensors, each: 1 11/16 × 1 11/16
11/16" (4.3 × 4.3 × 1.9 cm)
Manufactured by Sifteo Inc., USA

Many design and technology companies produce DIY kits for devices, smart objects, and robots that the user assembles as though with advanced sets of Lego bricks. Inspired by classic games such as chess, checkers, and mah-jongg, Sifteo Cubes are a hands-on interactive game system. Each cube contains a tiny computer chip and connects to other cubes, sensing their motion and position, through a wireless network to an application on a nearby computer. The cubes can be used in various games, including a spelling game in which they are rearranged until a word is correctly spelled, at which point they light up and highlight the word. David Merrill and Jeevan Kalanithi designed the cubes while graduate students at the MIT Media Lab, and they have since formed a company, with designer Brent Fitzgerald, to produce Sifteo Cubes, games, and software.

ric Schweikardt (American, born 1976)

///////////////////////////////

ubelets. 2010

///////////////////////////////

Recycled ABS, magnets, electronics,
nd copper, each: 1 5/8 × 1 5/8 × 1 5/8"
4 × 4 × 4 cm)
Manufactured by Modular Robotics, USA

ubelets are little modules that stick ogether with magnets to build smart objects; unlike the Bug Labs modular ardware (opposite), they require no pplication development. Working with Cubelets is much like building an evolving being block by block, with each block designed to perform a certain function. s the physical form takes shape, "the ehavior [emerges]," the designer says, like ... a flock of birds or a swarm of ees." Some blocks sense information bout light, heat, and distance, which is hen translated by blocks that act (rolling, driving, emitting a beam of light).

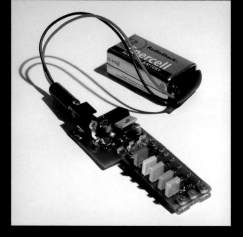

Ayah Bdeir (Lebanese, born 1982)

///////////////////////////////

littleBits. 2008

///////////////////////////////

Printed circuit board, analog components, and magnets, 13/16 × 13/16" (2 × 2 cm)
Manufactured by littleBits, USA

Ayah Bdeir's littleBits are a hardware library of preassembled circuit boards that connect to one another with magnets. Like Legos, which allow anyone to understand how to build structures without a complex engineering education, littleBits make a complex process intuitive, in this case assembling prototypes by snapping together electronic components. Thus littleBits allow nonexperts to engage with electronics, letting anyone get a feel for working with circuits. Users have made, for instance, a garage-door opener, a coffeemaker, a pair of blinking shoes, and a joystick.

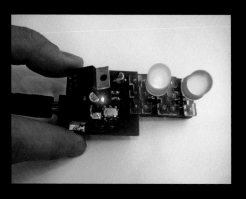

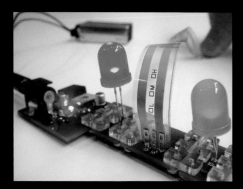

Bug Labs (USA, est. 2006)

////////////////////////////

BUG 1.3. 2009

////////////////////////////

Polycarbonate-ABS, polypropylene, stainless steel, brass, and silicon,
BUGbase: 2 1/2 × 5 × 1/4" (6.4 × 12.7 × 0.5 cm); BUGmodule: 2 1/2 × 2 1/2 × 3/16" (6.4 × 6.4 × 0.5 cm)
Manufactured by Bug Labs, USA

Bug Labs designs and produces modular hardware for building devices for such applications as remotely monitoring patients, detecting earthquakes, and hacking into a Toyota Prius and turning it into a mobile hotspot. Bug Labs provides the tool kit and the support, and users become the designers, programmers, and developers, producing unique devices to their own specifications. These applications can then be shared on the Bug Labs website, creating a crowdsourcing community.

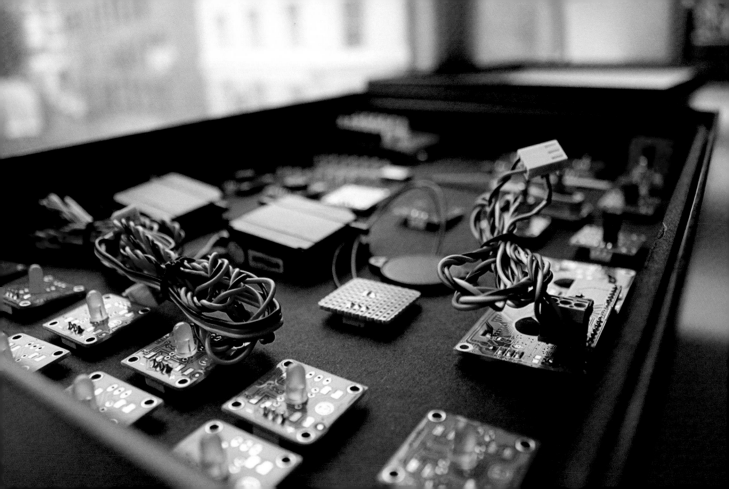

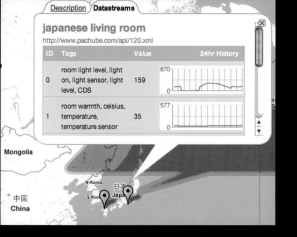

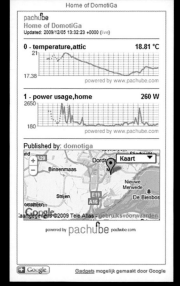

Usman Haque (British, born 1971)
of Connected Environments Ltd.
(UK, est. 2008)

//////////////////////////////

Pachube. 2009

//////////////////////////////

Custom software

Pachube, a network created by Usman
Haque, connects and shares data
collected by sensors from all over the
world. With it, anyone can track and
manage information coming from, Haque
says, "buildings, weather stations,
interactive environments, air quality
monitors, networked energy monitors,
virtual worlds and mobile sensor
devices," enabling direct, real-time
connections between any two or more
of them, across domains and industries
"[in] many-to-many connections: just
like a physical 'patch bay' (or telephone
switchboard)." Among Pachube's
applications Haque notes "[helping]
communities improve environmental
monitoring and quality of life; [helping]
companies turn networked products
into services with recurring revenue;
and [helping] cities and urban organizations capitalize on the benefits of
real-time urban sensor networks—
all of which are part of what is known
as the Internet of Things."

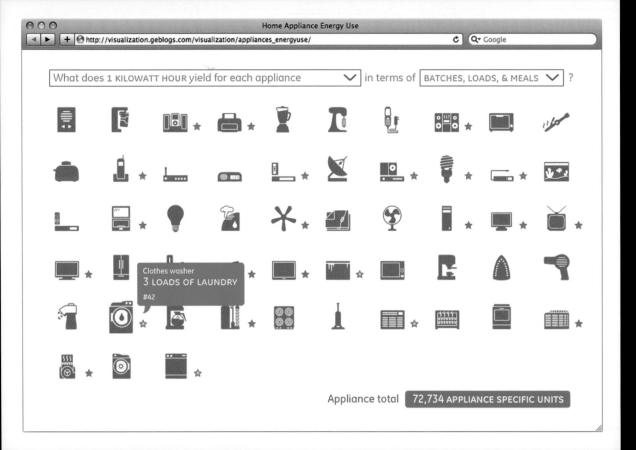

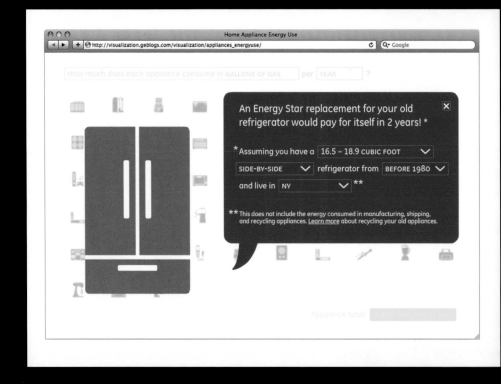

Lisa Strausfeld (American, born 1964),
Hilla Katki (American, born 1977),
Michael Deal (American, born 1987),
and Adam Suharja (American, born 1987)
of Pentagram (UK and USA, est. 1972)

/////////////////////////////

GE ecomagination: Home Appliance
Energy Use. 2010

/////////////////////////////

Illustrator and ActionScript software

As part of General Electric's ecomagination environmental-awareness and
education program, this energy-
visualization website helps put energy
consumption into perspective by translating abstract-seeming measurements—
watts and kilowatt-hours—into easily
understandable volumes, such as dollars,
gallons of gasoline, and hours of real time.
How much real-time video game play
is represented by each kilowatt-hour
of energy? Five hours. How much does
the electricity cost for a month's use
of a standard television in New York
State? $3.27. In Minnesota? $1.70.
Commonly used appliances appear in
a grid in descending order of wattage
consumption, cost, gas usage, or kilowatt-hour performance; energy usage
can be estimated by year, month, or day.
The program lets users know when an
upgrade to an Energy Star (a US government designation for energy efficiency)
appliance will save money—and how
long it will take for the savings to kick in.

Tim Holley (British, born 1985)
Industrial Design and Technology
(est. 1985)
Brunel University (UK, est. 1966)

/////////////////////////////

Tio. 2009

/////////////////////////////

ABS, TPU, printed circuit boards, and
electronics, 5 3/8 × 5 7/8 × 1 13/16"
(13.6 × 15 × 4.5 cm)

Tio is a bird-shaped light switch designed
to teach children not to waste energy.
Using a traffic stoplight's color progres-
sion and a series of increasingly angry
facial expressions, Tio lets children know
how long the lights have been on, so they
can decide when it is time to turn them
off. The accompanying website allows
them to see their energy-use patterns
and explains where energy comes from
and how harvesting it affects animals,
plants, and the larger environment.
Tio was developed for Onzo, a British
company that provides energy utilities
with data-capture and analysis services.

Matteo Signorini (Italian, born 1973),
Pascal Soboll (German, born 1974),
Martin Frey (German, born 1978),
Robin Bigio (Italian, born 1982),
Alexander Grots (German, born 1970),
Vicky Arndt (German, born 1974), and
Judith Hufnagel (German, born 1977)
of IDEO (USA, est. 1991)
Beatriz Lara (Spanish, born 1962),
Jesús Alejano (Spanish, born 1970),
Elena Alfaro (Spanish, born 1975),
Pascual de Juan (Spanish, born 1967),
Jorge Rodriguez Palomar (Spanish,
born 1970), Andrés Retortillo (Spanish,
born 1961), and Julio Pérez (Spanish,
born 1969)
of BBVA (Spain, est. 1999)

//////////////////////////////////

The Future of Self-Service Banking. 2010

//////////////////////////////////

ABS, polycarbonate, steel, and custom
and Windows Presentation Foundation
software, 8' 2 3/8" × 59 1/8" × 47 3/16"
(250 × 150 × 120 cm)
Manufactured by NCR, USA, and
Fujitsu, Japan

Automated teller machines, or ATMs,
first introduced almost fifty years
ago, now offer a wide range of banking
transactions but are still very limited
in terms of interface design. Among
the attempts to improve communication
between people and banking machines,
IDEO and BBVA's project combines
a new interface that stresses clarity
with a physical ATM design that stresses
privacy. Users stand behind an opaque
panel when using the machine, preventing
those waiting in line from seeing the
screen during transactions. Instead
of text prompts, the interface uses a
virtual banker, and user-friendly options
include a choice of which denominations
cash will be dispensed in.

Jack Dorsey (American, born 1976)

////////////////////////////////

Square. 2010

////////////////////////////////

ABS, permalloy, copper, PVC, and
carbon film resistor, 1 × 1 × 5/8"
(2.5 × 2.5 × 1.5 cm)
Manufactured by Square, Inc., USA

Square is a tiny attachment that can
be plugged into the headphone jack
of a smartphone or tablet to allow anyone
to accept a credit card payment. The
card is slid through the attachment;
signatures on touch screens stand in
for printed receipts. This simple idea is
as efficient and potentially transformative
as designer Jack Dorsey's previous
big idea: he is one of the coinventors
of Twitter.

Richard Hogg (British, born 1973)

////////////////////////////////

Barclays ATM animations. 2010

////////////////////////////////

Illustrator, Flash, and Photoshop
software

Fanciful cartoons—illustrated by
Richard Hogg and animated by Kwok Fung
Lam—appear on the Barclays ATM screen
at different points during transactions.
A giant blinking periscope asks customers
to report suspicious activity, an expand-
ing toolbox indicates the machine is out
of order, and thanks are lit up in various
languages (including Welsh) once the
transaction is completed.

Masamichi Oudagawa (Japanese, born 1964), Sigi Moeslinger (Austrian, born 1968), and Bruce Pringle (American, born 1967) of Antenna Design (USA, est. 1997)

////////////////////////////

JetBlue interface. 2004

////////////////////////////

Director, Photoshop, Illustrator, and Visual Basic software
Manufactured by IBM, USA

Masamichi Oudagawa (Japanese, born 1964) and Sigi Moeslinger (Austrian, born 1968) of Antenna Design (USA, est. 1997)
David Reinfurt (American, born 1971), Kathleen Holman (American, born 1962), and MTA New York City Transit (USA, est. 1953)

////////////////////////////

MetroCard Vending Machine. 1999

////////////////////////////

Vending machine: steel and other materials, 6' 7 7/8" × 41 11/16" × 26" (203 × 106 × 66 cm); interface: Director, Photoshop, Illustrator, and Visual Basic software
Manufactured by Cubic Transportation Systems, USA

The interfaces of both JetBlue's self-service check-in kiosk and the MTA's MetroCard Vending Machine are immediately familiar, greeting customers with clean and friendly design very much in character with each company, setting a favorable tone for the journeys about to begin. JetBlue's kiosk interface is sleek and serene, evoking clear skies, sophisticated travel, and the retro look of the film Catch Me If You Can (2002). The MTA's vending machine leads customers through the process of buying Metro-Cards in a manner that is efficient and no-nonsense, in a very New York spirit, suggesting colorful, never-boring transit ahead: the buttons on the screen are large (accommodating all hand sizes as well as hands covered in mittens or gloves) and the purchasing choices are clear (although the request for a zip code for credit card purchases leaves most tourists baffled); the machine itself is done up in bright, almost toylike primary colors, and with its enamel-coated steel, it is both graffiti- and scratch-proof.

(Canada 1963) and Cliff Kushler (American, born 1952)

////////////////////////////

Swype. 2010

////////////////////////////

C++ software

Swype, a text-input software for smartphones, is an offspring of the T9 mobile phone technology—also designed by Cliff Kushler and a partner in the 1990s—which made text messaging with a mobile phone's number keys easier by predicting what words were being typed. Swype replaces tapping repeatedly on touch screens with pressing a finger on the screen just once, on a word's first letter, and then swiping the finger in the direction of the next letter and then the next, until the software predicts which word is being spelled.

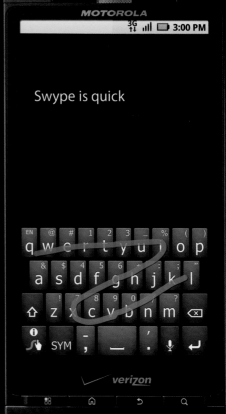

Ross Atkin (British, born 1982)
Innovation Design Engineering
Department (est. 1980)
Royal College of Art (UK, est. 1837) and
Imperial College London (UK, est. 1907)

////////////////////////////

MessSearch. 2009

////////////////////////////

Polystyrene, electronics, RFID reader, and webcam, 11 13/16 × 5 11/16 × 1 13/16" (30 × 14.5 × 4.5 cm)

In his belief that order can emerge from chaos, designer Ross Atkin developed MessSearch, a search tool for a physical desktop that is similar in form and function to a search tool for a digital desktop. The tool is used to tag desktop items, so that a user is able to search for and find them when needed, thus bringing organization to a desk that may seem unmanageable.

# Nervous Systems and Anxious Infrastructures

Jamer Hunt

It starts with a few pixels illuminated in the dark: "I am," a raspy metal voice intones, while the same text scrolls before my eyes.

> "I'm bi."
> And then more silence.
> "I'm off."
> "I am 18m."
> "I am hot."
> Lonely, mechanical voices declare from

the shadows:

> "I'm from Latvia."
> "I am freezin."
> "I'm still used to windows."
> "I am!!"
> Fragments of language fill the visual field,

and the voices, all synthetic, build bit by bit. These soon become waves of messages, filling the void with text clouds, clamorous with self-affirmation. Intermittent beeps fill the silences as swarms of messages whoosh through the space.

> The hair rises on the back of my neck. Suddenly, and for the first time, I can feel—actually feel—the Internet.
> And then all goes quiet again.

Stumbling across Ben Rubin and Mark Hansen's installation Listening Post (2002, fig. 1) is like discovering a hidden portal into the massively distributed World Wide Web. It is a simple configuration—a wall-size, suspended grid of programmable message boards—that displays phrases starting with "I am," drawn from a live Internet data feed. This is the technical back story, but the physical effect is anything but technological. In the darkened space a profound combination of utter loneliness and overwhelming copresence prevails. Isolated voices from everywhere and nowhere call out the simple affirmations of "I am." Alone in the shadows, you experience a shiver that is the uncanny play of presence and absence, many and none—of reaching a hand into cascading streams of data as they ebb and flow and eventually wash over you.

The designed, artificial world that envelops us is coming alive with communicative possibilities. There was a time when our tools of communication were distinct from our bodies: we spoke into a telephone wired into the walls of our home, or we hunted and pecked and clicked at a keyboard to type data into a personal computer. That era is vanishing as quickly as it arrived. Instead we are drifting into a new alignment, in both mind and body, with technology that is far more immersive, encompassing, and confounding. Surrounded by synthetic voices that talk to us and near-invisible sensors that observe and learn us, we are entering an age of uncanny technologies. These animated electronic encounters sketch the contours of an evolving landscape, illuminating the psychological and political implications of our warm, wet embrace of technology. We believe we are deft at negotiating the thinning boundary between human and machine, but in the thrumming traffic we are often left grasping at electronic shadows.

////////////////////////////////////

## Talk

What happens when a complex engineered infrastructure speaks to you? What does it feel like to communicate at a fundamental level with a network? Not just to listen but actually to communicate—to understand the intentionality of its discourse? In the twentieth century Louis I. Kahn famously asked, "What does the building want to be?" In the twenty-first century we must consider a new question and its corollary: What does the ATM want to say . . . and what do you do when it tells you?

The reinvention of our infrastructure has brought us to this new threshold of chattiness. The first phase of infrastructure development, during the rise of the earliest civilizations, consisted of roads, bridges, tunnels, and sewer and water systems. These were mostly feats of large-scale engineering, resulting in physical systems of linear complexity that linked us together, caused cities to explode in growth, and inspired migration on a global scale. In the second phase, copper cables and satellite dishes and then fiber-optic lines, server farms, transponders, and mesh networks catalyzed the flow of ideas, economies, and entertainment over the earth's surface with little connection to national boundaries or places of origin. The interconnection of the two first phases of infrastructure brings us to our present moment, in which we are designing systems that are soft, wet, emergent, and adaptive. We are creating new forms of nonlinear complexity—ecologies, biological systems, fuzzy logic—that can learn, develop, respond, and create. These technologies will be spatialized—that is, they will be everywhere, dispersed into our environment and immediately at our fingertips.

How we "talk" back to our electronic environment is evolving as well. Bound first to the mouthpiece and then to the punch card, keyboard, and mouse, we are now pinching and rotating (iPad), tapping our feet (Multitoe), waving our hands (SixthSense, g-speak), wiggling our retinas (EyeWriter, page 59), and otherwise dancing like honeybees to send messages back and forth. We are recalibrating the techniques of the body, fashioning gestural vocabularies to be used in an environment of ubiquitous computing, virtual reality, sentient computing, ambient intelligence, pervasive adaptation, an internet of things, or whatever other future states technologists dream up for us. In the process we are creating new microlanguages, new

Fig. 2
Jeff Hawkins of Palm, Inc.
Palm Pilot Graffiti. c. 1997

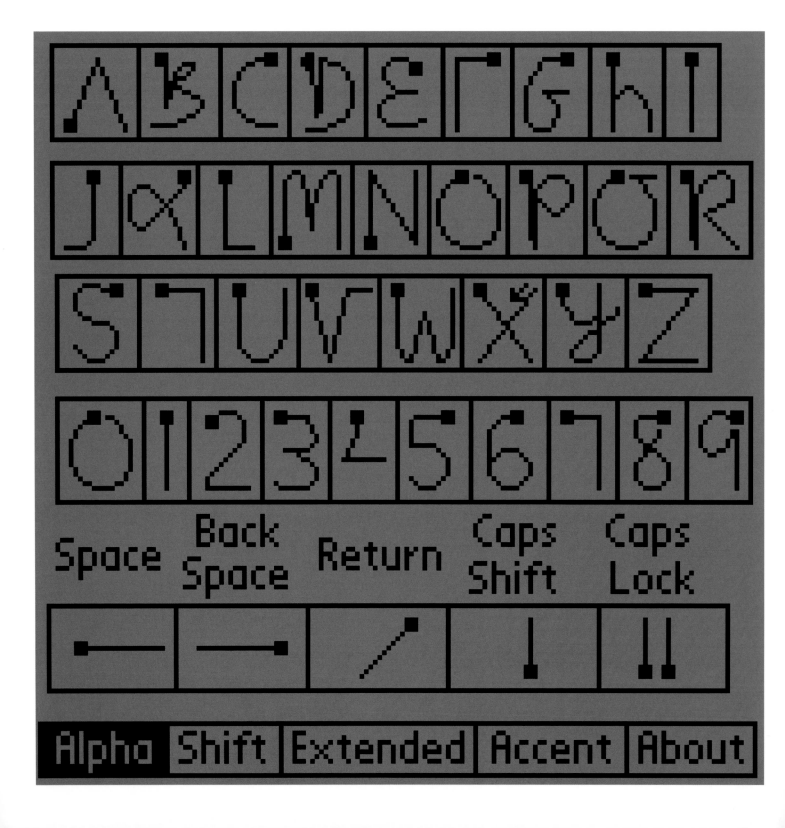

Fig. 3
Sprint PCS.
Claire. 2001

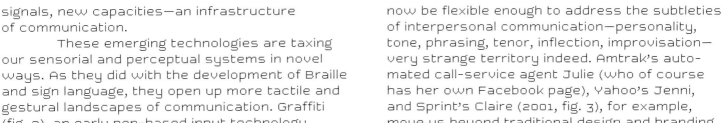

**Hi, I'm Claire, your Sprint PCS virtual Service Representative. I'm here to help you find answers to questions.**

To get started right away, click an item that interests you from the menu on the left.

To see an interactive demonstration about what you can do in this section, click PLAY.

PLAY

signals, new capacities—an infrastructure of communication.

These emerging technologies are taxing our sensorial and perceptual systems in novel ways. As they did with the development of Braille and sign language, they open up more tactile and gestural landscapes of communication. Graffiti (fig. 2), an early pen-based input technology, obliged its users to relearn the written alphabet (the software could not track the letterforms when the stylus was lifted in the middle of a letter), much as shorthand, decades earlier, forced onto our alphabetic system an alien construct that did not accelerate our habits of writing and thus became obsolete. New technologies repeatedly make fresh demands, asking us to learn new gestures, vocalizations, and eye patterns. The enduring ones eventually reconfigure our bodily techniques, transforming how we navigate physical space, focusing what is left of our powers of concentration, even organizing our patterns of thought.

The net impact of these changes has meant a transformation of the designer's job as well. The purview of the designer used to be mostly artifacts: buildings, bedrooms, posters, and toasters. Now it is more process based and includes scripting communication protocols, crafting personas, and inventing electronic surrogates. This means that designers must

now be flexible enough to address the subtleties of interpersonal communication—personality, tone, phrasing, tenor, inflection, improvisation— very strange territory indeed. Amtrak's auto- mated call-service agent Julie (who of course has her own Facebook page), Yahoo's Jenni, and Sprint's Claire (2001, fig. 3), for example, move us beyond traditional design and branding toward the creation of virtual personas capable of responding in real time with lifelike human qualities. And there's more to it; the voices have invented histories as well: Jenni apparently received a degree in art history from Berkeley and wanted a job in an art gallery but currently works as a bartender.[1]

What we say and how we say it may seem like natural and spontaneously occurring phenomena, but they rarely are. We all have strategies and scripts, unwitting combinations of speech that we reflexively deploy in our everyday encounters. This becomes increasingly true as businesses in our information- and service-based economy orchestrate the interac- tions between service employees and customers. Gerard Ralló's Reiterative Communication Aid (2010, page 66) insinuates itself into the tight spaces between unprompted and rote speech, forcing us to reconsider the usefulness of talking at all. This "aid" is a device with a built-in proces- sor that, when it detects familiar banter from an interlocutor, posts a generic reply on a screen worn around a user's neck, thus obviating the need to pay attention to the banalities of everyday conversation. "Most of the conversations we have through our life are redundant," Ralló has observed. "This fact clashes with modern praise of time efficiency and real-time data consumption. This device tracks conversations you have throughout your entire life, analysing your patterns of communication. Eventually, when a repeated pattern is detected, the device is able to replace you in that conversation, allowing you a freedom to explore anything and everything else."[2] While the design is obviously ironic and subversive (its obtrusive form is a giveaway), it is also a sly intervention that, by aping the constant stream of prescripted responses that we face—from the baristas at the coffee shop, from the call-center hotline, from the ticket agent dealing with our exasperated demands for a flight change—acknowledges the instrumental calculus of time, energy, and intention that we make as we navigate these encounters from one day to the next.

It is easy to get carried away by the current of technological determinism and imagine the remarkable leaps forward that these new interactions foreshadow. But we risk ignoring the thornier questions of control, determination, agency, responsibility, and accountability—unknowns that will continue to fog our clear vision of the future. The technological challenges are, perhaps, the easiest to resolve; it will be the ethical, moral, political, and emotional ones that we will continue to wrestle with.

The ubiquity of moments of interaction—of sites of speaking and listening—means that they will increasingly become contested arenas: who will have the power to initiate, respond, and ultimately control the conversation? The designers who plan, choreograph, and implement these interactions will have to subtly calibrate their presence in our lives, or else risk creating a din that drives us all into noise-cancelled, hermitic retreat. And the coming ubiquity of intelligent service agents—the Jennis and Claires of the world—will force us to confront their intentional, humanlike qualities. The conversation will undoubtedly shift in tone, rhetoric, and attitude, as well, as these technological surrogates become more obsequious or persuasive. A moment will arrive when they not only will have learned us but also will be preying on our social vulnerabilities and flattering our most shallow vanities to get what they want. And what do they want?

By now we have also all been unnerved by some well-dressed person on the street who appears to be talking to no one in particular, with the whisper-thin line between sanity and insanity only resolved when we finally catch sight of—or don't—an earpiece attached to one ear. Consider, then, what will become of the theater of our public spaces when we start waving our hands in the air to move screens around or spasmodically twitching and twittering to make our ambient technologies do their everyday work. It is not simply that we will look increasingly like those unhinged solitary wanderers who inhabit our public spaces; we will be creating, working, and playing within conditions that will be almost indistinguishable from mental illness itself, namely the dissolution of ego into space. Phantom screens will buzz and flit before our eyes. Voices will beckon us from all directions—the walls, the floor, our watches, our wallets. Wafting scents will trigger invented memories. Taps on the shoulder, squeezes on the arm, and—who knows?—stolen pats on the rear end will gently remind us, prod us, turn us on. Our own nervous systems will be entangled with other systems both hard and soft, making the untying of this knot even more complicated. We've certainly seen these scenarios before, in novels such as Neuromancer (1984) and films such as The Matrix (1999), but the potential fallout from these interactions and the impact on our psychical landscape have not been fully plumbed. The dissolution of our selves into the increasingly privately owned networks that blanket us will make us more paranoid, less confident that we can securely control or determine the boundaries between I and you, self and other, inside and outside; as we distribute and decentralize our subjectivity into prosthetic agents, we hold onto the hope that we won't lose sight of what distinguished us in the first place.

Anthony Dunne and Fiona Raby's Technological Dreams Series: No.1, Robots (2007, fig.4) explores these intertwined psychical and machinic states, featuring robots that flirt with the nuances of communication—with whom, why, and how. These robots do not do anything in particular, or rather do not do things in the manner in which we've come to expect robots to do things: as "technological cohabitants," as the designers call them, they share our spaces but perform only vexing functions. Robot 2, designed to manifest new behaviors over time, is, according to the designers, "very nervous, so nervous

Fig. 4
Anthony Dunne and Fiona Raby
of Dunne & Raby. Technological
Dreams Series: No. 1, Robots.
2007. Various materials,
dimensions variable

in fact, that as soon as someone enters a room it turns to face them and analyses them with its many eyes. If the person approaches too close it becomes extremely agitated and even hysterical."[3] Robot 4 is "very needy. Although extremely smart it is trapped in an underdeveloped body and depends on its owner to move it about."

     This intelligent but emotionally challenged robot is programmed initially to speak human languages, but it also has the capacity to evolve linguistically, so that "you can still hear human traces in its voice."[4] In other words, these robots come with cognitive and psychological dispositions that have nothing to do with problem solving and utility. They need us very deeply and yet they are fast forgetting about us, creating new languages that bear mere traces of our own. They are confounding in their irrationality and unpredictability. But the most troubling question that these objects raise is that of subjectivity: if the Robots have emotional capabilities, do they thus have souls?

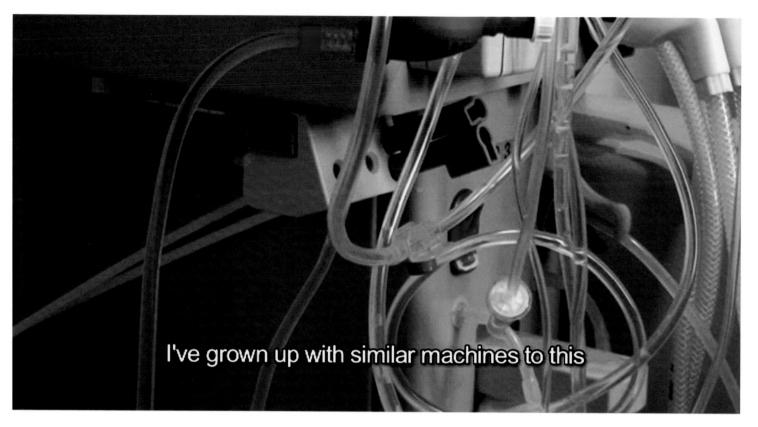

I've grown up with similar machines to this

Fig. 5
Revital Cohen. Design
Interactions Department,
Royal College of Art. The
Posthuman Condition. 2008.
Video (color, sound), 5:30 min.

/////////////////////////////////////////////////

Me

How can it be more human?
—The Future of Self-Service Banking[5]

I currently have nearly four thousand e-mails in my in-box.
Why? Because I might need to recall any one of them at some
future moment. My in-box has become my prosthetic memory,
freeing up space in my brain and releasing me from having
to commit to memory all those fussy details. In a similar
vein, I now think in terms of windows, sorting my daily tasks
into discrete panels. My operating system has infected my
cognitive processes, substituting machine operations for
human thought. There are ticklish psychological dimensions
to this that we had better not ignore.
        Revital Cohen's beautiful and meditative short film
The Posthuman Condition (2008, fig. 5) captures this self-
tightening knot in hyperreal detail, stepping back from specula-
tion and wandering deeply into the life-and-death implications
of our embrace of technology. The film is an interview with
long-term dialysis patients that shows, instead of the patients,
the machines that drain and recycle their blood. One disem-
bodied voice alludes to the machines whirring and humming in
the background, saying, "This is part of my body ... it's there
all the time"; another, describing the unpredictable quivering
of the machine's tubes, says, "You can almost see the blood
almost pulsing, and even the pressure gauge twitches a little
bit, the lines twitch as though they are alive."[6] Whether
we choose to plug in or not, our coupling with machines has
changed us, blurring the neat divide between us and them.

Science historian and theorist Donna Haraway, exploring the dissolution of this boundary as far back as 1985, prophetically declared, "Late twentieth-century machines have made thoroughly ambiguous the difference between natural and artificial, mind and body, self-developing and externally designed.... Our machines are disturbingly lively, and we ourselves frighteningly inert."[7]

It is worth pausing on the phrase "disturbingly lively." Sigmund Freud explored this precise disposition in his essay on the complex psychology of the uncanny. For Freud it was a term that described a sort of "creeping horror" or, more specifically, "that class of the terrifying which leads back to something long known to us, once very familiar."[8] It is a very particular feeling: the onset of dread in the presence of the almost familiar, in the haunting of the known by the unknown. Referring to Ernst Jentsch's earlier essay on the same subject, Freud continued, "Jentsch has taken as a very good instance 'doubts whether an apparently animate being is really alive; or conversely, whether a lifeless object might not be in fact animate'; and he refers in this connection to the impression made by wax-work, artificial dolls, and automatons. He adds to this class the uncanny effect of epileptic seizures and the manifestations of insanity, because these excite in the spectator the feeling that automatic, mechanical processes are at work, concealed beneath the ordinary appearance of animation."[9]

Poised at a shifting boundary between categories, Freud's uncanny aptly describes our present condition. What is lacking in Freud's analysis, however, is a reckoning with its politics. As we struggle with the creepy blur of the indistinct, our interactions are doubly fraught; they snare us in complex webs of global, privatized networks, where meaning, agency, and access are critical dimensions of human action. It will be important to keep our critical faculties and reflexes sharp in order to avoid ceding our social and political agency to invisible corporate entities.

Through this and other jostling interactions with sentient devices, we are unsettling the neat distinctions between humans and machines, us and them, public and private, and lively and inert. The uncanny—that disorienting, queasy apperception of some trouble hovering at the fluid boundary between categorical absolutes—may infect our relationship to these chatty technologies for some time. And as our "lifeless" networks come to life, as our ATMs become more "human," as we lose ourselves in the maw of adaptive systems, we risk the anxious dread of an uncanny everyday.

Notes

1.    Ian Urbina, "Your Train Will Be Late, She Says Cheerily," New York Times, November 24, 2004, www.nytimes.com/2004/11/24/nyregion/24voice.html.

2.    "Reiterative Communication Aid," GerardRalló, www.ideesabsurdes.net/wordpress/?p=367.

3.    "Technological Dreams Series: No.1, Robots," Dunne & Raby, www.dunneandraby.co.uk/content/projects/10/0.

4.    Ibid.

5.    The Future of Self-Service Banking, www.futureselfservicebanking.com. The Spanish bank BBVA worked with the design consultancy IDEO to explore new ways of designing the interaction between a user and an ATM in order to create a more "human" experience for bank customers (see page 44).

6.    "The Posthuman Condition," Revital Cohen, www.revitalcohen.com/project/the-posthuman-condition.

7.    Donna Haraway, "A Manifesto for Cyborgs: Science, Technology, and Socialist Feminism in the 1980s," in Elizabeth Weed, ed., Coming to Terms: Feminism, Theory, Politics (New York: Routledge, 1989), pp. 174–76; quoted in Anthony Vidler, The Architectural Uncanny: Essays in the Modern Unhomely (Cambridge, Mass.: MIT Press, 1994), p. 148.

8.    Sigmund Freud, "The Uncanny," 1919, in Studies in Parapsychology, ed. by Philip Rieff, trans. by Alix Strachey (New York: Collier Books, 1963), p. 20.

9.    Ibid., p. 31.

With another step up in scale, we move from the communication between people and objects to the communication between people by means of objects. The human body and mind are the central agents and subjects of study in this chapter, expressing and explaining themselves in ways previously unthinkable.

Some of the concepts and prototypes featured here are quintessential products of our time, mixing sarcasm and malaise about interpersonal communication with curiosity and an eagerness to overcome these obstacles creatively. Some alarmists fear that our reliance on digital communication has created a society that, despite exchanging information and thoughts around the clock in blogs and on social networks, can no longer articulate ideas and emotions; several of the design hypotheses that follow were generated to compensate for this inability, whether psychological or physical. At human scale, critical design is at its brightest, with highly concep-tual—albeit also highly descriptive—scenarios that explore the possible benefits and probable impacts of new technologies, often using dystopian conditions to heighten the questions' urgency. From Sascha Nordmeyer's plastic smile prosthesis for the socially awk-ward (page 64) to Gerard Ralló's range of communication interfaces that address the problems of the socially inept (pages 66–67), design-ers have been quick in pointing out the simultaneous absurdity and poetry of our present condition and of the possible remedies.

Not all the projects are speculative; some are exquisitely pragmatic, and the one prompted by the most urgent conditions is also the most lyrical: EyeWriter (page 59)—an interface that enables a paralyzed graffiti artist to tag buildings with his eyes—demonstrates that necessity and emergency can give rise not simply to particular solutions for extreme individual cases but rather to breakthroughs for society at large. This is not the only time that an idea developed to address a disability has provided the world with increased abilities. Digital technology follows the same historical rule.

Social networks are obviously critical to any discussion about technology-enabled interpersonal communication, but in a design catalogue, they appear as cause for design, not as subject. Although they so far have been particularly design impaired, they have provided several artists with opportunities for provocative meta-phors and visions, as in Hans Hemmert's platform attachments that make everyone the same height (page 70) and in the fluid collective game Tentacles (page 71).

P. A.

The texts in this chapter were written by Kate Carmody.

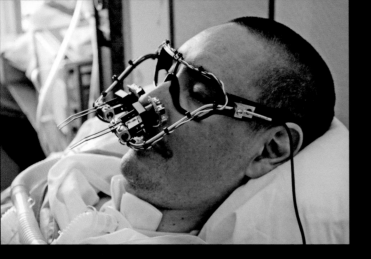

Zach Lieberman (American, born 1977),
James Powderly (American, born 1976),
Evan Roth (American, born 1978),
Chris Sugrue (American, born 1978),
TEMPT1 (American), and Theo Watson
(British, born 1981)

///////////////////////////

EyeWriter. 2009

///////////////////////////

openFrameworks and custom software,
eyeglasses, PlayStation Eye Camera,
IR pass filter, IR LEDs, battery clip,
resistor, zip ties, and flexible metal wire,
7 3/4 × 5 7/8 × 1 7/8" (20 × 15 × 5 cm)

In 2003 TEMPT1, a Los Angeles–based
graffiti artist and activist, was diagnosed
with amyotrophic lateral sclerosis (ALS),
which soon left him entirely paralyzed
except for his eyes. The EyeWriter
research project was born as a collaboration among TEMPT1, the members
of Free Art & Technology (FAT) lab, the
openFrameworks community, and Graffiti
Research Lab (GRL), with support from
the Ebeling Group production company,
the Not Impossible Foundation, and the
MFA Design and Technology program
at Parsons The New School for Design,
New York. The team equipped a pair of
inexpensive eyeglasses with eye-tracking
technology and custom-developed
software that could capture TEMPT1's
eye movements. From his hospital room,
wirelessly connected to a laptop and
laser-tagging apparatus installed in
downtown LA, the artist can paint graffiti
tags in color, which are then projected
at a superhuman scale in real time—
so that viewers see the glowing tag as

it is created—on buildings. The hardware,
software, and assembly instructions are
in the public domain, so that the power
of these creative technologies is widely
available, eventually leading to a network
of, as the designers envision, "software
developers, hardware hackers, urban
projection artists and ALS patients from
around the world who are using local
materials and open-source research to
creatively connect and make eye art."

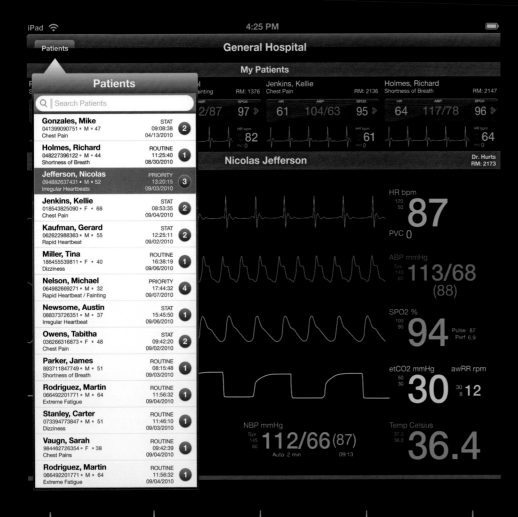

Trey Moore (American, born 1972)
and Kory Brown (American, born 1970)
of AirStrip Technologies (USA, est. 2004)

/////////////////////////////

AirStrip Patient Monitoring. 2010

/////////////////////////////

Custom software

AirStrip Patient Monitoring, a mobile-
device application, allows doctors and
other health care professionals to keep
track of patients from wherever they
are, providing real-time data about
a patient's status over a wireless
network. In an emergency, a plan can
be put into effect immediately, without
having to wait for the doctor to arrive
at the hospital to give directions. AirStrip
Technologies first gained recognition
in 2009 with AirStrip OB, an app for
real-time fetal-heartbeat monitoring.

James King (British, born 1982)
and Alexandra Daisy Ginsberg
(British, born 1982)
with iGEM 2009 Team
University of Cambridge
(UK, est. 1209)

////////////////////////////

E. chromi. 2009

////////////////////////////

Paraffin wax, aluminum, and polyethylene foam, acrylic case: 13 3/8 × 17 1/4 × 4 3/4" (34 × 43.8 × 12.1 cm)

The E. chromi project is the result of a collaboration between Royal College of Art Design Interactions graduates James King and Alexandra Daisy Ginsberg and the iGEM (International Genetically Engineered Machine) 2009 Team of the University of Cambridge. iGEM is a yearly competition, held at the Massachusetts Institute of Technology, in Cambridge, Massachusetts, between undergraduate student teams working in the field of synthetic biology. Synthetic biology is an area of scientific research focused on the possibility of redesigning, engineering, and constructing entirely new biological systems. The iGEM Team of the University of Cambridge, for example, took E. coli, bacteria found in the human gut (and generally harmless; only a few strains are dangerous enough to cause illness and death), and altered them so that they would change color when exposed to various chemicals produced by the body in the presence of different pathological conditions. King and Ginsberg collaborated with the team on potential applications for the engineered bacteria. The outcome was a new diagnostic system called E. chromi: a straightforward method, using the body's natural output, of visualizing a patient's internal conditions. The patient ingests a drink, much like a probiotic shake, laced with the engineered E. coli; the bacteria react with the enzymes, proteins, and other chemicals that are present in the gastrointestinal tract and turn different colors for different diseases, thus changing the color of the patient's feces. These colors are presented in King and Ginsberg's Scatalog, a collection of samples in a briefcase that demonstrate an array of E. chromi results in immediate visual terms. The designers give us access to the complex networks and systems of the human body.

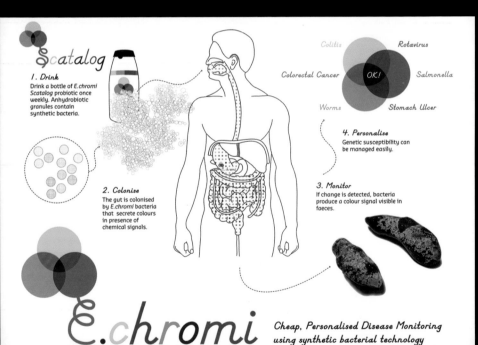

Scatalog

1. Drink
Drink a bottle of E.chromi Scatalog probiotic once weekly. Anhydrobiotic granules contain synthetic bacteria.

2. Colonise
The gut is colonised by E.chromi bacteria that secrete colours in presence of chemical signals.

3. Monitor
If change is detected, bacteria produce a colour signal visible in faeces.

4. Personalise
Genetic susceptibility can be managed easily.

Colitis — Rotavirus
Colorectal Cancer — OK! — Salmonella
Worms — Stomach Ulcer

E.chromi
Cheap, Personalised Disease Monitoring using synthetic bacterial technology

2009
Living Colour
E. chromi is a kit of BioBricks. Each part can modify E. coli bacteria to secrete one of six different colours. E. chromi uses the 2009 International Genetically Engineered Machine Competition.

2010
Arsenic Detector
Using E. chromi, the first biosensors appear for cheap testing of drinking water in the developing world.

2015
Colour Hunters
From canary-yellow M&Ms to melanin-coloured Coke, food colourings are made by bacteria. Professional Colour Hunters scour the biosphere, collecting genes that generate rare pigments to sell to industry.

2039
The Scatalog
Cheap, personalised disease monitoring now works from the inside out. Ingested as yoghurt, E. chromi colonise the gut. The bacteria keep watch for chemical markers of diseases and can produce easy-to-read warning signals.

O.L.F.
FREE THE RAINBOW
2049
Orange Liberation Front
A Dutch terrorist group protests against the patenting of their natural colour, orange. The OLF are threatening to detonate an antibiotic bomb at London Fashion Week, killing all colour in orange.

2069
Red Sky in the Morning. Google Health Warning
Google releases pollution-mapping bacteria that colour the sky red in zones of excess carbon dioxide. Diplomatic workers erupt as they drift across international airspace.

Marie-Virginie Berbet (French, born 1979)

/////////////////////////////

Little Black Box. Empathy Box. 2008

/////////////////////////////

PMMA, light-diffusion-control film, LEDs, and plethysmographic sensor, 7 3/8 × 9 1/4 × 7 1/4" (19 × 23.6 × 18.3 cm)

The Little Black Box, inspired by biofeedback techniques and named for a device in a Philip K. Dick story, visualizes our biological rhythms based on heart rate variability (HRV) and helps us control them. Marie-Virginie Berbet posits that this technology can be used to manage stress, eliminate sleep disorders, or enhance athletic performance, among other applications. Berbet cites research suggesting that HRV may demonstrate the mutual influence between brain and heart: interaction between the two plays a large role in regulating bodily functions, with changes in emotion reflected in changes in heart rhythm. Conversely, emotional states can be changed, for example, by using breathing exercises to modify the heart rate. A fingertip sensor detects a user's HRV, and the box then coordinates its light pulses and vibrations in time with it. The pulsing light can also be used to modify—rather than simply display—the HRV, by being programmed to slowly change, visually suggesting a variation in breathing pattern that the user can eventually generate without help. The inner state is thus externalized, bringing, as the designer says, the "feeling of the heart beating into the hands" and "[generating] a kind of self-empathy ... a singular interaction between [the] user and his own feelings."

Rizwan Bashirullah (Venezuelan, born 1974) and Hong Yu (Chinese, born 1977) of the Department of Electrical and Computer Engineering (est. 1910)
Christopher Batich (American, born 1943) of the Department of Materials Science and Engineering (est. 1959)
University of Florida (USA, est. 1905)
Neil Euliano (American, born 1964) of eTect, LLC (USA, est. 2009)

/////////////////////////////

Swallow-Signaling Pill (opposite, top left). 2010

/////////////////////////////

Hard gelatin capsule, biocompatible silver conductive ink, and silicon semiconductor chip, 7/8" (2.3 cm) high, 1/4" (0.9 cm) diam.

—

David Rose (American, born 1967) of Vitality (USA, est. 2004)

/////////////////////////////

GlowCap (opposite, top right). 2010

/////////////////////////////

ABS, bottle cap: 4 3/4 × 2 × 2" (12 × 5 × 5 cm); night light: 4 7/8 × 3 3/4 × 2 3/8" (12.5 × 9.5 × 6 cm)
Manufactured by Vitality, USA

Numerous studies tell us that patients are often unreliable about taking medications, both in clinical trials and in the treatment of chronic illness. With this in mind, the team of researchers behind the Swallow-Signaling Pill envisioned a "tattletale pill" prototype made of two separate parts: the pill itself, equipped with a tiny microchip and a digestible antenna, and an electronic device that communicates with it and can be integrated into a watch or mobile phone. The patient's device sends signals to a receiver kept by a doctor or family member, letting them know that the pill has been taken. The pill is powered by infinitesimal bursts of low-voltage electricity and requires no battery; the patient's stomach acid breaks down the antenna, and the microchip is passed through the gastrointestinal tract. David Rose has tackled the same issue with his GlowCap system, which employs both reminders for the patient and communication with pharmacies and doctors to ensure that prescription medication is taken properly. GlowCaps fit most standard prescription bottles and, once programmed, use light and sound to signal when it is time to take a pill. The GlowCap knows when the pill bottle has been opened and keeps track of the bottle's status via a wireless network. If the bottle is not opened at prescribed times, the patient receives a reminder by phone. GlowCaps also communicate with pharmacies about medication refills and send regular e-mail updates to family, caregivers, or doctors.

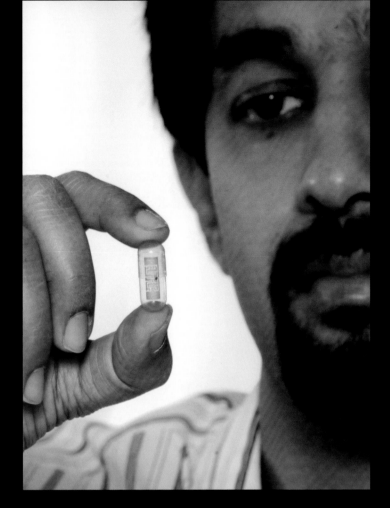

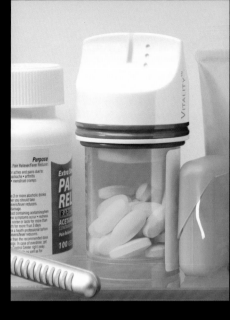

Department of Polytronic Systems
(est. 2001)
Fraunhofer EMFT (Germany, est. 1949)

////////////////////////////

Personal Health Assistant. 2010

////////////////////////////

Polyimide film, printed circuit board,
and electroluminescent pastes,
10 x 1 5/8 x 3/4" (25.5 x 4 x 1.9 cm)

Scientists at Fraunhofer, a German
research organization, are experimenting
with applications of smart plastics—
polymers impregnated with electronic
sensors that can monitor body functions
and respond to environmental changes.
The Personal Health Assistant, a sensor-
equipped wristband, has the potential
to be used in a variety of health care and
sports applications, such as detecting
and notifying pacemaker patients
of potentially damaging electronic
interference or warning athletes of
rising body temperature and impending
dehydration. The wristband's electroluminescent display automatically exhibits
information. The Personal Health
Assistant combines everyday products
with cost-efficient electronics and
demonstrates the possibilities for

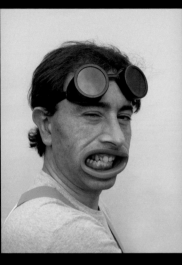
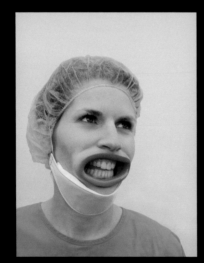

Sascha Nordmeyer (German and French, born Germany 1977)

////////////////////////////

Communication Prosthesis Portrait Series (Cyclist, Actress, Chef, Craftsman, Midwife, Politician, Model). 2009

////////////////////////////

Prosthesis: lacquered resin, 2 x 3 11/16 x 1 13/16" x (5.1 x 9.3 x 3 cm); photographs, each: 16 1/2 x 12 3/8" (42 x 31.5 cm)

This rigid prosthesis, shown in a series of portraits, covers the lips and exposes the gums, making communication easier and more explicit by forcing automatic facial expressions, almost grimaces. It was conceived for people who feel insecure about their appearance and their social skills and are therefore compelled to be excessively smart and communicative in every circumstance. As often happens with timid people, awkwardness is replaced by aggressiveness, and the exaggerated teeth-baring smile is a safe conversation-stopper.

Jonas Loh (German, born 1981)
Design Interactions Department
(est. 1989)
Royal College of Art (UK, est. 1837)

/////////////////////////////

Amæ Apparatus. 2010

/////////////////////////////

Aluminum, wood, leather, galvanic skin
response (GSR) sensor, smoke grenade,
switch, and glass tube, 13 3/4 × 7 7/8
× 5 1/2" (35 × 20 × 14 cm)

The suppression of feelings in the
workplace in the hope of greater
professional success, notes designer
Jonas Loh, has led to unusually high
rates of employee suicide; a particularly
troubling statistic comes from France
Télécom, where twenty-three employees
ended their lives over the span of
eighteen months in 2008 and 2009.
To counteract this stifling and dangerous
social conundrum, Loh created the Amæ
Apparatus, which makes a person's
feelings explicit. Loh calls it an early-
warning system for stressed-out people,
soliciting sympathy and allowing assistance to be provided in a timely manner.
Amæ, whose name comes from a subtle
Japanese concept describing the desire
for attention and care from a person
of authority, is worn like a backpack
and interprets the wearer's stress
levels through a skin sensor; color-coded
smoke erupts from a spout in a canister
to alert coworkers to various emotional
states.

Gerard Ralló (Spanish, born 1984)
Design Interactions Department
(est. 1989)
Royal College of Art
(UK, est. 1837)

////////////////////////////

Devices for Mindless Communication.
2010

////////////////////////////

Reiterative Communication Aid (top)
Acrylic and electronics, 7 × 10 1/4
× 12 5/8" (19 × 26 × 32 cm)

Personal Adviser for Reintegration
(center)
Acrylic and electronics, 8 1/4 × 11 3/8
× 13 3/8" (21 × 29 × 34 cm)

Conversation Challenger (bottom)
Acrylic and electronics, display:
3 × 6 3/4 × 3 1/4" (7.5 × 17 × 8.4 cm);
device: 3 × 2 5/8 × 3 7/8" (7.5 × 6.6
× 10 cm)

Gerard Ralló imagines what sort of help
we will need with communication in the
future as certain skills are strengthened
by developing technology and others
erode. The Reiterative Communication
Aid addresses the fact that we would
be better off without most of the idle
conversations we find ourselves dragged
into. The device, worn around the neck
and displaying a screen, tracks the
wearer's conversations over time; once
a back-and-forth pattern is established,
the screen provides automatic answers
to mundane questions so the wearer
does not need to. Conversely, the
Personal Adviser for Reintegration
preserves the habit of what the designer
calls "sporadic, banal conversations
with no aim behind them" for future
generations who have lost the ability
to engage in small talk. It, too, is worn
around the neck, with the display screen
positioned so the wearer can quickly
read prompts for benign topics and tepid
questions, thus ensuring the survival
of polite conversation without requiring
the user to think. The Conversation
Challenger embodies the designer's
theory that our access to unlimited
information will cause us to lose interest
in each other as human beings. The
device listens to a conversation and
offers related content culled from the
Internet, forcing a choice between
another person and the machine. With
it, the designer asks if it is "really possible
for someone [to] be more interesting
than everything else?"; the Conversation
Challenger's answer is generally "no."

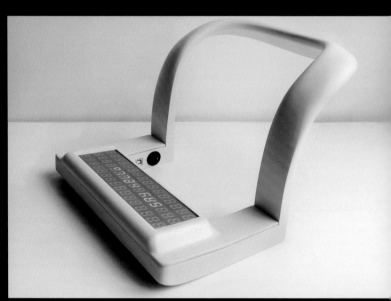

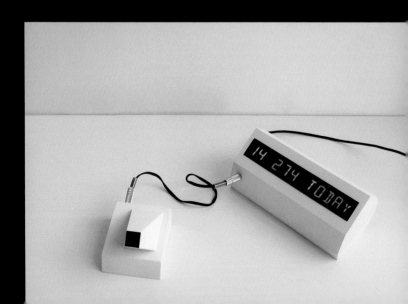

Gerard Ralló (Spanish, born 1984)
Design Interactions Department
(est. 1989)
Royal College of Art
(UK, est. 1837)

//////////////////////////

Expressions Dispatcher. 2009

//////////////////////////

Aluminum, acrylic, foam, fabric, and electronics, helmet: 11 3/4 × 8 7/8 × 12 3/4" (30 × 22.6 × 32.5 cm); remote control: 3 7/8 × 3 1/2 × 1 1/4" (10 × 9 × 3.5 cm)

Gerard Ralló's Expressions Dispatcher puts our reactions to daily situations into the hands of someone else—a life coach of sorts. The device is a two-part system—a helmet equipped with a screen that covers the wearer's face and displays various emoticons, and a remote control device in the hands of an expert who follows the wearer around and has complete power over which emotions are displayed. The responsibility for creating our self-image and how we are perceived is thus passed to an individual who is removed from our immediate emotional state and can analyze an appropriate response.

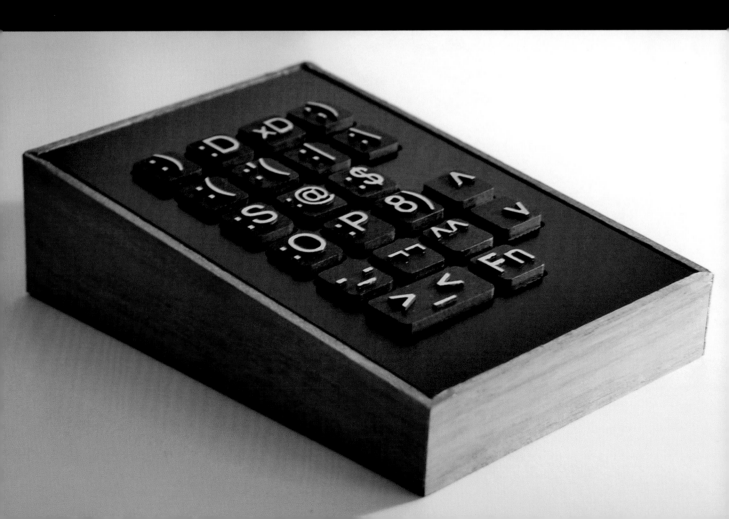

Gunnar Green (German, born 1978)
Design Interactions Department
(est. 1989)
Royal College of Art (UK, est. 1837)

///////////////////////////

Call Me, Choke Me. 2008

///////////////////////////

Leather, aluminum, plastic, and
electronics, 1 1/2 × 6 1/4 × 5 7/8"
(4 × 16 × 15 cm)

This device, a collar designed to be
worn around the neck, ties mobile-
phone activity to the practice of erotic
asphyxiation. With each phone call or
text message, whether or not it is picked
up or responded to, the collar tightens.
The callers and senders are unaware of
the game but still part of it. The pleasure
and pain of being constantly sought
after—normally expressed with frequent
neurotic glances at our device screens
and by hypocritical and empty complaints
about feeling drained—are embodied
by Gunnar Green in a sadomasochistic
contraption that subtly demonstrates
one of the tenets of contemporary
interaction. The wearer can loosen
the collar at any time by pulling a string.

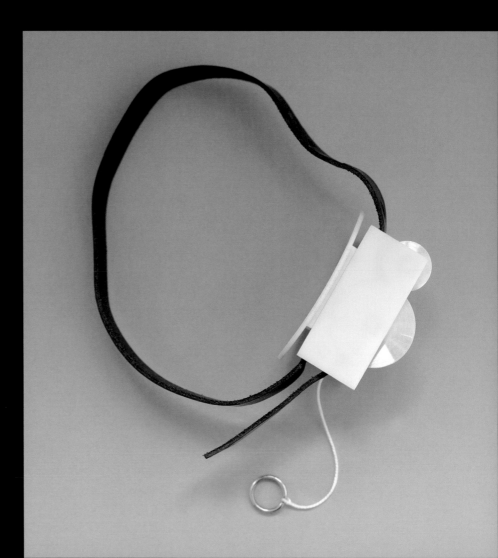

Key Portilla-Kawamura (Spanish
and Japanese, born Spain 1979),
Ali Ganjavian (Azerbaijani and
Iranian, born Iran 1979), and Pablo
Carrascal (Spanish, born 1984)
of kawamura-ganjavian
(Spain, est. 2006)

////////////////////////////////

Earshell. 2010

////////////////////////////////

Polypropylene, 1 1/2 × 3 1/8 × 3 3/4"
(3.9 × 8 × 9.4 cm)

"We [have used] earrings as symbols
of distinction since time immemorial,"
the designers of kawamura-ganjavian
tell us, "however they are not particularly
useful items." In response they have
designed the Earshell—a sound-
enhancement device that is also an
elegant adornment and dramatizes the
interest of the listener.

Adi Marom (Israeli, born 1974)
Interactive Telecommunications Program
(est. 1979)
Tisch School of the Arts (est. 1965)
New York University (USA, est. 1831)

////////////////////////////////

Short++. 2010

////////////////////////////////

Aluminum, electronics, and Arduino
and HTML software, elevated: 7 × 4 3/4
× 9 1/2" (17.8 × 12 × 24.1 cm)

Designs by Adi Marom and Hans Hemmert
(following page) explore how daily
functions and especially face-to-face
communication can change simply by
tweaking and tinkering with people's
height. Marom's robotic footwear extends
and contracts via an iPhone application,
so that the wearer becomes taller or
shorter to fit various needs and moods—
from reaching a higher supermarket shelf
to smelling a flower on a tree branch;
height thus becomes what the designer
calls an "interactive variable."

Hans Hemmert (German, born 1960)

///////////////////////////////

Level. 1997

///////////////////////////////

Polystyrene, rubber, and Velcro,
1 1/2–19 5/8" (4–50 cm) high

Hans Hemmert's shoe extenders,
produced in various heights, make
everyone 6 1/2 feet (2 meters) tall.
The extenders made their debut
at an event thrown in conjunction
with <u>Personal Absurdities</u>, a 1997
exhibition at the Galerie Gebauer
Berlin. At that party, everyone saw
eye to eye.

Michael Longford (Canadian, born 1960)
of Mobile Media Lab (est. 2007)
York University (Canada, est. 1959)
Geoffrey Shea (Canadian, born 1958)
of Mobile Experience Lab (est. 2006)
Ontario College of Art and Design
(Canada, est. 1876)
Rob King (Canadian, born 1982)
of Canadian Film Centre Media Lab
(Canada, est. 1997)

////////////////////////////

Tentacles 1.0. 2009

////////////////////////////

Objective-C and Processing software

Tentacles is a multiplayer game designed
to be played in a public space on a giant
screen that displays players' locations
via iPhone or iPod touch. Players begin
the game in the dark at the bottom of the
ocean, each controlling a squidlike form
evolving out of the primordial ooze and
hunting for life-sustaining microorganisms
called tenticules. As each creature eats,
it grows and is confronted with other
growing creatures, representing other
players, that can steal its tentacles and
deprive it of nutrients. Players must make
a choice, the designers say, to "'share'
or 'scare'"—to decide if they are out for
themselves or willing to be part of the
larger whole, making for a dynamic and
philosophical public game.

Revital Cohen (Israeli, born 1981)
Design Interactions Department
(est. 1989)
Royal College of Art (UK, est. 1837)

/////////////////////////////

Phantom Recorder. 2010

/////////////////////////////

Glass, leather, electronics, and steam,
11 3/4 × 19 3/4 × 13 3/4" (30 × 50
× 35 cm)

Revital Cohen designs speculative,
metaphysical objects that examine the
relationship between the natural and
artificial. The Phantom Recorder explores
the phenomenon of the phantom limb: an
amputee's sensation that a missing limb
is still attached to the body and functioning. "The phantom owner is suddenly
endowed with a unique and personal
appendage," Cohen explains, "invisible
to others and sometimes capable of
extraordinary hyperabilities." This
physical hallucination is often treated
as a hindrance and corrected through
therapy, but Cohen feels that attempts
to alleviate it "tend to overlook poetic
functions of our body." What if, she
wonders, the sensation could be har-
nessed and used at will? The conceptual
interface Cohen created in response to
this inquiry would connect the part of the
brain that thinks it is controlling the
missing limb to electrodes in a neural-
implant device. This device could be
activated to record or cause particular
sensations. The potential for new
ways to understand the communication
between mind and body goes further,
Cohen says: "Could we use this
technology to record illusions of the
mind? What if our imagination could
be captured through our nerves?"

Revital Cohen (Israeli, born 1981)
Design Interactions Department
(est. 1989)
Royal College of Art (UK, est. 1837)

/////////////////////////////

Artificial Biological Clock. 2008

/////////////////////////////

Glass, resin, nickel-plated brass, and
electronics, 5 7/8 × 6 3/4 × 5 7/8"
(15 × 17 × 15 cm)

Revital Cohen addresses the contentious
subject of modern reproductive technology with her Artificial Biological Clock.
In vitro fertilization and related methods,
she explains, are making it hard to retain
a realistic view of how long a woman may
put off childbearing. Here Cohen con-
trasts natural and artificial by highlighting
contemporary social pressures and
expectations that dictate a woman's
reproductive vitality, rather than her
natural body rhythms. In past eras
women's bodies and reproductive cycles
were thought to be in harmony with the
lunar cycle—if this ever was true, it is
no longer so, Cohen theorizes, because
of "artificial light and contraceptive
hormones." She says that "along
with the growing pressure to develop
a career," habits of modern life are
"distorting the body's reproductive
signals." A woman no longer in touch
with her body's rhythms could rely on
the Artificial Biological Clock to remind
her of her fertility's "temporary and
fragile nature." The clock is fed information via an online service from her doctor,
therapist, and bank manager. When
these complex factors align perfectly,
the clock lets her know that she is
ready to have a child.

/////////////////////////////

## 3

Pear wood, glass, resin, gold-plated
brass, powder-coated steel, and
acrylic tubing, 12 5/8 × 9 1/8 × 11 3/4"
(32 × 23 × 30 cm)

and also including a Guilt Adjustor,
speaks to the emotional and psychological effects of the potentially devastating
genetic information we now have access
to. The Disclosure Case, which makes
reference to one of the key ethical
issues raised by genetic profiling, allows
potential inheritors of a trait to decide
for themselves if they want to know
their fate; traditional heirlooms of
precious metals, an echo of recent
treatments for cancer that have relied
on gold and silver, are kept alongside
audio messages from relatives that
disclose inherited genetic traits. This
box, inspired by Pandora's, is left for
the next generation to open.

Designers search for the meaning of life in their own empirical and suggestive ways. Some narrate life from birth to death—as Jason Rohrer does in his oh-so-short video game Passage (page 76)—and others zero in on the most minute and mundane moments, such as toothbrushing or procrastinating—as Benjamin Dennel does in his witty poster (page 79) and David McCandless does in his Hierarchy of Digital Distractions (page 78). No task is too menial and no ritual is too unassuming when it comes to a deeper understanding of our position in the universe; relived and visualized, even small gestures acquire a dramatic humanity when elevated by design.

The question of the meaning of life is so enormous and profound—and life itself so difficult to perceive, moving quickly from the endless summers of youth to maturity—that we must rely on synthesis and description, qualities characteristic of visualization design, in order to capture its amazing range. Scientists and statisticians have long used visualization design to make sense of complex behaviors gathered in large data sets; here, designers employ it to help us make sense of the ultimate mystery.

In some cases this daunting task is approached through narrative, such as Christien Meindertsma and Julie Joliat's gripping bound documentary, PIG 05049 (page 82), a deadpan investigation of the deconstruction and afterlife of a slaughtered pig. In its apparent lack of ideology, PIG 05049 says more about the inscrutability of corporations, the dangers and nasty surprises lurking in products, the adulteration of consumer society, and humanity's loss of innocence than any sermon or proclamation would. PostSecret (page 86) lets us peek into the darkest corners of the human soul. In this mail-based project, people unload their deepest secrets anonymously, expecting neither judgment nor absolution. The haikulike confessions have the power to haunt the readers much as they have haunted the individuals who contributed them.

When data gathering and interpretation are not enough, designers turn to religion. The thoughtful projects at the end of this chapter connect religious practices and rituals with contemporary technology, which is either embraced or rejected. Along with the major religions considered here—Christianity, Islam, and Judaism—designers also consider science, another belief that requires a leap of faith.

P. A.

The texts in this chapter were written by Kate Carmody.

5

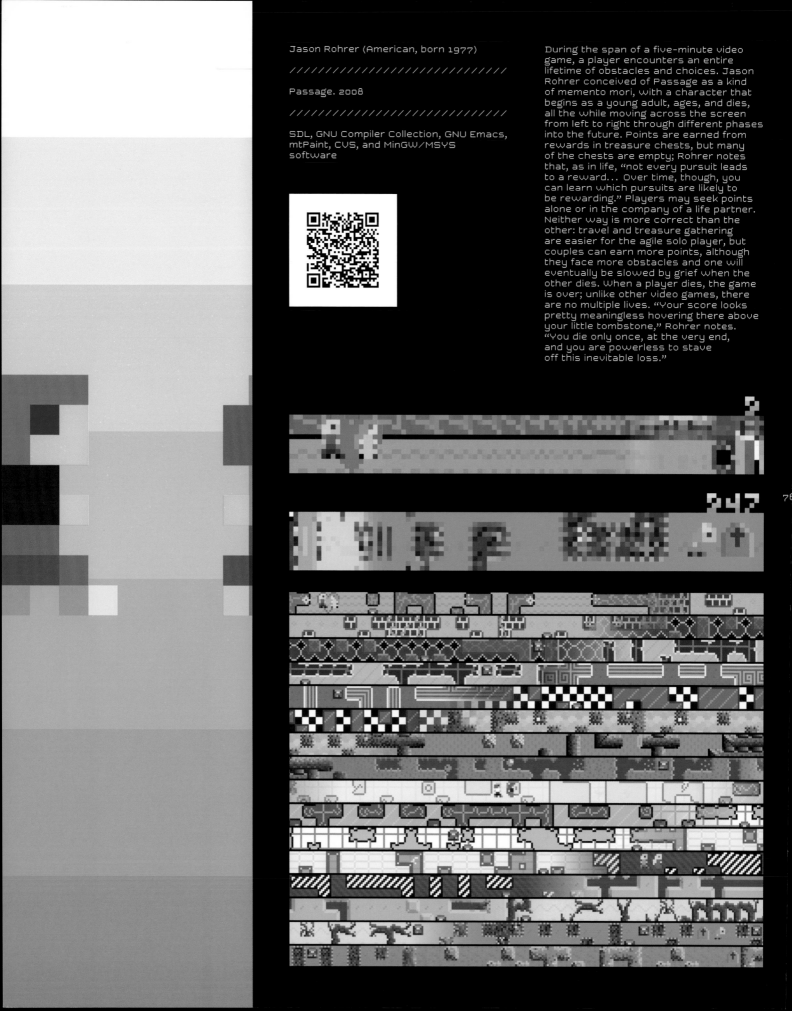

Jason Rohrer (American, born 1977)

//////////////////////////////

Passage. 2008

//////////////////////////////

SDL, GNU Compiler Collection, GNU Emacs, mtPaint, CVS, and MinGW/MSYS software

During the span of a five-minute video game, a player encounters an entire lifetime of obstacles and choices. Jason Rohrer conceived of Passage as a kind of memento mori, with a character that begins as a young adult, ages, and dies, all the while moving across the screen from left to right through different phases into the future. Points are earned from rewards in treasure chests, but many of the chests are empty; Rohrer notes that, as in life, "not every pursuit leads to a reward... Over time, though, you can learn which pursuits are likely to be rewarding." Players may seek points alone or in the company of a life partner. Neither way is more correct than the other: travel and treasure gathering are easier for the agile solo player, but couples can earn more points, although they face more obstacles and one will eventually be slowed by grief when the other dies. When a player dies, the game is over; unlike other video games, there are no multiple lives. "Your score looks pretty meaningless hovering there above your little tombstone," Rohrer notes. "You die only once, at the very end, and you are powerless to stave off this inevitable loss."

Nicholas Felton (American, born 1977)

////////////////////////////

The 2009 Feltron Annual Report. 2010

////////////////////////////

Four-color letterpress, 10 x 8"
(25.4 x 20.3 cm)

Every year since 2005, Nicholas Felton has produced a report about himself based on his life's quantifiable experiences. His 2009 report is the most extensive yet, containing information provided by every person with whom the designer had a substantial face-to-face encounter. The information, collected via online survey, formed a database of his personality and habits, from facts (where he went, what he drank) to more subjective material (his mood). People in 179 distinct relationships, such as dentist, friend/esteemed colleague, ex-wife, and grill master, reported what they perceived to be Felton's state of mind: "Earnestly industrious," "Unhurried and relaxed," "Pensive (but not in a lame way)." The section "Mood: An assessment of demeanor" charts the designer's temperament during his encounters along a scale of happiness and sadness. The report is thus an objective visualization of deeply personal relationships. Felton's project shows us what happens when a year's worth of isolated bits of information is looked at in total; when this data is visualized, what may seem like inconsequential details aggregate into a narrative. The end result of Felton's 2009 report is a limited-edition signed and numbered book, and Felton has recently launched a website that allows anyone to collect personal data in a similar fashion. His 2010 report is devoted to his father, who passed away in September of that year.

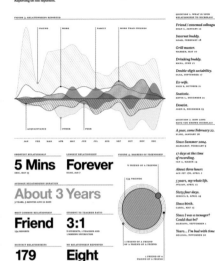

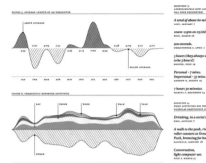

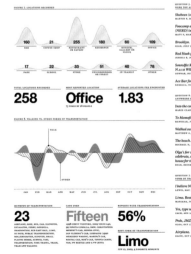

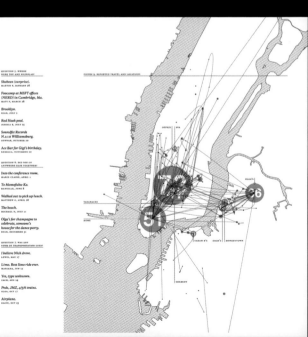

David McCandless (British, born 1971)
of Information Is Beautiful (UK, est. 2009)

/////////////////////////////

The Hierarchy of Digital Distractions.
2009

/////////////////////////////

Illustrator software

David McCandless used his own
experience to create a pyramid diagram
of the interferences constantly gnawing
at our attention span in this socially
networked, data-consuming world.
Devices and websites, represented
by logos, are sorted by how potentially
distracting they are, stacked according
to which activities and notifications
are more likely to cause us to abandon
whatever we are doing: a call on the
landline trumps Facebook, at least until
the arrival of a text message. McCandless
has also calibrated the relative importance of different kinds of e-mail,
tweets, and Facebook notifications,
all of which hover between the bottom
of the pyramid, representing "Any kind
of actual work," and the top, marked
"Partner shuts the lid of laptop on
your fingers." McCandless also takes
on topics of global importance in his
visualizations, as he does on page 137.

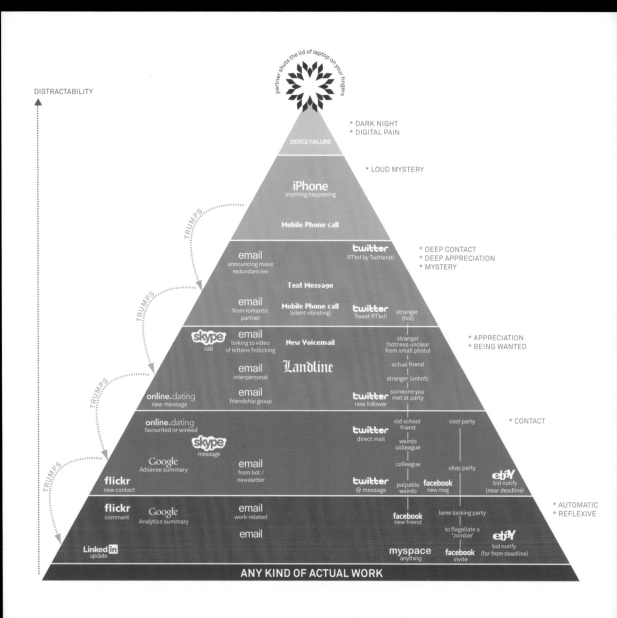

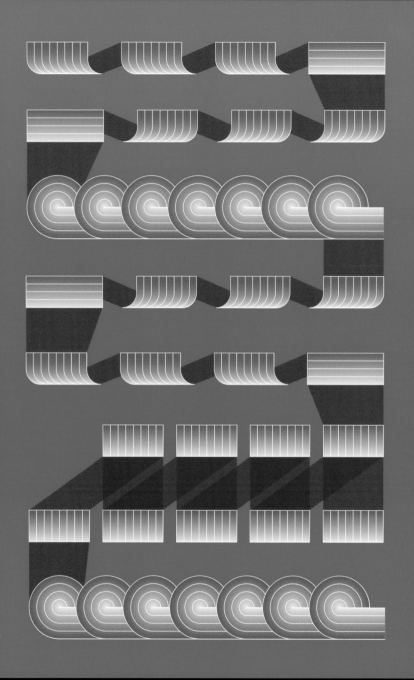

# MY WHEEL OF WORRY, MAY 2010

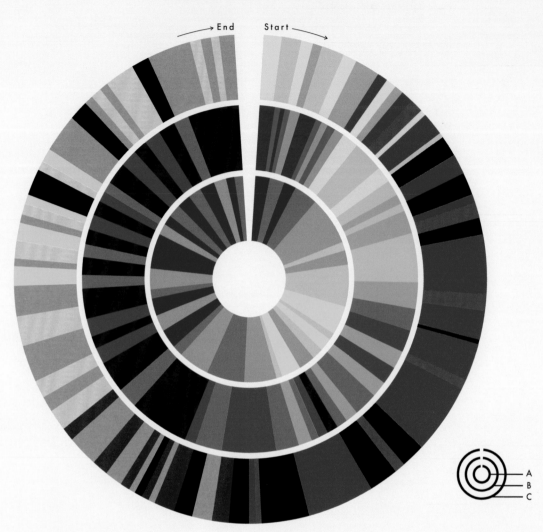

→ End    Start →

## A. SUBJECTS OF CONCERN WHILE FALLING ASLEEP

■ Loneliness    ■ Death    ■ Money    ■ Bedbugs    ■ The New York Knicks

## B. LOOKING AT MY CREDIT-CARD STATEMENT MAKES ME ...

■ Hope the next text is a contract offer from the Yankees.
■ Concerned about how I will retire by age 34.
■ Regret buying that limited-edition "Star Wars" VHS boxed set.
■ Wonder if Donald Trump has ever even eaten instant ramen.
■ Avoid ads for newfangled gadgets that can do "everything."
■ Justify getting a bigger TV because it "keeps me company."
■ Annoyed when stinking-rich people complain about anything.
■ Whiny, irritable and always thirsty for eight (cheap) beers.
■ Remind myself how much worse some people have it.

## C. THOUGHTS WHILE SCRATCHING A LOTTERY TICKET

■ I'll take the brownstone with a hoop in the backyard!
■ Who doesn't need a second laptop just for chatting?
■ I will spend $100 on albums every week from now on.
■ You need to have something to give before you give back!
■ What would I do with all my free time?
■ Is being "not rich" more punk?
■ What's a beach house when you have the Internet?
■ I have everything I need. (Except height.)
■ Rich or not, there's always a reason to feel bad.
■ The first thing I will buy is a better brain!

Andrew Kuo (American, born 1977)

///////////////////////////////

My Wheel of Worry. 2010

///////////////////////////////

Offset lithography, 10 3/4 × 8 3/4"
(27.2 × 22.3 cm)

Andrew Kuo presents his inner worries,
arguments, counterarguments, and
obsessions in the form of charts and
graphs. In the three-tiered graph My
Wheel of Worry (opposite), originally
published in the May 16, 2010, New York
Times Magazine, Kuo illustrates the
things in his life that concern him and
his specific feelings about each. On
the graph's innermost ring Kuo shows
what causes him anxiety in the moments
before sleep (loneliness, death, money,
bedbugs, and the New York Knicks); in
the middle ring he charts his very specific
reactions to his credit card statement;
on the outermost ring, what he thinks
about as he scratches a lottery ticket.
In this chart and others, Kuo brings the
graphic language of scientific fact to
the irrational emotions associated with
everyday life.

Mayo Nissen (German, born 1986)
Copenhagen Institute of Interaction
Design (Denmark, est. 2007)

///////////////////////////////

Visualising Household Power
Consumption. 2009

///////////////////////////////

Processing software

Mayo Nissen's poster visualizes a
home's power usage over twenty-four
hours and compares it to an average
of data collected over four days.
The point is not simply to understand
energy-usage patterns but also to give
narrative shape to our everyday activities. The power data on the graph, which
was recorded at one-minute intervals,
reconstructs the activities of a given
day in its spikes and lulls; the designer
muses, "Was that spike at 3am a one-off
nighttime cup of tea...and can boiling the
kettle just once really use so much
power? That consistent peak must be
dinnertime. Is that wave in the graph,
visible at night, the fridge on its cycle,
running all day every day?" The chart's
light gray lines show each minute of each
day; the thick black line represents the
average energy used over four days; and
the red line is what is known in statistics
as a "smoothed average," revealing
broader usage patterns.

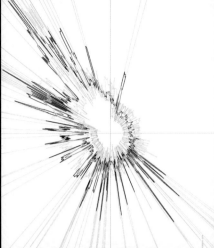

Jennifer Kay (Scottish, born 1986),
Jacek Barcikowski (Polish, born 1981),
and Martina Pagura (Italian, born 1983)
Copenhagen Institute of Interaction
Design (Denmark, est. 2007)

///////////////////////////////

Sidetrack. 2010

///////////////////////////////

Wood, acrylic, paper, ink, and electronics
25 9/16 × 27 9/16 × 23 10/16"
(65 × 70 × 60 cm)

Sidetrack, built from modified turntable
and printer parts, is based on research
showing that work-at-home professionals have trouble separating their
home and work lives, and in particular
that they spend most of their time
at their desks and not in other parts
of their homes. Areas throughout the
home (the kitchen, the office) are tracked
by sensors connected to a rotating table.
As the user moves from room to room,
the table plots a pattern, drawn by
pens attached to a moving arm, disclosing
what the designers call "pockets of
time" being devoted to various tasks.
Distractions, in this case, are not the
problem but are encouraged as healthy
breaks in rather monotonous days.
Each day is recorded on a separate
paper disk, allowing users to learn
from their own patterns.

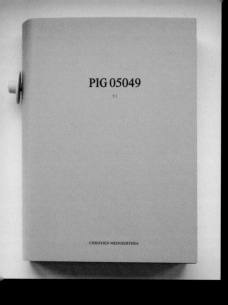

Christien Meindertsma (Dutch, born 1980)
and Julie Joliat (Swiss, born 1979)

/////////////////////////////////

PIG 05049. 2006

/////////////////////////////////

Offset lithography and plastic, 7 11/16
x 5 7/8 x 1 9/16" (19.5 x 15 x 4 cm)
Published by Flocks, the Netherlands

For PIG 05049, Christien Meindertsma tracked all the products made from a single pig over the course of a three-year study and then published the results in the form of a book, designed with Julie Joliat. Pig no. 05049, which Meindertsma selected at random from a commercial farm in the Netherlands, was used in 185 different products, each one pictured. These include the expected foodstuffs as well as nonfood items such as photographic film, toothpaste, and even the glue used in the book's binding. The work visualizes the complexity of the meat-processing industry, as well as how many points of contact we have with animal products without being aware of them. This visual catalogue of one animal's afterlife explores the remove of the relationship between humans and animals, and consumers and products. The book is in the collection of The Museum of Modern Art, New York.

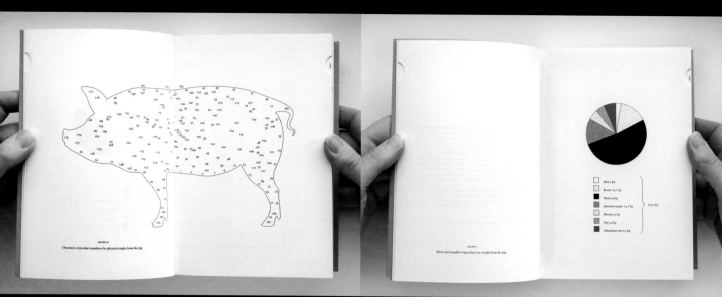

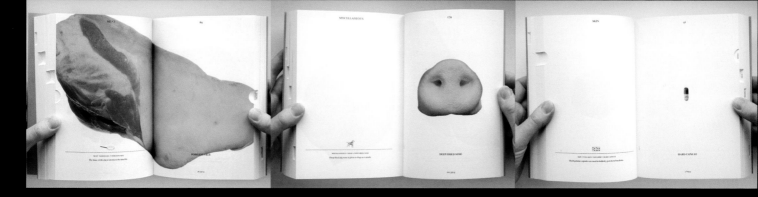

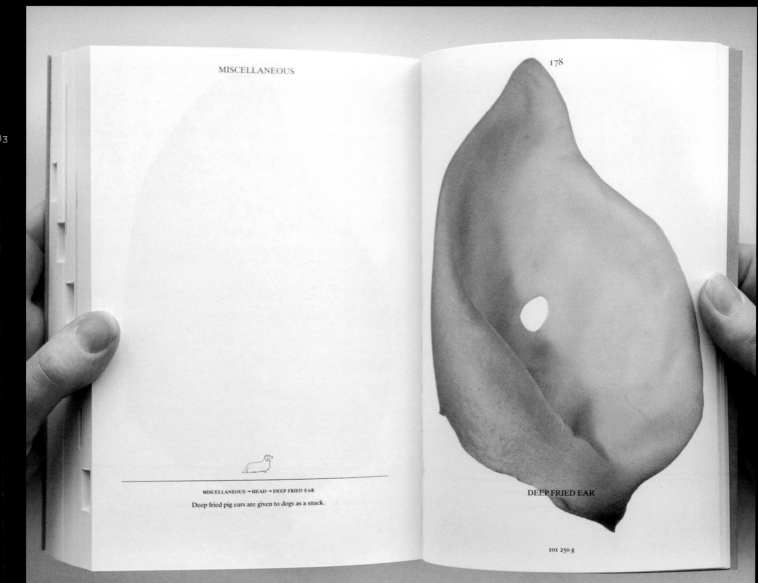

MISCELLANEOUS

178

MISCELLANEOUS → HEAD → DEEP FRIED EAR

Deep fried pig ears are given to dogs as a snack.

DEEP FRIED EAR

101 250 g

James Auger (British, born 1970)
and Jimmy Loizeau (British, born 1968)
of Auger/Loizeau (UK, est. 2000)
Reyer Zwiggelaar (Dutch, born 1963)
and Bashar Rajoub (Jordanian, born 1974)
of the Department of Computer Science
(est. 1970)
Aberystwyth University (UK, est. 1872)

/////////////////////////////

Happylife. 2010

/////////////////////////////

High-resolution thermal-image camera,
Corian, stainless steel, electronics, and
mechanical and computer components,
15 3/4 × 39 3/8 × 3 1/2" (40 × 100
× 9 cm)

Reyer Zwiggelaar and Bashar Rajoub
have been developing new profiling
technology based on biometric data,
in which a camera equipped with sensors
detects changes in a person's mood
and emotion by taking thermal images
of his or her face. By analyzing facial
expressions, eye movements, pupil
dilation, and other physiological changes,
the camera may be able to predict future
criminal activity. With Happylife, designers
James Auger and Jimmy Loizeau have
adapted this technology for keeping the
peace at home. The designers added
a visual display with facial-recognition
software, so that the camera could
differentiate between members of a
family. A dial, one for each family member,
registers current and predicted emotional
states, based on data accumulated over
the years by the machine. The designers
have imagined complex scenarios in
which the Happylife system might have
a significant impact on a family's life, and
with writer and poet Richard M. Turley,
they have created vignettes to illustrate
such situations: "It was that time of the
year. All of the Happylife prediction dials
had spun anti-clockwise, like barometers
reacting to an incoming storm. We
lost David 4 years ago and the system
was anticipating our coming sadness.
We found this strangely comforting."
The designers hope to install the system
prototype in an actual family's home
to further their research.

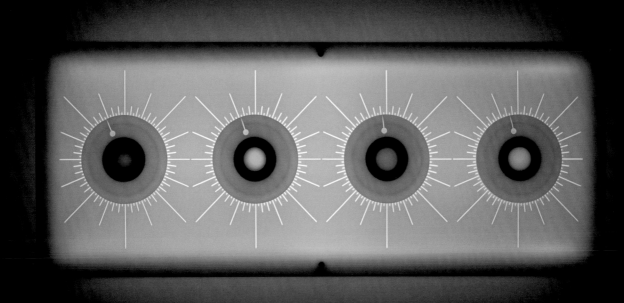

Michiko Nitta (Japanese, born 1978)
Design Interactions Department
(est. 1989)
Royal College of Art (UK, est. 1837)

/////////////////////////////

Hyperreal Everyday Life. 2006

/////////////////////////////

Headphones, CD player, foam, and
electronics, 7 7/8 × 5 7/8 × 5 7/8"
(20 × 15 × 15 cm)

This device alters the way in which
we view our lives, transforming our
mundane everyday activities into
epic achievements by adding a thrilling
sound track and cropping the wearer's
vision so that life has the proportions
of a movie screen.

We Are What We Do (UK, est. 2004)

/////////////////////////////

Historypin. 2010

/////////////////////////////

Python, Google Maps, and OAuth software

We Are What We Do, an organization
based in London, encourages small but
effective social change. As part of a
campaign to get people from different
generations communicating with each
other, the organization created Historypin
in collaboration with Google. This website,
where historical photos and stories are
added to Google Maps's street views,
acts as both a visualization of the past
and an archive. Each generation learns
something in the process; young people
ask older people for photos and stories,
and older people learn from younger
people how the technology works.

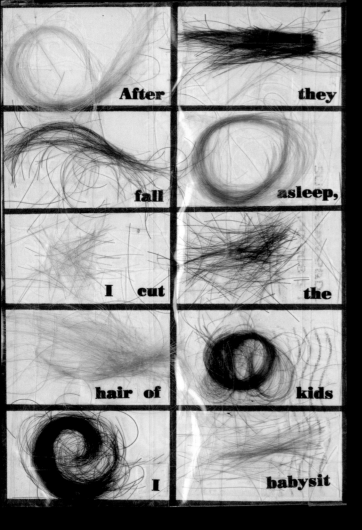

After they fall asleep, I cut the hair of kids I babysit

you told me your darkest secret and my heart ached because I realized I couldn't possibly love you any more

Frank Warren (American, born 1964)

////////////////////////////

PostSecret. 2004

////////////////////////////

Various materials, dimensions variable

PostSecret began in 2004 when Frank Warren left three thousand postcards in public places, each asking whoever found the card to mail him a secret. "Slowly," he says, "secrets began to find their way to my mailbox"; he shared the anonymous secrets and accompanying artwork online and in exhibitions and books. After a few months, Warren stopped passing out postcards, but the secrets kept coming, often on homemade cards. To date he has received close to half a million secrets, running the emotional gamut from serious, scary, and moving to funny and optimistic. Both ends of the project—sharing a secret with the world and reading one from a stranger—have proven cathartic. Warren feels the project's popularity is best summed up by something a participant wrote: "The things that make us feel so abnormal are actually the things that make us all the same."

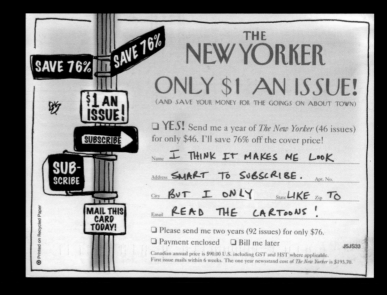

THE NEW YORKER

SAVE 76%   SAVE 76%

$1 AN ISSUE!

SUBSCRIBE ▶

SUB-SCRIBE

MAIL THIS CARD TODAY!

ⓔ Printed on Recycled Paper

ONLY $1 AN ISSUE!
(AND SAVE YOUR MONEY FOR THE GOINGS ON ABOUT TOWN)

❑ YES! Send me a year of *The New Yorker* (46 issues) for only $46. I'll save 76% off the cover price!

Name  I THINK IT MAKES ME LOOK

Address  SMART TO SUBSCRIBE.  Apt. No.

City  BUT I ONLY  State LIKE  Zip TO

Email  READ THE CARTOONS!

❑ Please send me two years (92 issues) for only $76.
❑ Payment enclosed   ❑ Bill me later   J5JS33

Canadian annual price is $90.00 U.S. including GST and HST where applicable.
First issue mails within 6 weeks. The one year newsstand cost of *The New Yorker* is $193.70.

Interaction Research Studio (est. 2000)
Goldsmiths (est. 1891)
University of London (UK, est. 1836)

//////////////////////////

Prayer Companion. 2010

//////////////////////////

Photopolymer resin, dot-matrix display,
and printed circuit board, 13 3/4 × 8 3/4
× 5 1/2" (35 × 22 × 14 cm)

Developed for the nine Poor Clare Sisters
who live at a monastery in York, UK, the
Prayer Companion is a communication
device with a very explicit purpose: it
alerts the nuns to issues that need their
prayers. The nuns, whose everyday lives
have changed little since medieval times,
have taken vows of enclosure, and their
only connection to the outside world
is through occasional access to Catholic
newspapers, mail, and limited use of
the telephone and computer. Designed
to be understated and unobtrusive,
the Prayer Companion subtly scrolls
a ticker tape of issues across its top;
its small screen can only be viewed
from above and close-up, thus minimizing
its distracting potential. The device was
designed specifically for the nuns and
is the only one of its kind. "Goldie,"
as the nuns call it, sits on a table in a
hallway that they often pass through,
scrolling news as well as the feelings
of anonymous strangers whose blog
entries are aggregated by the website
We Feel Fine. The nuns have told Bill
Gaver, of the Interaction Research
Studio, that "it has been valuable
in keeping [our] prayers pertinent."

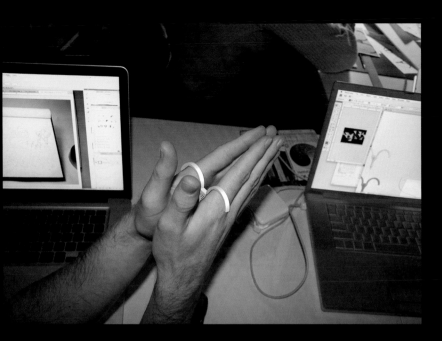

Jae Yeop Kim (Korean, born 1980),
Ting Yuin Chien (Taiwanese, born 1985),
Scott Liao (Taiwanese, born 1983),
and Dustin York (American, born 1981)
Media Design Program (est. 1973)
Art Center College of Design, Pasadena
(USA, est. 1930)

////////////////////////////

The Messenger. 2010

////////////////////////////

Resin and silver and gold paint, 2 × 2
× 1/4" (5 × 5 × 0.5 cm)

The Messenger was created while the
designers were studying the perceived
barriers between faithful and scientific
outlooks, often thought to be at odds
with one another. The Messenger
operates on the assumption that people
pray when in need of help, and it imagines
a system where help could be provided
and faith could create an opportunity
for action. The user holds the device
and prays into it, so that the prayer
is recorded and then sent via satellite
to a database that catalogues it.
Scientific and faith-based organizations
can listen in and try to provide help
where it is needed, such as water
in a drought, or medicine for the
sick. It is important to note that the
Messenger "does not attempt to subvert
or replace any God," as the designers
explain, but rather "[reinforces] the
idea that when we pray, our community
as well as our deity is listening."

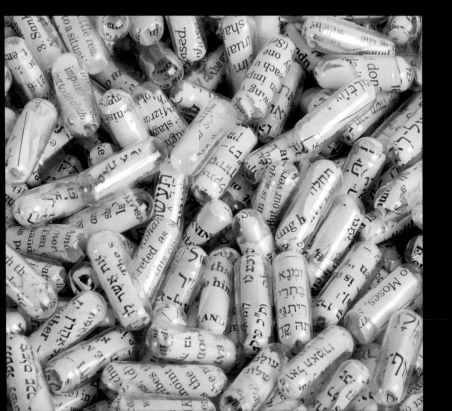

Johanna Bresnick (American, born 1973)
and Michael Cloud Hirschfeld (American,
born 1975)

////////////////////////////

From Mouth to Mouth. 2006

////////////////////////////

Paper and gel capsules, 7/8" (2.2 cm)
high, 1/4" (0.6 cm) diam.

This project is a very literal interpretation
of a passage in the Old Testament:
In Ezekiel 3, God instructs Ezekiel to
eat a scroll of lamentations so he can
then speak His words to the people of
Israel. By encapsulating in digestible pills
the entire text of Leviticus, one of the
five books of the Torah, the designers
suggest a comparison between medicinal
and religious prescription, as well as
the idea of many people ingesting the
same knowledge and then interpreting
it differently, even questioning it. The
entire text was divided, so that only
a fragment went into each vegetable-
based capsule, which were placed
all together on a koshered table and
displayed in the exhibition Reinventing
Ritual: Contemporary Art and Design
for Jewish Life at The Jewish Museum,
New York, in 2009.

Soner Ozenc (Turkish, born 1980)
of Soner Ozenc Product Design Studio
(UK, est. 2006)

////////////////////////////////

El Sajjadah. 2005

////////////////////////////////

Electroluminescent sheet, 27 5/8
× 47 1/4" (70 × 120 cm)

A Muslim's prayer rug ensures that the
space for prayer, which takes place five
times per day, is clean and separated
from other activities. Soner Ozenc has
created a rug that points the praying
person in the direction of Mecca. He
embedded in the rug a compass module
that connects with electroluminescent
printing on its surface; the carpet pattern
grows brighter and brighter as it is
turned in the correct direction.

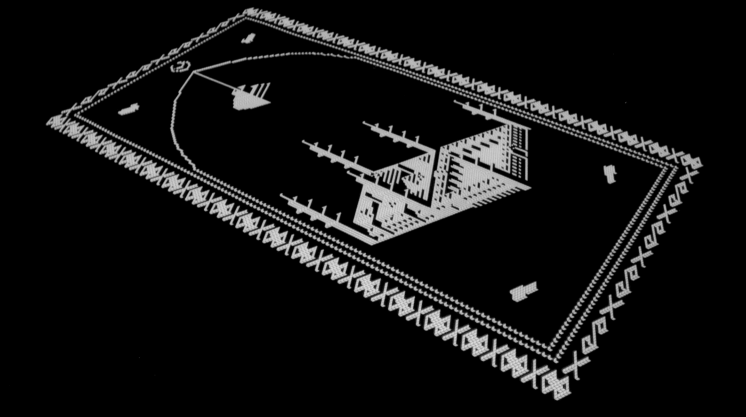

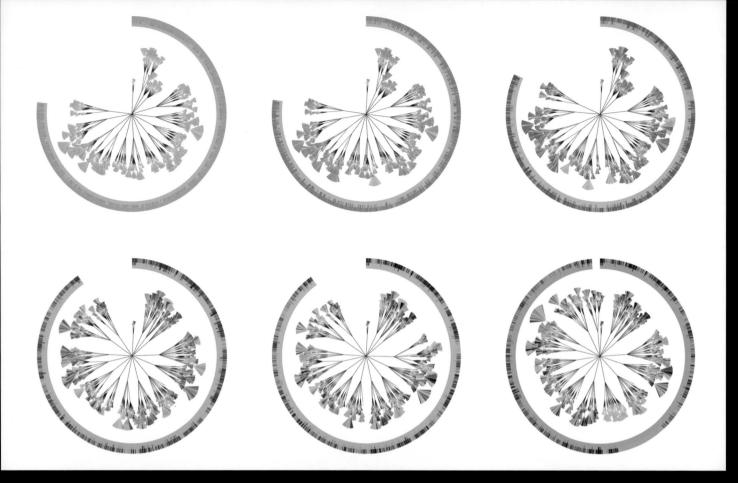

Greg McInerny (British, born 1977)
of Microsoft Research, Cambridge
(UK, est. 1997)
Stefanie Posavec (American, born 1981)

/////////////////////////

(En)tangled Word Bank. 2009

/////////////////////////

C++, R, Processing, and Illustrator
software

This visual comparison of the six editions
of Charles Darwin's <u>On the Origin of
Species</u> shows the changes Darwin
made to the texts during his lifetime.
Using data from online versions of the
books, the designers created six wheels,
each representing a different edition,
with each chapter divided into subchap-
ters, paragraphs (represented by a leaf
shape), and sentences (represented
by a smaller "leaflet"). The sentences
are colored blue or orange based on
whether or not they will appear in the
next edition—on whether or not they
will survive. Changes representing
scientific advances, adjustments in
the author's thought process, and
conflicting sections in the text become
apparent, with subtleties as well as
major changes immediately revealed.

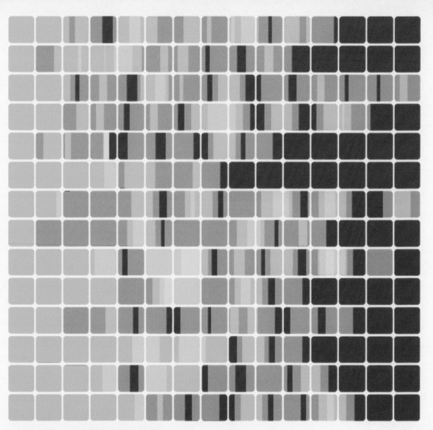

marker rs1800497

# Avoidance of Errors

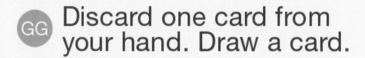

GG Discard one card from your hand. Draw a card.

Frank Lantz (American, born 1963),
Kevin Slavin (American, born 1969),
Kevin Cancienne (American, born 1975),
Kati London (American, born 1976),
Mark Heggen (American, born 1982),
Demetri Detsaridis (American, 1975),
Jesen A. Fagerness (American, 1973),
and Mike Essl (American, born 1974)

/////////////////////////////////

Helix. 2011

/////////////////////////////////

Helix is a two-player trading-card game currently under development. Players send in swabs of saliva; the designers send it out to be analyzed and then generate a customized fifty-card deck from each player's specific DNA. With these cards, two players can engage in tabletop warfare, pitting their personal resources against each other in duels that reward strategy and decision making but are limited by genetic reality. Customized down to the most detailed level, the deck becomes a literal, pocket-sized copy of genetic code. But only part of the story is told with cards—a genetic tendency (obesity, alcoholism, longevity) may be present in a player's deck, but having the trait doesn't necessarily mean that it is expressed. The deck allows players to become shadow versions of themselves, with all their genetic cards on the table, and in the game, as in reality, life depends on how the cards are played, not on which cards are dealt. The effects of any trait depend on the player; the challenge of the game is how to contend with or take advantage of it. A player with a great deck can still lose if the game is played without strategy, and a skilled player with a weaker deck can win.

# Design Wonder Stories: When Speech Is Golden

Alexandra Midal

Unless they were deaf and dumb, anyone at all could use this mode of transmission, which required no apparatus at all. An electric battery, two vibrating plates, and a wire would suffice.
—Charles Bourseul[1]

A few years ago Georges Charpak, a Nobel Prize winner in physics, related that he used to visit ethnographic museums in search of ceramics and other baked clay items . . . in order to listen to them. With the utmost seriousness, he said he thought that, like the wax disk Thomas A. Edison used to "capture" words, the grooves traced in ancient ceramics might have recorded the voices of their time.[2] The only thing not yet invented was the apparatus that would allow them to speak. He did not achieve his goal.

When Achille Castiglioni designed the Rompitratta switch (fig. 1) for VLM in 1968, he paid the most attention to the sound the switch made when turned on and off.[3] The switch contains an essential value beyond its basic simplicity: a new unity of form and sound. In the Rompitratta's click, as well as in the sneeze of James Chambers's Gesundheit Radio (2010, page 25), meant to get rid of troublesome dust, and in the neurotic complaints of the Robots in the Technological Dreams Series (2007) by Dunne & Raby, design does away with the strictly necessary and takes on psychological and sensorial values. Such is true of Robot 4 (fig. 2), which, because it cannot move itself, whimpers when it wants to be moved. In addition to breaking with the customary servility of the robot, this vocal insistence on obtaining satisfaction suggests that the machine has evolved into a being almost equal with humankind; in contrast to previous notions of the robots, which the designers note would have been made to speak human languages, "over time they will evolve their own language. You can still hear human traces in its voice."[4] These robots have a power equal to that of the spirits that haunted objects in the movie Poltergeist (1982).

Why does a designer strive to make objects speak? Is it to stimulate a range of sensations? If the history of design is based on significant constructions meant, above all, to be useful, then to render them anthropomorphic, to endow them with emotions and give them speech diminishes the primacy of rational and functionalist values and overturns this history. This concept goes beyond style, era, and discipline: the interpretation of design's modernity cannot ignore this "other" design, which shifts design's history toward a new horizon.

How and by what subtle modifications can an ordinary object be transformed into an entity?

J. G. Ballard describes this movement particularly well in the story "The Thousand Dreams of Stellavista" (1962), in which a young married couple lives in a house equipped with sensory memory cells, which adjusts its mood to the pleasures and anxieties of those who inhabit it.[5] The psychotropic house is gradually transformed into a theater of deadly passion where scenes between its previous inhabitants, contained in the house's memory, are constantly being replayed. The house is trembling, tumultuous, ailing—convulsing and twisting to the point of threatening the couple's lives. Inhabiting a space populated by objects that reproduce human acts and feelings replaces design's reassuring functionalist origins with empathy and emotion.

An environment perceived through psychosensitive vibration corresponds to the notion of an architecture of the intimate as advanced by Étienne Bonnot de Condillac in Traité des sensations (Treatise on the Sensations, 1754) and then by Nicolas Le Camus de Mézières in Le Génie de l'architecture, ou L'Analogie de cet art avec nos sensations (The Genius of Architecture; or, The Analogy of That Art with Our Sensations, 1780). "Every nuance, every gradation, affects us. The arrangements of forms, their character, and their combination are thus

Fig. 1
Illustration of the Rompitratta switch by Steven Guarnaccia, from Achille Castiglioni, with texts by Paola Antonelli, 2000

Fig. 2
Antony Dunne and Fiona Raby of Dunne & Raby. Robot 4 from Technological Dreams Series: No.1, Robots. 2007. English oak, 32 × 18 7/8 × 6" (75 × 48 × 158 cm)

an inexhaustible source of illusion," Le Camus wrote, echoing Jean-François de Bastide's La Petite Maison (The Little House, 1763), a novel of seduction in which sensualist architecture occupies the primary role.[6] Le Camus celebrated the erotic-emotional tensions of space by nourishing himself with libertine literature and with the harmonic architecture of the Jesuit Louis Bertrand Castel's clavecin oculaire (ocular harpsichord) and Charles Le Brun's illustrations for his treatise on the passions.[7] "Affectations" or "sensations," to use Le Camus' terms, arise from a concept of space that emphasizes emotional states.

Modernism claimed the values of functional orthodoxy for design, with affect as an improbable traveling companion. This affective "other" design, supposedly disengaged from the progressive realm of technology, introduces the flexibility of psychological, pathological, and individual atavisms; it may suggest a postmodernist inclination, but above all it suggests a rethinking of the complexity of the foundations of design itself. A relationship between design and speech produces an illusion—a powerful lure and a speculative and hypothetical exchange in which, as Adolf Loos wrote, describing a perfectly integrated space, "In the family's room . . . every new piece is absorbed immediately. Such a room is like a violin. One can get to know a violin by practicing on it, a room by living in it."[8] This relationship challenges the modernist, functional convention of design in favor of something more open and emotional, thus opening up new directions for the discipline.

/ / / / / / / / / / / / / / / / / / / / / / / / / / / / / / / / / / / / / / / / / / / / / / / / / / / /

A Theater of Imaginary and Domestic Fiction

My purpose here has less to do with underlining the modernist misunderstanding about the equation of functionalism and design than with acknowledging the diversity of conjunctions between design and fiction.

An appetite for the imaginary is particularly present in the work of Noam Toran. Since 2008 he has been assembling, in collaboration with Onkar Kular and Keith R. Jones, The MacGuffin Library, a stunning archive of objects, each of which generates its own fiction. Kutsenov's Steps (fig. 3), for example, is a miniature reproduction of the Odessa Steps from Sergei Eisenstein's Battleship Potemkin (1925), but what is depicted here is not those famous steps but an empty stand-alone structure endowed with buttresses. A text accompanying the objects weaves together fact and fiction, mutating to become a MacGuffin—a banal object that plays a dramatic role, an imaginary object given body by industrial modes of production. These MacGuffins activate a narrative that questions the history of design, subtly shifting from function toward fiction.

By encouraging us to reconsider the relationship between discourse and form and between formalization and formulation, Toran reiterates the meaning of "giving form to something," which is etymologically related to "fiction."[9] In his design work he shifts the dominant definition of industrial design in order to develop apparatuses that reveal other possibilities in the realm of intimate domesticity.

With this marriage of spatialization and affect, rationalization is replaced with mechanisms of empathy and meaning

Fig. 3
Noam Toran, Onkar Kular, and
Keith R. Jones. Kutsenov's
Steps from The MacGuffin
Library. 2008. Polymer resin,
3 1/8 × 3 1/8 × 13 3/4"
(8 × 8 × 35 cm)

THE EUPHONIA, OR SPEAKING MACHINE.

Fig. 4
Illustration of the Euphonia
automaton from Illustrated
London News, 1846

THÉÂTROPHONE

Fig. 5
Jules Chéret. Théâtrophone.
1890. Lithograph, 48 15/16 ×
34 3/8" (124.3 × 87.3 cm)

and with the glorification of the psyche. What presides, curiously,
among these empathic, psychological objects is the telephone.

/////////////////////////////////////////////////

"It DOES Speak": Between Silence and Logorrhea, the Secret
History of the Telephone[10]

On July 2, 1875, Alexander Graham Bell and Thomas A. Watson
invented the telephone. "I wanted to hear it talk," Watson
explained in his autobiography.[11] We might wonder if he was
admitting to the desire to hear the telephone speak rather
than someone speaking on it.[12]

   Communication was an integral part of Bell family history.
Bell's grandfather invented a system to alleviate stuttering, and
his father taught elocution and created a system of phonetic
notation. The young Bell became a professor of vocal physiology
and elocution at Boston University and in 1874 conceived an
artificial head capable of pronouncing words, a work in the
lineage of speaking automatons such as the Marvelous Talking-
Machine, or Euphonia (1845, fig. 4), created by the astronomer
Joseph Faber: a woman's head that could speak when pedals
and keyboard were moved, much like playing a piano; each touch
produced a different syllable, allowing the machine to utter
words in a mechanical, indeed, absent, tone and even sing.[13]

   The family tradition culminated in the birth of the
telephone, which united technology, design, and communication
in the unusual form of a small setup, almost eight inches in length,
equipped with wires and a transmitter-receiver that allowed
a person to speak and listen to someone else. In order to
demonstrate the power of the telephone, Watson and Bell liked
to have people use it to listen to recorded theatrical spectacles.
This idea was later perfected by Clément Ader with the
Théâtrophone (fig. 5), which at the Exposition Internationale
d'Électricité in Paris in 1881 linked the Opéra de Paris to
the homes of Parisian subscribers.[14] Evening performances
at the Palais Garnier, the Opéra Comique, the Musée Grévin,
and the Théâtre Français were also transmitted at a distance
to an enchanted public. But in spite of its capacity for seduction
and then-unequaled technology, the telephone is one of the
forgotten systems in the quasi-encyclopedic research conducted
by Siegfried Giedion, the historian of the origins of the mechanization of design.[15] In reconstructing the genesis of industrialization,
relying on documents and patents registered by engineers or
inventors, both famous and not, Giedion makes no mention of
the tools of communication, neither the telephone nor the
phonograph.

   The telephone brought the infiltration of the outside
world into the home, an unheard-of noisy invasion of interiority.
The dream of recording and transmitting the voice has given
structure to visions from the Telephonoscope proposed by Albert
Robida in his novel The Twentieth Century (1882) to the apparatus described by Edward Bellamy in Looking Backward (1888)
to the science fiction inventions of Hugo Gernsback or in the
musical comedy Just Imagine (1930) by David Butler. Thus
this disruptive innovation—which should not be relegated solely
to the realm of modern science fiction—sheds light on the meaning of societal transformations. By intertwining mechanization

and works of art in his analysis of design, Giedion persuades us that the process of mechanization is an artistic act. And one only need think of Marshall McLuhan's idea that the proliferation of technology creates upsetting new environments to see that the only valid antidote is to rely on counterenvironments—namely, art—to oppose the intrusion of a speaking object and the repercussions of its presence, especially since this intrusion extends into our internal worlds.

New light on the telephone's invention is shed by the fact that Bell was the son and the husband of hearing-impaired people, and that young Edison had scarlet fever as an adolescent and was hard of hearing as a consequence. Do we assume it is a coincidence that Bell and Edison were both attuned to the deprivation of the senses? And thus registered the patents for the telephone and for the phonograph, the telegraph, the Vitascope, and the Kinetoscope?

The invention of the telephone can also be seen as a way of thinking about strange and idiosyncratic behaviors: Bell was in the habit of carrying around a dead man's ear, while Watson, entirely enamored of the world of mediums and spiritualism, was described as someone "susceptible to the unearthly curls, spectral cats, and nocturnal horses. He was haunted from the start, invaded and possessed."[16] The bizarre led to the extraordinary, underscoring that one of the telephone's great achievements was the successful new affinity between technology and the paranormal. In his autobiography Watson added that the invention of the telephone was also in part aimed at establishing contact with his deceased brother; as children they had promised each other to find a way to communicate if one of them died, an attempt that testifies to a tension between communication design and the occult. Moreover, the phenomenon of a parallel communication with the dead undermines the dynamic of technical rationalism and formalism associated with design and attempts to unite reason, aesthetics, and the psychological experience. The telephone abolishes physical frontiers, including those that separate the private domestic sphere and mental landscape, transforming identity and behavior in a metamorphosed environment. Like the spatialization of affect described by Le Camus, Loos, and others, Bell and Watson's position substitutes the activity of the psyche for the stranglehold of rationalization.

Around the same time, in 1895, Henry van de Velde was having a similar change of heart, putting forward the idea of a house that would reflect the spirit or humor of its inhabitants: "There is an absolute correlation between man in particular and the house, the room in which he lives."[17] He thus created a cartography of sensory connections between subject and environment. Returning to these ideas allows us to reconsider design in light of the emergence of a new, modern, and intensely psychological individual, one capable of amplifying vibrations and movements in new spaces of sensual and sensorial representation.

////////////////////////////////////

Silence and Delegation

This new perception forms a contrast with the quiet claims of functional design, such as those contained in Jasper Morrison and Naoto Fukasawa's recent manifesto, Super Normal (2006), among other declarations that celebrate simplicity and soberness.[18] The cover of the book displays a Moka Express, the famous espresso maker designed by Alfonso Bialetti. This classic of Italian coffee culture, an aluminum pot that can be placed directly on the stove, has not changed since its invention in 1933; four million of them are produced and sold every year. It is an industrial icon that sets the tone for Super Normal's defense of anonymous objects devoid of the psychological element.

A metaphor for the apparent affective silence of functional, anonymous design is found in ventriloquism, which first appeared in performances by Fred Russell in 1896. The ventriloquist is invoked regularly by artists and architects as the figure that connects body and abstract discourse, provoking the frisson of being willingly fooled by illusion.[19] A similar suspicion marked the reactions of those who first listened to Edison's phonograph; they skeptically assumed it was duplicity, a ventriloquist behind the mechanism. Taken at its extremes, on the one hand, technological innovation could not be understood as such and must be a magician's sleight of hand, thus establishing a correlation between technology and magic, with somebody hiding in order to perform a trick. On the other hand, remote technology does perform an act of disembodiment, so that the telephone, like the phonograph, suggests the existence of spirits. Cinematic works have repeatedly explored this theme, showing the complexity of the ventriloquist and creature dyad, torn between the silence of the man who cannot express his emotions and the chatter of the disrespectful marionette. This is the case of the relationship in James Cruze's intriguing film The Great Gabbo (1929, fig. 6), incarnated by Erich von Stroheim and his marionette. Beyond the obvious mise en abyme, this example finds a surprising echo in the history of design: I would suggest

or for art galleries, whereas from the beginning a parallel path of design had been opened in the realm of reflection and illusion. Reclaiming this alternate history allows design to escape modernist determination, whether critical or partisan. Returning to the spiritualist and prosthetic origins of the telephone dismantles the foundations of the preeminent silent stylistic codes, which serve industrial normalization, and places them in an infinitely more psychological environment. Even if this act is called auditory hallucination—or, indeed, schizophrenia—I propose that we listen carefully to these polyphonies of design.

In this light, design may revive a particular idea of the body and nervous system: the desire to fuse the psyche and domesticity. The possibility of generating sensations to inanimate objects revisits Heinrich Wölfflin's psychoaesthetic conception in Prolegomena to a Psychology of Architecture (1886), which he borrowed from Robert Vischer's theory of empathy, that asks, "How is it possible that architectural forms are able to express an emotion or mood?"[21] The analysis of the work of art was thus opened to the united influence of aesthetics, spatiality, and psychology, showing that mood, or Stimmung, was and is the raison d'être of design. Design's desire for Stimmung, occupying the interstices of previous historical analyses, is neither rhetorical nor tactic, and it opens onto other possibilities. The series of past encounters of design and Stimmung recounted here does not posit a return: it reveals the more nuanced contours of an alternate and intense history, and it changes the established modernist history of design. It holds a promise for the discipline's future, one disengaged from functionalism and able to forge a new conception of design and design history.

that speech is embodied in fictional or inanimate objects, and the silence of the designer replaces a discourse that has been largely rejected.

This echo is found in Toran's Subliminal Furniture (2003, fig. 7), which depicts trivial situations of incommunicability. One member of a couple uses a hidden keyboard to convey subliminal messages to the other, thus imposing his or her will. Manipulative and grating, this hypnotic arrangement annihilates any form of dialogue.

To a certain extent, this metaphor illustrates the situation of design. During the 1980s designers renounced political engagement and abandoned the theory of the discipline. Drawing on the sociology of Jean Baudrillard, the anthropology of Marcel Mauss, behavioral science, and the semiotics of Roland Barthes, among other sources, they found themselves unable to theorize about their work and flirted with the human sciences, which, to use Ettore Sottsass's description, "opened a broader horizon, as if we had emerged from design's town center and headed toward new, uncertain peripheries."[20] In return, designers invited the social sciences to consider their work as case studies, under the aegis of the transdisciplinary.

The examination of design from the theoretical perspective of other disciplines left a lasting mark: an inability to claim disciplinary autonomy. The opening of design to theories from anthropology, sociology, and other areas of study turned out to be an obstacle to the articulation of its own history, theory, and criticism. Without enough theoretical publications and critics, everything seemed to push designers to produce objects one after the other, as if they were merely technicians with a skill, for industry

← Fig. 6
James Cruze. <u>The Great Gabbo</u>. 1929

Fig. 7
Noam Toran. Subliminal Furniture. 2003. Digital video (color, sound), 10 min.

Notes

1.      Charles Bourseul, "Transmission électrique de la parole," <u>L'Illustration</u>, August 26, 1854. Trans. by Jeanine Herman.

2.      Georges Charpak, "Les Sons fossiles," in <u>Mémoires d'un déraciné, physicien, citoyen du monde</u> (Paris: Odile Jacob, 2008), pp. 67–69.

3.      Achille Castiglioni, "The Object I'm Proudest Of? A Switch for an Electric Lead I Designed 30 Years Ago," in Sergio Polano, <u>Achille Castiglioni: Complete Works</u> (Milan: Electa, 2001), p. 252.

4.      "Technological Dreams Series: No. 1, Robots," Dunne & Raby, www.dunneandraby .co.uk/content/projects/10/0.

5.      J. G. Ballard, "The Thousand Dreams of Stellavista," <u>Amazing Stories</u> 36, no. 3 (March 1962); reprinted in <u>The Complete Stories of J. G. Ballard</u>, introduction by Martin Amis (New York: W. W. Norton, 2009), pp. 305–20.

6.      Nicolas Le Camus de Mézières, <u>Le Génie de l'architecture, ou L'Analogie de cet art avec nos sensations</u>, 1780; published in English as <u>The Genius of Architecture; or, The Analogy of That Art with Our Sensations</u>, trans. David Britt (Santa Monica, Calif.: The Getty Center for the History of Art, 1992), p. 71.

7.      "By a well-conceived and ingenious device, he constructed an instrument that gave a concert of colors, while at the same time producing another in sound. Colors succeeded each other harmonically and struck the eye with the same enchantment and, to a man of education, a pleasure as great as any that the ears can enjoy in sounds combined by the most able musician." Ibid., pp. 72–73. Charles Le Brun delivered his treatise as a lecture in 1668; many of his drawings of human faces can be found in Jennifer Montagu, <u>The Expression of the Passions: The Origin and Influence of Charles Le Brun</u> (New Haven: Yale University Press, 1994).

8.      Adolf Loos, "Die Interieurs in der Rotunde," <u>Neue Freie Presse</u>, June 12, 1898; translated in "Interiors in the Rotunda," in <u>Spoken into the Void: Collected Essays, 1897–1900</u>, trans. Jane O. Newman and John H. Smith (Cambridge, Mass.: MIT Press, 1987), p. 24.

9.      The word "fiction" derives from the Latin <u>fingere</u>, which means "to touch with one's fingers" or "handle," and by extension, "to shape."

10.     William Thomson, quoted in Anton A. Huurdeman, <u>The Worldwide History of Telecommunications</u> (Hoboken, N.J.: John Wiley & Sons, 2003), p. 163.

11.     Thomas Augustus Watson, <u>Exploring Life: The Autobiography of Thomas A. Watson</u> (New York: D. Appleton, 1926), pp. 69–70.

12.     On Watson's belief that the telephone itself is speaking, see Avital Ronell, <u>The Telephone Book: Technology, Schizophrenia, Electric Speech</u> (Lincoln: University of Nebraska Press, 1989), p. 257.

13.     On Alexander Graham Bell's talking head, see Herbert Newton Casson, <u>The History of the Telephone</u> (Chicago: A. C. McClurg, 1910), p. 15.

14.     One such subscriber, in 1911, was Marcel Proust. See Proust, entry for February 21, 1911, in <u>Lettres à Reynaldo Hahn</u> (Paris: Gallimard, 1956), p. 199.

15.     See Siegfried Giedion, <u>Mechanization Takes Command: A Contribution to Anonymous History</u>, 1948, reprint ed. (New York: W. W. Norton, 1969).

16.     Ronell, <u>The Telephone Book</u>, p. 276.

17.     Henry van de Velde, <u>Aperçus en vue d'une synthèse d'art</u> (Brussels: Monom, 1895); cited in Pascal Rousseau, "Home Sweet Home: La Maison utérine, antre primitif de la modernité," <u>Exposé</u>, no. 4 (2004): 92.

18.     Naoto Fukasawa and Jasper Morrison, <u>Super Normal: Sensations of the Ordinary</u> (Baden, Switzerland: Lars Müller, 2007).

19.     Philippe Parreno invokes the ventriloquist in <u>Le Cri ultrasonic de l'écureuil</u> (<u>The Ultrasonic Scream of the Squirrel</u>, 2006), an hour-long performance with the ventriloquist Ronn Lucas, during which the performers' voices mingled in a disturbing fashion, blurring the identity of each speaker. See also Mark Wigley, "The Art of Listening to Architecture," in Cynthia C. Davidson, ed., <u>Eisenman/Krier: Two Ideologies</u> (New York: Monacelli Press, 2005).

20.     Ettore Sottsass, <u>Sèvres, le temps d'un voyage</u> (Paris: Bernard-Chauveau, 2006); quoted in Anne-Marie Fèvre, "Tel père, Memphis," <u>Libération</u> 3 (January 2008), www.liberation.fr/culture/0101604876-tel-pere-memphis. Trans. by Jeanine Herman.

21.     Heinrich Wölfflin, preface to <u>Prolegomena zu einer Psychologie der Architektur</u> (Munich: Dr. C. Wolf & Sohn, 1886); published in English in <u>Empathy, Form, and Space: Problems in German Aesthetics, 1873–1893</u> (Santa Monica, Calif.: The Getty Center For the History of Art, 1994), p. 149.

Because of its density and complex infrastructures and systems, the city relies on communication for its own sheer survival. It is an environment of continuous negotiation and navigation, based on codes of behavior that are timeless—the basic laws of human cohabitation—but often unwritten. Rather, these codes demand relentless adaptation and renewal. Politicians are certainly responsible for this delicate, dynamic balance, as are the engineers, experts, and consultants they rely on, but the responsibility lies first and foremost with citizens.

Designers have an important role in this. With their inventions—of all kinds, at all scales—they can enhance clarity, civility, and engagement by involving citizens in maintaining the codes that keep the city alive. Designers can also stimulate the flow of communication that is the vital lymph of the urban organism. This chapter shows the changed role of designers—from creators of form and function to enablers, inspirers, and facilitators—in particular detail.

Using technology, designers enhance a sense of neighborhood (page 101), connect us with street life, and put us in touch with our local government (page 102), all the while helping us communicate effectively, feel pride in our cities, and find inventive ways to get along, as in the community-forming projects Garden Registry (page 110) and Southwark Circle (page 110). Technology can also help tourists understand new places at a glance (page 105), through digital information systems as well as physical ones, and enables authorities to coordinate routine and emergency conditions (page 103). But the city can also communicate in a very low-tech and primal fashion, through its views—its ancient projections of civic personality—and (loud) sounds and (pungent) smells (page 106). Designers master the high and low with dexterity, bringing them together when human needs call for it.

P. A.

The texts in this chapter were written by Azzurra Cox.

CITY

Andy London (American, born 1968) and
Carolyn London (American, born 1972)
of London Squared (USA, est. 1999)

/////////////////////////////

The Lost Tribes of New York City. 2009

/////////////////////////////

Digital video (color, sound), 3 min.

In this stop-motion animation, various
objects on the streets of New York
City—among them a public telephone,
a manhole cover, newspaper boxes—
come to life, with voices taken from the
filmmakers' interviews with New Yorkers
and tourists. The result is a kind of urban
ethnographic research: conversations
with a wide and representative range
of people about their hopes and identities
and how they relate to New York. Some
of the interview subjects speak with
heavy accents, some don't; some tell
jokes, others wax wise and philosophical.
The filmmakers' skill with the stop-motion
effects allows the objects to embody
the voices in a vibrant way. The Lost
Tribes of New York City is both comic
and poignant, showcasing the city's
remarkable diversity while at the same
time emphasizing the common experience
that connects its various tribes.

Poke (UK and USA, est. 2001)

////////////////////////////////

BakerTweet. 2009

////////////////////////////////

Arduino board and web content
management, 9 13/16 × 3 7/8 × 3 7/8"
(25 × 10 × 10 cm)

By simply pressing a button, the
bakers at Albion Cafe in the Shoreditch
neighborhood of London can signal that
something delicious has just popped
out of the oven. Designed by Poke,
a company with an office across the
road from Albion, BakerTweet makes
modern technology mimic a traditional
local encounter, like word passing from
neighbor to neighbor, or the smell of
fresh bread in the street attracting
customers to the bakery. The small,
plain metal box ("bakery-proof," the
designers say, to withstand the heat
and mess of the kitchen) is equipped
with a dial, a button, and a screen
interface, and it sends subscribers
real-time notices on Twitter; the
system can be customized online
every day to reflect what the bakers
plan to make. A hungry follower in
the neighborhood can stop by right
when the goods come out of the
oven, and the bakery can let customers
know when the treats are at their
absolute peak. This seamless line of
communication between bakers and
customers, in turn, renders the city
more intimate. For the duration of the
exhibition <u>Talk to Me</u>, MoMA's Cafe 2
will broadcast the arrival of baked
goods via BakerTweet.

Mayo Nissen (German, born 1986)
Copenhagen Institute of Interaction
Design (Denmark, est. 2007)

/////////////////////////////

City Tickets. 2010

/////////////////////////////

Kiosk, electronics, solar panel, and paper,
70 1/2 × 14 1/2 × 11" (179 × 37 × 28 cm)

City Tickets capitalizes on a common
(and somewhat dull) mechanism of urban
infrastructure—the kiosks that have
replaced parking meters—to open a
direct channel of communication between
citizens and local authorities. At brightly
colored City Tickets kiosks, which also
dispense parking permits, people can
report problems, suggest improvements,
and give general feedback. The kiosks
generate short forms, printed as
standard-format receipts, that can be
then mailed free of charge to the right
city department, where they are entered
into a public database; the receipts
are printed with hyperlocal maps
indicating the exact location of a problem
and enabling the city to respond more
efficiently. Once the reports are listed,
citizens can track their progress through
the system, including a projected date
of completion, online, by phone, or at
the original kiosk. Citizen participation
is encouraged, and transparency and
accountability are increased. With its
innovative and affordable repurposing of
existing urban infrastructure, City Tickets
demonstrates the effective interplay
among service, interaction, and design.

Electronic Ink, Inc. (USA and UK, est. 1990)

/////////////////////////////

911 Command Center Radio Control Application. 2006

/////////////////////////////

Creative Suite, Flash, and Windows Presentation Foundation software

The 911 Command Center is an emergency-response interface that helps dispatch critical resources more efficiently and with fewer errors. Unlike traditional interfaces, which present an overwhelming amount of high-stakes information with equal weight, Electronic Ink's design uses color, animation, and relative sizing to make critical calls more prominent and render priorities intelligible at a glance. Active radio channels, for example, are animated to attract responders' attention, and dormant channels are collapse so that irrelevant data and functions do not distract. This new interface improves awareness, clarity, and accuracy in emergency response to such a great degree that one major American city has already adopted it (the company prefers not to reveal which one), as have various industries, such as airlines, that depend on mission-critical environments.

...think (Canada, est. 1999)

////////////////////////////////

...eezing Bus Stop. 2007

////////////////////////////////

...yl, battery, proximity sensor, MP3
...r, digital timer, audio amplifier,

At first glance, Rethink's bus-shelter
advertisement for Vancouver's Science
World seems rather ordinary: a white
background with a large orange circle
and Science World's blue logo. There
is also a button labeled "Press here and
we'll explain"; observers who comply
are "sneezed" on by the advertisement,
a realistic effect created with sound
and a spritz of water at face level.

Applied Information Group (UK, est. 2002)

////////////////////////////////

Legible London. 2007

////////////////////////////////

Stainless steel, aluminum, PVC, vitreous enamel, polyester film, and Optiwhite glass, 7' 6 1/2" × 27 1/2" (230 × 70 cm)

Henry C. Beck's iconic diagram of the London Underground from the 1930s clearly presents the city's subterranean transit lines, but until now there has been no comprehensive mapping of its pedestrian routes. In 2005 the designers of Applied Information Group (AIG) identified thirty-two different signage systems for pedestrians, creating "visual noise rather than reliable, coordinated information." In an effort to make the city easier to navigate for the 2012 Olympic Games, the mayor's office and Transport for London have begun a campaign called Legible London and commissioned AIG to design a user-friendly pedestrian way-finding system. AIG's design for the maps and signs, the result of extensive research, is focused on the needs of pedestrians. Maps are placed to match the user's orientation and include three-dimensional (and therefore more recognizable) renderings of landmarks and details such as whether the streets are cobblestone or asphalt; concentric circles identify locations within five-minute and fifteen-minute walks. The system is also integrated with public transport networks to get both residents and

tourists to destinations near and far. Legible London was launched in 2007 with a prototype in the West End and in 2009 expanded into three more neighborhoods; it has been a great success, with some surveys showing that most Londoners would like the system to be available across the city. Legible London renders an exceptionally complex city more accessible and transparent, enabling both efficiency and exploration, and has the added benefit of encouraging walking, thus addressing environmental and public-health issues.

Sissel Tolaas (Norwegian, born 1962)

Berlin, City Smell Research. 2004

Glass and smell simulation, each bottle:
5 7/8 × 7 1/16 × 2 3/8" (15 × 18 × 6 cm)

"Smell immediately locates you in a space," says artist, designer, chemist, and odor theorist Sissel Tolaas. "It gives you new tools to perceive your surroundings." Throughout her career Tolaas has worked provocatively with smell, applying headspace technology—used in the perfume industry to capture and synthesize natural scents—to render essences ranging from the objectionable (sweat, rotten fish, dog feces) to the everyday (fresh laundry, kebabs, shoe shop) and put them into an archive of more than seven thousand scents. From this archive she has created fragrances that do not adhere to the usual definitions of what smells good or desirable; instead, her aim is to stimulate emotional responses, evoke memories, and re-create places in all their chaos and specificity. While conducting her City Smell Research, which was presented at the Berlin Biennale in 2004, Tolaas worked in various Berlin districts to distill an essential scent for each one, creating an olfactory map of the city. The scents are contained in bottles that physically recall the city map and compass points. This work is not simply the charting of a landscape of smell; it also explores the potential of smell as information that enhances and subverts the physical and symbolic boundaries of the urban ecosystem.

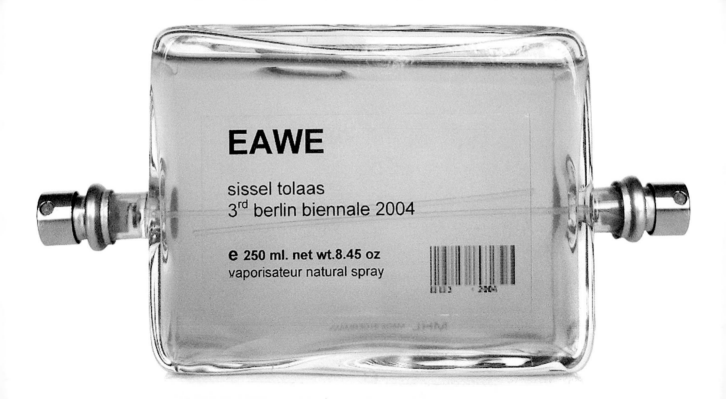

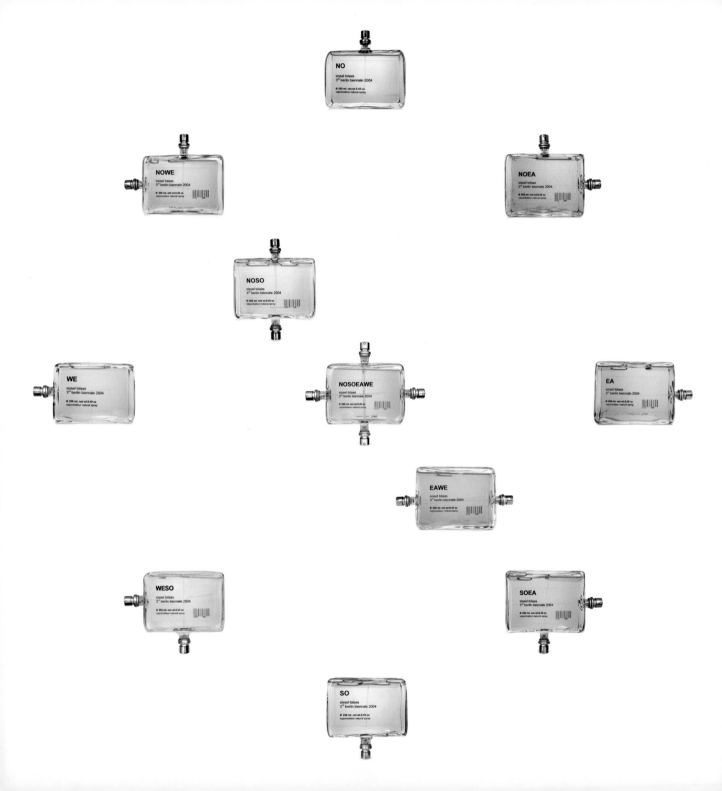

SENSEable City Lab (est. 2003)
Massachusetts Institute of Technology
(USA, est. 1861)

//////////////////////////////

TrashTrack. 2009

//////////////////////////////

MATLAB and Processing software

The removal chain that takes trash from garbage can to processing and recycling facilities is more complex than we can imagine: as globalization increases, waste from Los Angeles can resurface as carpeting in Alabama or even clothing in China. TrashTrack gives us some insight into the process, revealing the hidden infrastructures of urban trash removal. Waste products from households, businesses, and government offices in New York, Seattle, and London were tagged with custom-designed, nontoxic chips and the signals from the tags were overlaid in real time onto satellite maps to demonstrate the objects' physical journey. Carlo Ratti, director of SENSEable City Lab, likens the project to the tracing of nuclear molecules through the human body in order to learn how systems work. To raise awareness, SENSEable City Lab exhibited the project results at The Seattle Public Library and The Architectural League of New York in 2009, showing the maps alongside footage of waste-disposal and recycling facilities by video artist and photographer Armin Linke.

Armin Linke (Italian, born 1966)

//////////////////////////////

Computer Dump Guiyu China. 2005

//////////////////////////////

Chromogenic color print, 59" x 6' 6 11/16"
(150 x 200 cm)

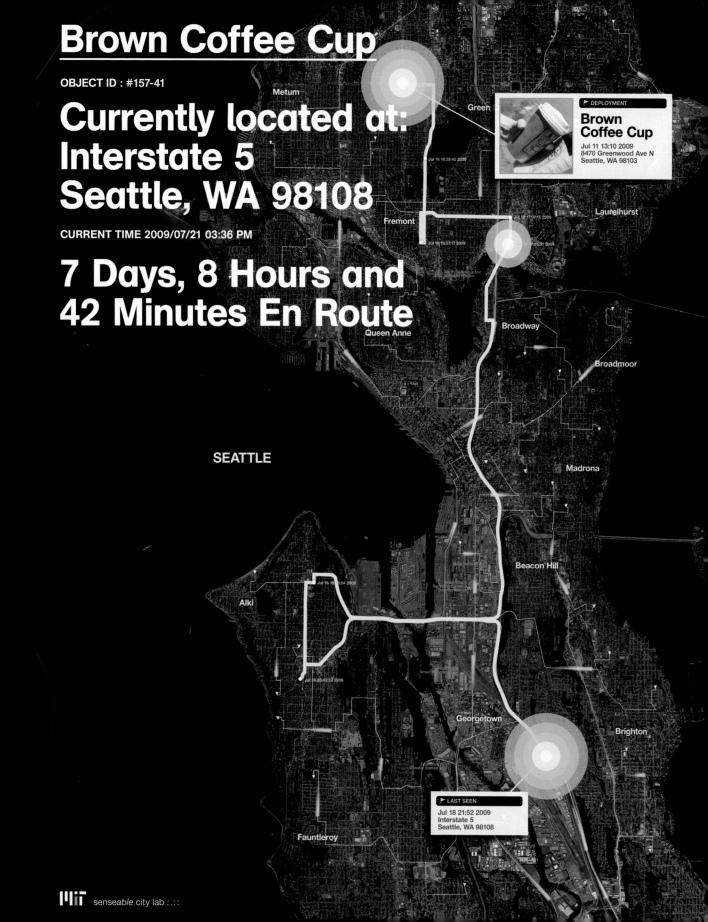

# Brown Coffee Cup

OBJECT ID : #157-41

## Currently located at: Interstate 5 Seattle, WA 98108

CURRENT TIME 2009/07/21 03:36 PM

## 7 Days, 8 Hours and 42 Minutes En Route

▶ DEPLOYMENT

**Brown Coffee Cup**
Jul 11 13:10 2009
8470 Greenwood Ave N
Seattle, WA 98103

SEATTLE

Metum
Green
Fremont
Laurelhurst
Queen Anne
Broadway
Broadmoor
Madrona
Beacon Hill
Alki
Georgetown
Brighton
Fauntleroy

▶ LAST SEEN

Jul 18 21:52 2009
Interstate 5
Seattle, WA 98108

MIT   *senseable* city lab :.::

Amy Franceschini (American, born 1970)
of Futurefarmers (USA, est. 1995)

//////////////////////////////

Garden Registry. 2008

//////////////////////////////

Flash, Flex Builder, PHP, and MySQL
software

Garden Registry is an online map and
social network where users can add their
own gardening sites and identify potential
future locations in San Francisco. The
registry includes everything from window
boxes and terraces to yards, community
gardens, and vacant plots, creating
what the artist group Futurefarmers
calls an "important portrait of land use."
The site also maps the city's micro-
climates, indicating which areas are most
suitable for which vegetables according
to the amount of direct sunlight and
moisture they receive. Gardeners can
let each other know about their surplus
produce so that they can benefit from
and contribute to a broader exchange
of locally grown food.

Southwark Circle CIC (UK, est. 2009)

//////////////////////////////

Southwark Circle. 2009

//////////////////////////////

Custom software

In the UK, as in many countries, the
elderly population is growing at a much
faster rate than other groups. Research
by the design group Participle has
shown that the keys to good quality
of life for senior citizens are rather basic:
a regular social network of at least six
people and freedom from worrying about
physically challenging problems, such
as changing lightbulbs. Southwark Circle,
a membership organization based in
the London borough of the same name,
mobilizes public, private, and volunteer
resources to help seniors take care
of household chores, forge stronger
social and neighborhood connections,
and contribute their own skills to the
Circle community. Southwark Circle
was created in collaboration with
Participle and tested by more than
250 seniors and their family members,
and the service was launched in 2009.
It is an alternative model for senior
care, one that moves away from formal
government-run or social services
and toward community.

Emily Read (British, born 1982)
and Chen Hsu (Taiwanese, born 1982)

////////////////////////////

Homeless City Guide. 2007

////////////////////////////

Illustrator software

To deliver vital information more effectively to the urban homeless— a decentralized population with little access to mobile technology—designers Emily Read and Chen Hsu revived the centuries-old language of the hobo code. The homeless can use this series of simple symbols to communicate with each other about safety, shelter, and free food by inscribing them with chalk on sidewalks, buildings, and other surfaces. The code, reproduced in each issue of the Pavement, a London-based magazine for the homeless, forms a common language that is both inconspicuous and highly directed. Read calls the language "a means of exposing the hidden potentials of the city and making these more accessible to the homeless" and "a new, informal avenue of communication," one that also makes reference to the very roots of language and civilization.

1

# HOMELESS CITY GUIDE

⌂ squat

▢ empty building

⊡ dangerous neighbourhood

⊡ danger

⌄⌄ guard dogs

@↓ an attack happened here

⊔ good place to drink / smoke

⊗ unfriendly place

⊘ friendly place

⊔ soup run (with rating)

Ⓟ strong police presence

°°° potential for work

≡ good food thrown away here

•— safe for sleeping

10→ message board x mins that way

⋔ security guard

↻→ you'll get moved on here

step 1

step 2

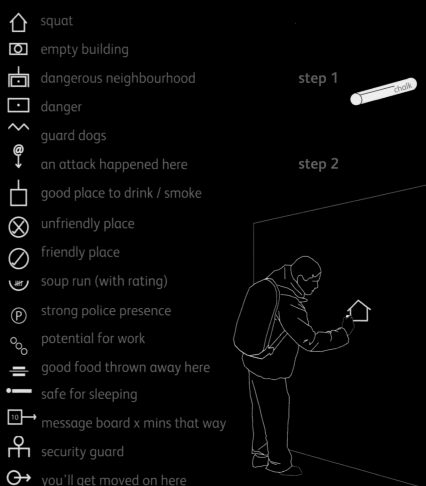

## MAKE YOUR MARK AND HELP OTHERS TO READ THE CITY
Make non permanent marks to keep the system up to date and stay within the law.

Jeroen Beekmans (Dutch, born 1985) and
Joop de Boer (Dutch, born 1978)
of Golfstromen (the Netherlands, 2007)

/////////////////////////////////

Gentrification Battlefield. 2010

/////////////////////////////////

After Effects software

In this video game trailer, longtime inhabitants of a neighborhood fight for possession against advancing hipsters and yuppies. The game takes place in Amsterdam-Noord, a real-life neighborhood that has become a symbolic stage for class and social conflict in the Netherlands, with artists and cutting-edge institutions existing alongside a sizable immigrant community. The neighborhood has Amsterdam's highest unemployment rate and highest percentage of right-wing voters. Jeroen Beekmans, one of the game's designers, notes that urban redevelopment in the area has led to "garages and dancing schools losing terrain to creative start-ups with molded concrete floors and apple-green chairs." In Gentrification Battlefield, which has the retro aesthetic of a PlayStation 1 game, you can either be Timo, a hipster driving a Volkswagen van, or Sjaan, an elderly resident threatened with eviction; the neighborhood battlefield is rendered complete with key landmarks. By presenting the process of gentrification as a real battle, the game provides insight into the political and social complexities of the issue. Golfstromen is planning to turn the concept into a real game.

Christian Zöllner (German, born 1981),
Patrick Tobias Fischer (German,
born 1980), Thilo Hoffmann (German,
born 1980), and Sebastian Piatza
(German, born 1985)
of VR/Urban (Germany, est. 2008)

////////////////////////////

SMSlingshot. 2009

////////////////////////////

High frequency radio, Arduino board,
laser, batteries, plywood, and ash wood,
14 3/16 × 8 5/16 × 1 5/8" (36 × 21 × 4 cm)

The SMSlingshot marries the traditional
weapon with digital technology, splatter-
ing information onto facades and other
surfaces that then serve as public
screens. The battery-powered device is
a wooden slingshot with a display screen,
keypad, and laser. Users can store and
type text messages and then release the
slingshot to blast them onto surfaces,
where they appear within a splash of
color and linger as long as the performers
decide, and the text is tweeted at the
same time. VR/Urban considers the
SMSlingshot an intervention against
increasingly commercialized urban space,
which is thus reclaimed and occupied
through virtual tags. The device fuses
a prehistoric tool, vibrant urban art, and
innovative technology into a product that
encourages interaction, information, and
empowerment in the city.

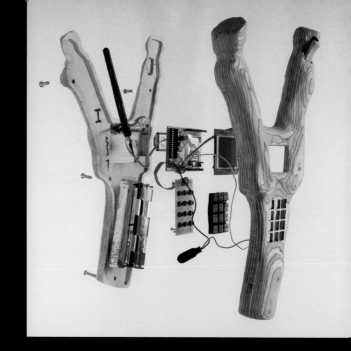

Evan Roth (American, born 1978)

////////////////////////////////

Graffiti Taxonomy. 2009

////////////////////////////////

'AEIOU', Paris
Two-color screenprint, 35 3/4
x 17 3/4" (90.8 x 45.1 cm)

'S', New York
Two-color screenprint, 30
x 24" (76.2 x 61 cm)

Evan Roth has catalogued characters
from graffiti tags found in New York
and Paris and assembled them into
comprehensive taxonomies of particular
letters. The result is an organized study
of stylistic expression, depicting range,
commonalities, and deviations in letterforms. For the Paris project, Roth isolated
the ten most commonly used letters
(A, E, I, K, N, O, R, S, T, U) for further
study. Eighteen tags, shown in both
uppercase and lowercase letters,
were chosen to represent the diversity
and range of each specific character,
from simple to ornate. The Fondation
Cartier pour l'art contemporain, which
commissioned Graffiti Taxonomy for the
exhibition <u>Born in the Streets—Graffiti</u>
in 2009, displayed these tags on the
museum's exterior, transforming the
building into a canvas and learning tool.
Roth's cataloguing of each letter of the
alphabet in New York is ongoing; on his
website he calls for leads from the public,
thus crowdsourcing the hunting and
gathering of specimens.

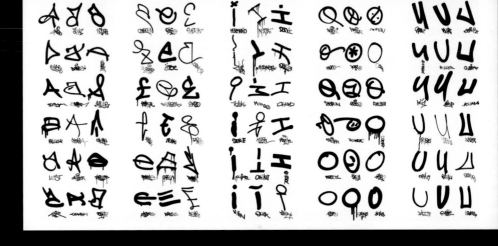

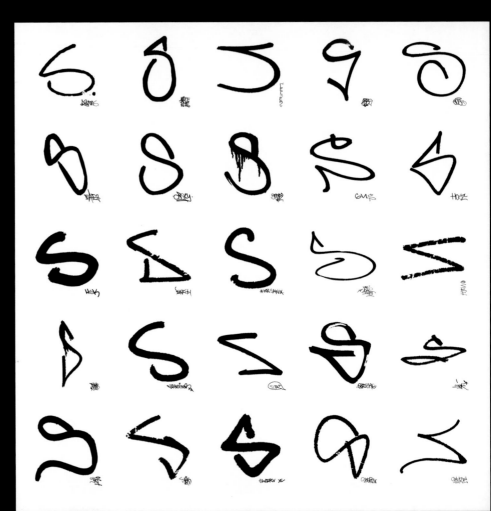

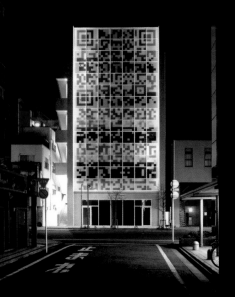

Naoki Terada (Japanese, born 1967)
and Kenichi Hirate (Japanese, born 1980)
of Terada Design Architects (Japan,
est. 2003)
Alexander Reeder (American, born 1978),
Nao Tokui (Japanese, born 1976),
and Taeji Sawai (Japanese, born 1978)
of Qosmo, Inc. (Japan, est. 2009)
Izumi Okayasu (Japanese, born 1972)
of Izumi Okayasu Lighting Design
(Japan, est. 2005)

/////////////////////////////

N Building facade. 2009

/////////////////////////////

Aluminum, double-glass panels, ceramic print, LEDs, and Vectorworks, Barcode Robo, Xcode, and Logic Pro software

The N Building, located in a shopping district near Tokyo's Tachikawa station, has a uniquely interactive facade. Instead of the signs and billboards that are usually attached to commercial buildings, a large QR code forms the N Building's skin. The QR code takes passersby to relevant online information about the building, including notices and updates from its retailers and tweets from shoppers. This virtual yet tangible interaction between building and person is a novel, enhanced experience of the physical, in which, as the designers say, "the facade of the building disappears, showing those inside who want to be seen."

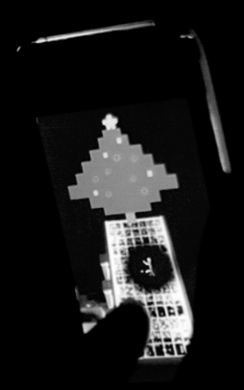

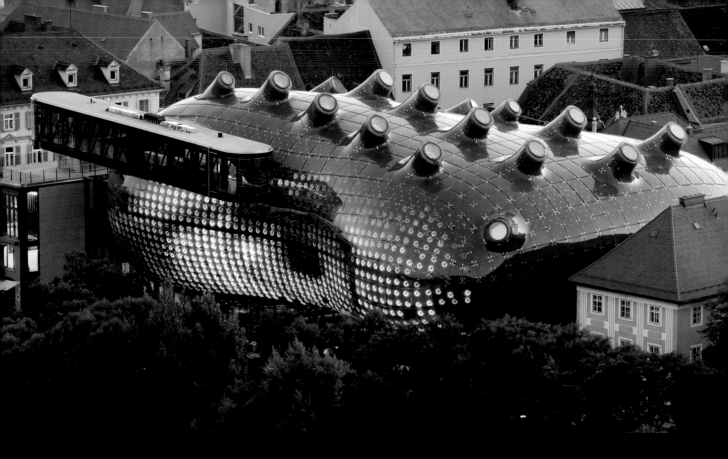

Jan Edler (German, born 1970)
and Tim Edler (German, born 1965)
of realities:united (Germany, est. 2000)

/////////////////////////////

BIX Communicative Display Skin. 2002

/////////////////////////////

Plexiglas, wood, steel, fluorescent tubes,
and electronics, panel: 31 1/2 × 43 1/2
× 11 3/4" (80 × 110.5 × 29.8 cm)

BIX is a permanent light-and-media
installation for Kunsthaus Graz, Austria,
the biomorphic art museum designed
by Peter Cook and Colin Fournier,
which opened in 2003. BIX consists
of a Plexiglas facade with 930 fluorescent
tubes on the building's eastern side.
The facade thus functions as an oversize,
undulating urban screen, with each
light ring adjustable for brightness
and functioning as a pixel in a dynamic,
low-resolution art gallery, as if the
building were tattooed with larger-than-
life images, text, and film sequences.
The designers want BIX to act as "an
architectural 'enabler' enhancing the
building's communicative possibilities"
as well as its range and identity. Through
manageable and inexpensive technology,
this modular system embodies a vision
of architecture as a changing, moving,
and performing medium and demonstrates an accessible, eco-conscious
(for its era) integration of media surfaces
in urban landscapes. A BIX panel is in
the collection of The Museum of Modern
Art, New York.

Jacques Herzog (Swiss, born 1950)
and Pierre de Meuron (Swiss, born 1950)
of Herzog & de Meuron (Switzerland,
est. 1978)

////////////////////////////

Allianz Arena skin. 2005

////////////////////////////

ETFE foil extendable panel and other
materials, deflated panel: 9' 10 1/8"
x 6' 2 13/16" (300 x 190 cm); fully inflated
panel : 32' 9 11/16" x 15' 1 1/8" (10 m
x 460 cm)

Nicknamed "ring of fire," the Allianz
Arena, designed for Munich's two
local soccer teams, features an outer
membrane constructed of 2,874 inflated
ETFE foil panels. Each panel contains
four lights that can be illuminated in
white, red, or blue, so that the panels
can be independently lit with the colors
of the home team. The stadium glows
red for FC Bayern München, blue for
TSV 1860 München, a checkerboard when
they play each other, and white for the
German national team or other matches.
Thus the arena wears the team colors,
embodying and magnifying the energy
of the spectators inside it.

Area/Code (USA, est. 2005)

/////////////////////////////

ConQwest. 2003

/////////////////////////////

Custom software

Area/Code designs games that draw on the stylized social interaction of play to investigate systems and landscapes, both real and imaginary. ConQwest and Crossroads both engage with urban space. ConQwest, designed for Qwest Wireless, was the first large-scale use of Semacodes, optic codes (like QR tags) scanned by mobile phones. The game is a team-based treasure hunt designed for high school students: players move through the city collecting treasure by taking pictures of unidentified Semacodes with their telephones and securing territory by moving their team totems into specially delineated zones. The players' locations and status are shown on the game's website in real time, turning it into a spectator event. The game's 2008 debut in Minneapolis was a big success, and since then Qwest has staged the game in ten more American cities, making it an annual event.

////////////////////////////

Crossroads. 2006

////////////////////////////

Custom software

Crossroads, developed for Boost Mobile handsets and designed for the Van Alen Institute, a nonprofit architectural organization, is a two-player, GPS-enabled street game. Players claim Manhattan intersections as they advance, but it is not a matter of simply moving forward and conquering: Crossroads draws on the traditions of the second line, a New Orleans brass band parade whose spontaneous and random routes cross neighborhood as well as social and cultural boundaries. To engender that same spirit of improvisation, the game includes the character Baron Samedi (also known as Papa Bones), a disruptive spirit who moves independently and introduces chaos: control of any intersection flips to the other player when he appears at it. The Baron can be diverted via offerings placed at intersections in another nod to traditional New Orleans culture. In Crossroads, Area/Code combines real and imaginary opponents in an urban game that pays homage to one place-based culture by re-creating it somewhere else.

Toby Barnes (British, born 1973)
and Matt Watkins (British, born 1973)
of Mudlark (UK, est. 2009)

////////////////////////////////

Chromaroma. 2010

////////////////////////////////

Illustrator and Flash software
and advanced wireless services (AWS)
spectrum band

Chromaroma uses an existing
infrastructure—London's transportation
systems—as a platform for a real-time
game. Commuters sign up to play using
their Oyster cards, a form of electronic
ticketing used in Greater London, and
then are grouped into one of four teams,
where they rack up points with each
journey and strategically complete
specific tasks and missions. Some
missions rely on an evolving story line
(such as a diamond heist or a ghost hunt),
and others have players altering their
daily routines (getting off a stop earlier
or going all the way to the end of the line)
in order to gain a new perspective on
the city. The players' physical movements are recorded by their Oyster cards
and can be charted on three-dimensional
interactive maps and published on
Twitter or Facebook, making everyday
journeys into social experiences.
Chromaroma thus injects the often
mundane process of commuting with
a sense of playfulness, encouraging
people to explore the city and ally
themselves with strangers. Since it
does not rely on smartphone technology,
the game is accessible to anyone
with an Oyster card; the design
company Mudlark hopes eventually
to expand Chromaroma to other
cities around the world.

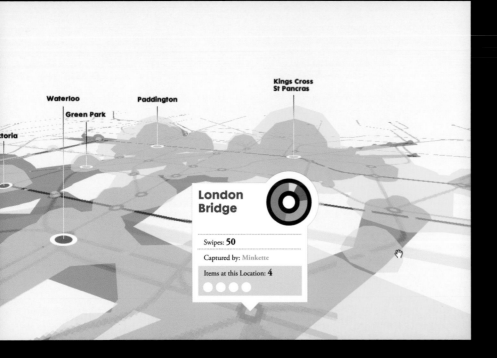

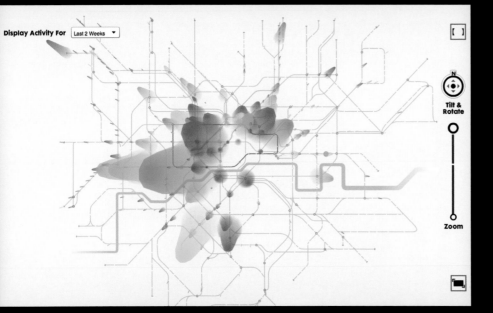

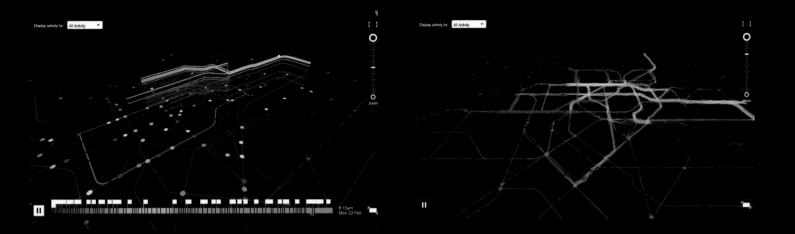

1

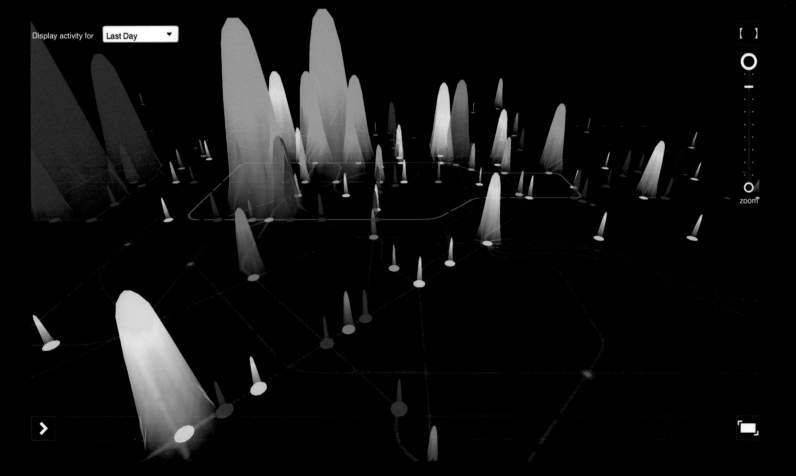

Pedro Miguel Cruz (Portuguese,
born 1985) and Penousal Machado
(Portuguese, born 1970)
of the Centre for Informatics
and Systems (est. 1991)
University of Coimbra (Portugal,
est. 1290)
João Bicker (Portuguese, born 1961)
of Ferrand, Bicker & Associados
(Portugal, est. 1998)

//////////////////////////////

Visualizing Lisbon's Traffic—7am,
10am, and 6pm (top left, bottom right,
bottom left). 2009

//////////////////////////////

Processing software

Pedro Miguel Cruz, Penousal Machado,
and João Bicker mapped the GPS
coordinates and velocities of 1,534
taxis circulating throughout Lisbon
over one month, using data provided
by MIT Portugal's CityMotion project,
and then condensed the data into an
animation representing an average single
day to produce a dynamic visualization
of the city's traffic. Coordinates and
velocities are grouped by second and
coded by color; thickness and color
correspond to traffic intensity, with
warm colors indicating sluggish traffic
and cool colors indicating traffic moving
quickly, making it is easy to spot areas
likely to be bottlenecked. As a novel
way of expressing useful everyday
information, the project suggests
applications for future mobile decision-
making technology and presents an
elegant image of the city and transport
network as a pulsating protozoan
organism—with a metabolism that
shifts depending on the time of day.

1

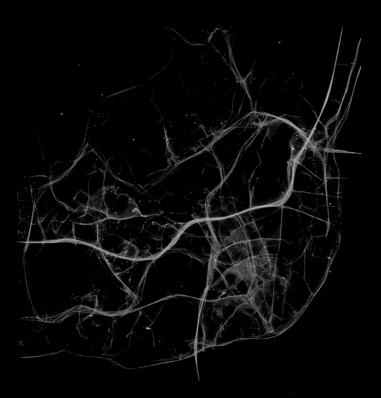

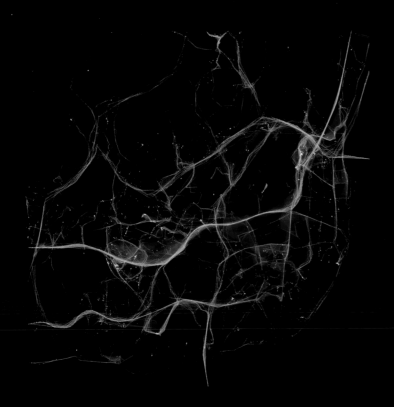

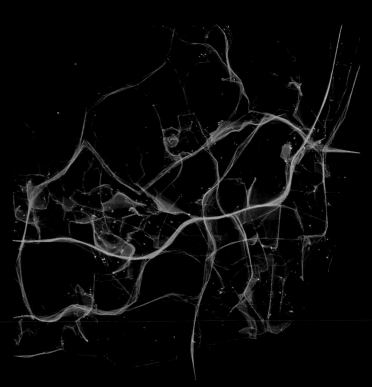

Michal Migurski (Polish, born 1977)
of Stamen Design (USA, est. 2001)

\\\\\\\\\\\\\\\\\\\\\\\\\\\\\\\\

Walking Papers. 2009

\\\\\\\\\\\\\\\\\\\\\\\\\\\\\\\\

Python, VLFeat SIFT, PHP, FPDF,
Modest Maps, GDAL, and OpenStreetMap
Potlatch software

Walking Papers is an interface that makes
a complex process (digital mapping) and
a democratic service (OpenStreetMap,
a free and editable map of the world)
transparent and approachable. Users
select the places they wish to annotate
and print out a map, which is tagged with
QR codes that will link the map back to
OpenStreetMap's database; they then
take to the streets, penciling in data as
they go. This information is scanned and
uploaded (or sent by mail) to the Walking
Papers site and traced into OpenStreet-
Map. In this way, participants help
detail maps of their own neighborhoods
with useful, eye-level data—restaurants,
post-office boxes, ATMs—without
expensive equipment or extensive
knowledge of the technology. Stamen
Design notes that the process combines
mapping with "web-service opportunism
and old-fashioned undigital fulfillment."
Although designed with the amateur
mapper in mind, Walking Papers has
proven useful in extraordinary situations,
such as after the earthquake in Haiti
in 2010, when the existing mapped
infrastructure was largely destroyed
and locating relief camps, hospitals,
and other services was a vital task.
Its usefulness in that context has
endured: data on the Walking Papers
website shows that, a year after
the earthquake, maps of Haiti still
accounted for almost twenty-five
percent of total uploads. Walking Papers
is a process both personalized and
collective, and the physical papers
it produces are artifacts of exploration.

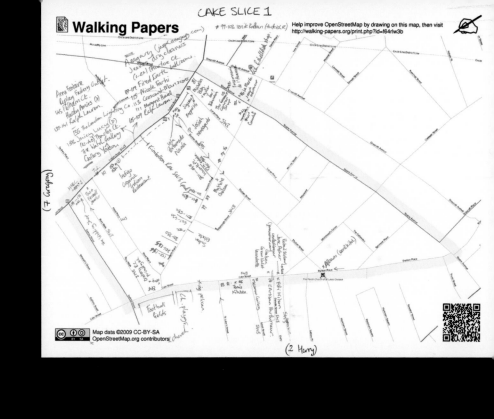

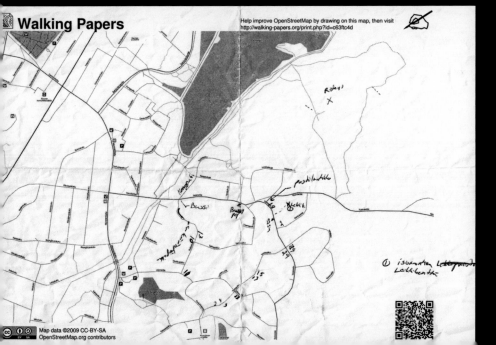

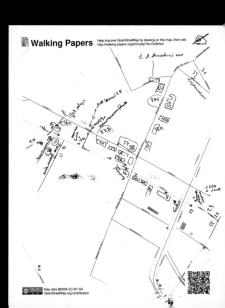

Aaron Straup Cope (Canadian
and American, born Canada 1971)
of Stamen Design (USA, est. 2001)

////////////////////////////////

prettymaps, Beijing (top left), Manhattan
(bottom left), and Tokyo (opposite). 2010

////////////////////////////////

Polymaps, Mapnik, and TileStache
software

prettymaps are interactive maps that
integrate data from freely available
sources into multidimensional renderings
of different places. The application pulls
geographic data from open-mapping
projects—including street-level data
from OpenStreetMap, land-formation
data from Natural Earth, and place-
specific data from Flickr—and plots
them atop one another. Users can view
the maps at varying degrees of detail,
zooming from a view of the world to
a view of a single neighborhood. They are
visually striking, with cities transformed
into colorful abstractions, but the shapes
are recognizable for anyone already
familiar with the terrain.

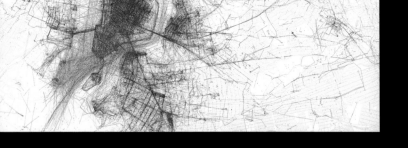

represented in blue, and someone whose photos are taken within a limited time period is assumed to be a tourist and represented in red; photographers whose status can't be determined are represented in yellow.

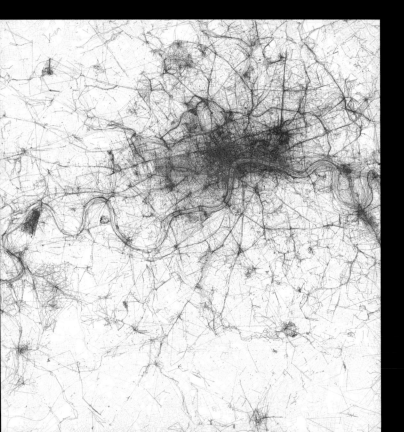

Jack Schulze (British, born 1976),
James King (British, born 1982), and
Campbell Orme (British, born 1982)
of BERG (UK, est. 2005)

/////////////////////////////

Here & There. 2009

/////////////////////////////

Offset lithography, 39 3/8 × 27 5/8"
(100 × 70 cm)

In this horizonless perspective, the
streets of New York suddenly fold
upward, creating a double view of
the city. BERG's Here & There map of
Manhattan is inspired by gaming technology, satellites, and, the designers say,
the idea that "the ability to be in a city
and to see through it is a superpower,
and it's how maps should work."
The maps, created using sophisticated
modeling software, start in the fore-
ground with a three-dimensional image
of buildings that graphically bends as the
buildings extend into the distance, thus
displaying remote areas of the city in plan
view. This puts the viewer in two places
at once, above and in the city, able to
visualize urban space as a continuous
medium. BERG has produced two
Manhattan maps—one looking uptown
from Third Avenue and Seventh Street,
and one looking downtown from Third
Avenue and Thirty-fifth Street. The
designers hope in the future to explore
how enriching the maps with local
information, such as bus routes, might
make them useful as way-finding devices.
For now, the maps present a mind-
bending visualization of the city—indeed,
one that seems to belong in a dream.

# Conversations with the Network

Khoi Vinh

The design world that I came up in—the graphic design industry at the end of the last century—was fundamentally about fashioning messages: ornamenting and embellishing content so that a core idea, product, or service could be more effectively consumed. Even if a designer felt compelled to obscure the content, as was the style of the postmodern discourse that dominated the field at the time, the operative notion was that design was still elementally about the transmission of messages.

It took nearly a decade of working in digital media before I understood that this idea was fundamentally at odds with the new arche-type inherent in networked technology. To be sure, digital media is conducive to communication; in fact, the Internet is perhaps the greatest multiplier of communications that the world has ever seen. With its enormous and pervasive reach it transmits ideas across great distances with great speed, among a large number of people, and in unbelievably rapid succession, all as a matter of course. In many ways such free-dom and efficiency have drastically democratized communication, obsolescing the more deliberate, thoughtful pace that communication took when mediated by graphic design. But in this new world designers are critical not so much for the transmission of messages but for the crafting of the spaces within which those messages can be borne.

To understand this difference, it's helpful to look back at the predigital world and recognize that the predominant notion of how design worked was this: every design solution was the product of a visionary who birthed and nurtured an original idea, a radical insight, or an inspired revision. The designer gave it life and labored over it, so that the original inspiration evolved into a complete and definitive work. There was no design without the designer.

It was a useful construct through which to comprehend design: the idea that a single person (or small group of people) was responsible for a design solution allowed hopeful young designers like me to understand this mystery as something achievable on human terms. It made inspiration knowable and potentially reproducible, provided role models, archetypes to aspire to. If genius could be embodied in a single person, then anyone might be a genius, or at least, with work and discipline, could learn from the ways of their design heroes. These heroes could be interviewed, written about, studied, even encountered in the real world at lectures and conferences. They walked among us; if we were lucky we might even come to know them personally.

In this model the designer was something of a storyteller, and the finished design functioned as a kind of narrative. The designer created the beginning, middle, and end, leading the audience through something immersive, wondrous, bracing, satisfying, and/or inspiring. Thus the core product, whether an advertise-ment, magazine article, or consumer object, would be transformed into a visual story: an ad for a museum might become a map of the human body, an interview with a musician might become a travelogue of an alternative mindscape, a jar of pasta sauce might evoke a classical age lost to contemporary sensibilities. Whatever the conceit, the audience was beholden to the designer's grand plan, experiencing the design according to those original intentions. The closer the audience's experience to the designer's original script, the more effective the designer.

Many of the greatest designers in history have been measured by their ability to tell compelling stories. As an aspirant to the trade, I marveled at Alexey Brodovitch's groundbreaking midcentury work in the pages of Harper's Bazaar. Brodovitch forged hypermodern tales of glamour from expertly art-directed photography, type, and graphic elements. In each magazine spread he juxta-posed models in unexpected poses with inventive layout, commanding the narrative as effectively as the magazine's editors and writers; in many ways his was the hand that compelled each issue into a coherent whole.

In my early career I also pored over David Carson's deconstructive work from his signature stints as art director at Beach Culture and Ray Gun. With blown-out type and nearly unreadable text, Carson practically usurped the narrative in favor of his own creative agenda, privileging the relationship between designer and reader while demoting the relationship between the writer and reader; he abstracted his own reading of the content into an unconventional, heady brand of visual narrative, something that spoke to the unique persuasive power that designers possessed.

These were my heroes: Brodovitch, Cipe Pineles, Paul Rand, Alexander Liberman, M. F. Agha, and other originators of the visual storytelling methods still plumbed by designers today, as well as Carson, Rudy VanderLans, Why Not Associates, Ed Fella, P. Scott Makela, Neville Brody, and the rest of the graphic-design insurgents who were then at the frontiers of design authorship. It's not easy to rationalize such diverse bodies of work into a coherent influence, but what they had in common was that they were all storytellers.

As I pursued a career in interaction design, I saw it as my duty to carry this sensibility over to a new platform. The Internet was then, and today remains, a young medium, and I reasoned that it could only benefit from a century's worth of design conventions and lessons accumulated in the analog world. And in this I made a fundamental miscalculation.

The designer as author, as craftsperson bringing together beginning, middle, and end, becomes redundant in a space in which every participant forges his or her own beginning, middle, and end. And that is exactly what happens in networked media. The narrative recedes, and the behavior of the design solution becomes prominent. What becomes important are questions that concern not the author but the users. How does the system respond to the input of its users? When a user says something to the system, how does the system respond?

Where analog media thrived on the compelling power of narrative, digital media insists on much less linear modes of communication. Instead of the one-to-many model that dominated the last century—for example, a magazine article written by a single journalist and encountered by thousands of readers—the Internet is a many-to-many platform, a framework in which everyone talks to everyone and every utterance might inspire a reply. It is a conversation rather than a broadcast.

Although we are approaching the commercial Internet's third decade, it feels like we are still in an evolutionary phase, still coming to grips with this transition from narrative to conversation. We remain preoccupied by the residual power of brands built upon aging narrative authorities: the major broadcast networks, the major publishers, and the major record labels and film studios. Yet few of these industries have achieved truly comfortable footholds in the new landscape; they continue to grapple with the new digital paradigm—sometimes elegantly, often fitfully, occasionally with tremendous intolerance.

In part this transitional difficulty can be blamed on the superficial resemblance that digital interfaces can share with artifacts of the analog world: pages, headlines, paragraphs, logos, icons, and photographs are just as common in digital products as they are in print products. Graphic communication appears to be a thread common to both analog and digital worlds, so for many, like me, who came from the former, it has only been natural to try to apply narrative thinking to the latter. But to understand digital media as a form of narrative is to misread the problem entirely.

Digital media is not a printing press; it does not yield publications but objects of a new kind—some people call them products, a decidedly commercial (and not altogether objectionable) term, but I prefer experiences. The great experiences of this new medium have no beginning, middle, and end; there is no narrative arc for Google, no measurable breadth for Facebook, no climactic resolution for Twitter. Of course the companies that brought these experiences to life have a narrative of their own: they were founded one day in the not-too-distant past and they will fold one day in the unforeseen future. But in the day-to-day interactions of countless millions of people, these experiences exist as a continuum.

Certainly they are a coherent environment of pages, headlines, paragraphs, logos, icons, and photos, but they are also an amalgam of invisible user cues, organizational structures, intentional and unintentional system responses, ambient content, constantly regenerating activity, and, most important, reflections of each user, in the content, in the ornamentation, in the very personality of the experience.

To design these systems is to anticipate what cannot be planned, to create a framework in which the unexpected can be expected to happen. The designer's job is not to execute the vision of one person but to establish the conditions under which rich, rewarding conversation can happen. This work occurs at many different levels, from the prompts for user input and the character of system output to the channels for peer dialogue and the continual iteration that takes place over a product's life cycle.

Take the search function. A user enters a term in a search field, and the system reflects back the user's intention and then some; it must respond in a manner that acknowledges the thrust of what was requested, but it must also provide more—more accuracy, more depth, more variety. Just as a conversation between two people must move forward, search results must reiterate what one participant says to the other while simultaneously sharpening and broadening the subject of discussion.

The search function is perhaps the most common interaction performed today, across every subject, under the aegis of many different brands, and in countless contexts. Yet it is quite often thoroughly unsatisfying, mostly because few systems can participate in sufficiently rewarding search-based conversations with their users. I might argue that in spite of its critical importance, searching is so difficult a problem that it has required the most overwhelming combination of human intellect and raw computing power to design a search experience that can adequately converse with users: Google. Its success is well known, but it's still worth emphasizing how thoroughly Google's effectiveness has shaped the Internet experiences designed in the first decade of this century. Designing systems in such a way that their core content is transparent to Google—that is, so that it will be found by Google's remarkably effective search—became a nonnegotiable design principle for countless digital products.

Perhaps because of its inherent difficulty and the fact that few sites have the resources to do it well, searching, in most digital experiences, is designed only as a supplemental feature. In recent years more and more digital experiences have come to rely on the more readily available power between peers; social networks have become so expansively propagated that the conversations between users on these networks threaten to eclipse the primacy of search in terms of directing traffic. Conversations on Facebook and Twitter—status updates, tweets, and other fragmentary bits of communication—can contain within them recommendations, references, asides, and links to other content and Internet destinations that are much richer and more powerful than search results because they originate from trusted sources. As a result we are entering an age in which these conversations can be more effective at driving attention and commerce than results provided by Google and other search engines.

Designing for social media is an exercise in negating the designer's authorial privilege. Experiences that hope to reap the rewards of rich social interactions must be incredibly modest in demonstrating the storytelling skills of the designer, because they are very much in the business of creating the conditions under which these rewarding conversations can happen. They must allow the narrative to recede and the behaviors of the system to come forward.

The most popular social networks— and social networks are always measured in popularity—have been paragons of neutrality. There is a brand presence at Facebook, of course, but it is decidedly less prominent than the artistic showmanship in the pages of any major print magazine. The design of its predecessor, Myspace, was distinguished only as a platform for some of the most uninhibited, aesthetically unsound user customization ever brought into the world. And Twitter, that unpredictable outlet for billions of stray thoughts, may be a harbinger of design to come: a design practically without a design. For many users Twitter is experienced through third-party client software; the Twitter logo and the Twitter brand are all but invisible, yet at the same time the experience is indelibly Twitter. This is what digital design looks like when it does away with the biases of the analog world.

But social networks must do more than allow for conversation between users. If they were simply bulletin boards for motivated users on the networks, if their only design challenge was to let those who would talk be heard, they would be something very different. They must also allow for passive conversation, for the thousands of users who pass through a posting without speaking up. These lurkers may mark a post as a favorite, or they may make the implicit endorsement of republishing it, or they may forward the post to their own networks; although they take no explicit action, the simple fact of their having viewed a post is automatically recorded. These ghostlike tracks are also a kind of conversation; they say something back to the original poster as well as to themselves—their presence is participation in itself. Designers who create social experiences must anticipate these marginal but critical behaviors, and there can be a multitude of them—enough so that there is little or no room for the designer to execute expressions of his or her ego. As a design

challenge, social media is still new; it is significant in its implications today but will only become more and more so as social networks become more prevalent, more complex, and more diffuse.

In the last decade of the twentieth century it was clear that the Internet would transform everything; now that this has nearly come to pass, it is becoming increasingly evident that social media will do so as well. But part of that transformation is a sense of continual renewal, and this is the last and perhaps the most significant way in which digital media transforms the work of the designer: the designer's challenge is to create a framework for the user to engage in conversation, but the designer is also now charged with engaging the user in conversation through the framework itself. Design solutions can no longer be concluded; they're now works in progress, objects that continually evolve and are continually reinvented. A designer creates a framework for experience, the user conducts experiences within that framework, and through feedback—both explicit and implicit—the designer is expected to progressively alter that experience to reflect the user's usage patterns, frustrations, successes, and unexpected by-products. In the language of digital products: iterate, iterate, iterate, and then iterate some more. Each iteration, each new version of the product, each modified or optimized function, each newly added feature set are all parts of the conversation between the designer and the user. When an inveterate user of a digital product encounters a new change, she is listening to the object talk to her.

Over the course of the twentieth century our perception of the world has been changed by momentous technological breakthroughs, among them air travel, telephones, television, satellites, and the Internet. Faraway people and places have suddenly come within reach, if not physically, then via video or audio. The world might seem to have shrunk, but in reality these innovations have progressively added layers of understanding and communication, making that same world deeper, richer with new metaphysical and expressive dimensions. The addition of virtual worlds, such as the myriad sites and artificial environments supported by the World Wide Web, has further diversified our choices for inhabitation, with interesting social and cultural consequences; among the most revealing examples are those that emerge in the so-called God games, video games in which players engage in building new worlds or even new civilizations.

What most of these technologies have in common is the fact that they are based on systems and rely on network connections, just like the natural world, and understanding their design should be and often is a requirement for those building the elements that come together to constitute these physical and virtual worlds, from designers and architects to engineers and television executives. For those who are not willing or able to understand systems but still need access to them, there are interfaces that function as zones of engagement and exchange.

One of design's foremost directives is to bring technological breakthroughs up or down to a comfortable and understandable human scale. The projects in the following chapter, which deal with both natural and artificial systems at all dimensions, feature efforts to render highly complex phenomena—such as the way trees work (page 135), the consequences of global warming (page 137), the proportions of the solar system (page 146), or the cycles of human migrations (page 141)—in clear, elegant, and therefore human interfaces.

P. A.

The texts in this chapter were written by Azzurra Cox.

WORLDS

Chris Woebken (German, born 1980)
and Kenichi Okada (Japanese, born 1980)
Design Interactions Department
(est. 1989)
Royal College of Art (UK, est. 1837)

/////////////////////////////

Animal Superpowers: Ant and Giraffe.
2008

/////////////////////////////

Ant: fiberglass, virtual-reality glasses,
and microscopes, gloves: 3 3/4 ×
6 5/16 × 8" (9.5 × 16 × 20 cm), helmet:
9 3/8 × 12 3/16 × 7 11/16" (24 × 31
× 19.5 cm); giraffe: PVC, mirrors, and
voice changer, 18 1/8 × 8 11/16 ×
9 3/8" (46 × 22 × 24 cm)

Animal senses, like our own, have
evolved in reaction to specific contexts
and survival needs, and they often go
above and beyond the limited sensory
capacities of humans. Birds, for example,
use magnetic fields to determine their
migration routes, ants communicate
via scent trails, and dogs can sense
impending earthquakes. In an effort
to make these abilities comprehensible
to us, Chris Woebken and Kenichi Okada
have designed a series of experiential
sensory enhancements for children.
The ant apparatus, a helmet with gloves
attached, displays the world through
an ant's eyes: microscopes in the gloves
magnify minuscule surface details to fifty
times their regular size and transmit the
images to the helmet. The giraffe device
raises the wearer's line of sight, simulating for a child the physical perspective
of an adult, and also deepens the
voice. Although these prototypes
were specifically made as responses
to the curiosity of children, in a broader
sense they present us all with ways
to stretch our own limited human
interactions with the world.

Alex Metcalf (British, born 1980)
Design Products Department (est. 1999)
Royal College of Art (UK, est. 1837)

/////////////////////////////

Tree Listening at Royal Botanic
Gardens, Kew, England. 2008

Tree Listening at Fermynwoods,
Northamptonshire, England. 2009

/////////////////////////////

Installation with copper, plastic, stainless
steel, aluminum, glass, headphones,
amplifier, and wood, dimensions variable

Alex Metcalf's Tree Listening installation
reveal to us what happens inside a
tree, where water and nutrients ascend
from roots to leaves through a complex
hydraulic system of xylem tubes in the
trunk. To create a sensory glimpse into
this system, Metcalf designed a listening
device, powered by solar energy, that
is placed on a tree trunk, linked to an
amplifier, and connected to a series of
headphones that hang from the branches
of trees in various locations in London
and around the United Kingdom. Through
the headphones, passersby can listen to
a tree's inner workings—"a quiet popping
sound," Metcalf describes, produced
by the water passing through the xylem
cells, as well as "a deep rumbling sound"
in the background, produced by the tree
movements. Through the device, the
tree bark is figuratively stripped away,
revealing a unique soundscape that
enhances our appreciation and understanding of trees. The installation
joins science and art in a multilayered
interaction with the natural world.

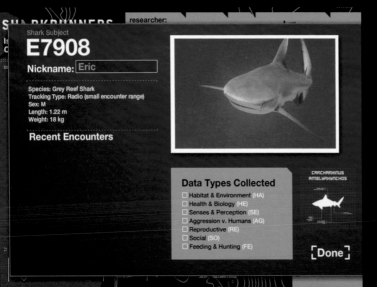

Area/Code (USA, est. 2005)

///////////////////////////

Sharkrunners. 2007

///////////////////////////

Custom software

Sharkrunners, designed for the twentieth anniversary of the Discovery Channel's Shark Week, is an online role-playing game about oceanic exploration and research with a twist: it incorporates telemetry data from real sharks tagged with GPS transponders. At the start of the game, players align themselves with a specific research agenda, choose a crew, and pick a home port. They take control of fictional research vessels with the goal of encountering sharks, using advanced observation techniques to gather high-quality data and earning more funding for research; the sharks move in real time, and the research vessels move at a true-to-life pace. Players receive e-mail/text alerts when their vessels are within range of an encounter, and they can try one of a series of approach techniques, each carrying risks and payoffs. This ongoing game is enriched by a website and online forum, where players can discuss strategy, honor the holders of fund-raising records, review shark news and research, and become part of a global community committed to learning about and preserving the species.

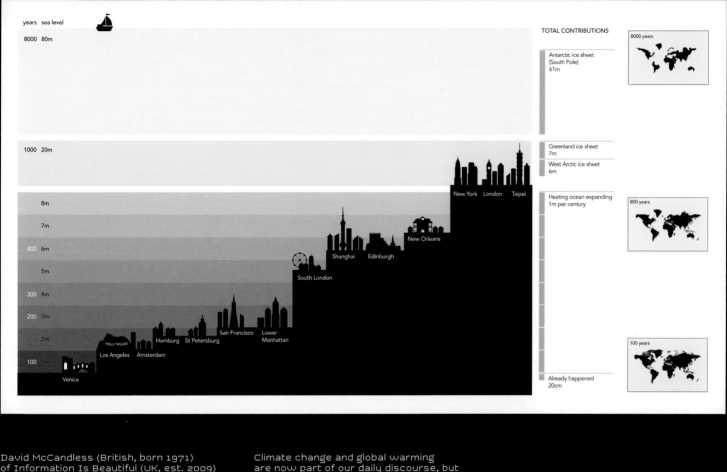

David McCandless (British, born 1971)
of Information Is Beautiful (UK, est. 2009)

//////////////////////////////

When Sea Levels Attack! 2008

//////////////////////////////

Illustrator software

Climate change and global warming
are now part of our daily discourse, but
scientific predictions about their effects
can still be perplexing and abstract:
a three-foot sea-level rise, for example,
is meaningless without a link to our
everyday lives. David McCandless's
explicit graphic demystifies and contextu-
alizes this information, clearly showing
when and how much sea levels are
predicted to rise and which major cities
around the world will be most affected.
The interface, familiar to anyone who can
read a bar graph, grounds the information
in the real world. McCandless, an enthusiastic, self-taught information designer,
put aside a writing career to dive into the
visualization of natural, human, political,
and scientific phenomena (see also
page 78). His work is collected in a book
and on his website, which has a devoted
following.

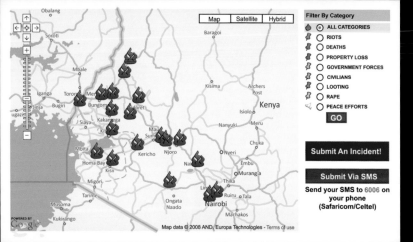

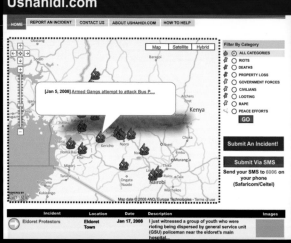

Erik Hersman (American, born 1975),
David Kobia (Kenyan, born 1978),
Ory Okolloh (Kenyan, born 1975), and
Juliana Rotich (Kenyan, born 1977)

/////////////////////////////

Ushahidi. 2008

/////////////////////////////

Linux, Apache, PHP, MySQL, Kohana
Framework, jQuery, and FrontlineSMS
software

Ushahidi, which means "testimony"
in Swahili, is a free web-based tool
for collecting, visualizing, and mapping
information. It was launched in Kenya
in 2008, when a disputed election
caused riots to erupt across the country.
The website enabled citizens to report
incidents and identify safe spaces, using
their mobile phones, on the geographic
platforms Google Maps, Yahoo! Maps,
OpenStreetMap, and Microsoft Virtual

Earth, effectively building a corps of
forty-five thousand citizen journalists;
the data was aggregated and mapped for
anyone who needed it. Ushahidi has since
grown into an open-source platform
used worldwide in times of crisis; it has
proven to be a vital tool in vastly different
contexts, from the 2010 earthquakes in
Haiti and Chile and the 2011 earthquake
and tsunami in Japan, when targeted and
effective humanitarian relief was enabled
by its aggregated data, to a winter storm
in Washington, DC, in January 2010, when
Ushahidi provided information about road
blockages and available snow plows.
Using Ushahidi, communities of activists,
news and relief organizations, and
concerned citizens can track changing
information as it emerges, making nimble
response possible. The platform applies
the logic of crowdsourcing to crisis
management and humanitarian work,
creating a new paradigm for aid: victims
supplying real-time, on-the-ground
information to a linked global volunteer
community that orchestrates appropriate
relief efforts.

13

Jan Gerber (German, born 1980) and
Sebastian Lütgert (German, born 1972)
of The Oil of the 21st Century
(Germany, est. 2007)
Alternative Law Forum (India, est. 2000)
CAMP (India, est. 2007)
Majlis (India, est. 1991)
Point of View (India, est. 1998)

/////////////////////////////

Pad.ma. 2008

/////////////////////////////

Python, JavaScript, HTML, TurboGears,
jQuery, Ogg Theora, and OXD b software

Pad.ma (short for Public Access Digital
Media Archive) is a web-based archive
of annotated video content—primarily
clips, footage, and unfinished films,
largely from urban India—that aggregates
material that might otherwise be lost
in the editing process and filmmaking
ecosystem. The result is a singular
collection of footage, much of it fragmentary, that provides glimpses into places

and narratives. Pad.ma currently contains
more than six hundred of what the
website calls video "events" on a range
of subjects, including "changing city-
scapes, street and domestic life …
protests, chance meetings, police
raids, train-rides … conversations
with community, state, and corporate
interests … [and] found footage."
The entire collection, densely tagged
by timeline, location, and theme, can be
viewed online and is free to download
for noncommercial use. Pad.ma's
community of users includes independent
filmmakers, activists, and artists who
can contribute material to the archive
without worrying about whether or not
it is finished; the site's focus on linking
and reuse proposes a new kind of
viewing and contextualization. Pad.ma,
its creators say, "expands upon the
perhaps inevitable destiny of all video
in digital form: that it becomes possible
to distribute, share, annotate, reuse,
and reinterpret it, even as the original
'author's' intentions expire, and
contexts change."

Matt Jones (British, born 1972),
Matt Brown (British, born 1980),
Tom Armitage (British, born 1982),
Matt Webb (British, born 1978),
Paul Mison (British, born 1970), and
Phil Gyford (British, born 1972)
of BERG (UK, est. 2005)
Max Gadney (British, born 1973)
of BBC (UK, est. 1922)

/////////////////////////////

BBC Dimensions. 2010

/////////////////////////////

Illustrator, Photoshop, SVG, HTML,
JavaScript, CSS, PHP, MySQL, and Google
Maps API software

The BBC Dimensions website takes landmark events and phenomena and superimposes them onto a satellite view of any city, neighborhood, or area. The Apollo 11 moon landing, for example, an event of great historical significance, covered an area smaller than the average parking lot, and the 2010 floods in Pakistan spanned a region equivalent to half of the Eastern Seaboard of the United States. Users pick from a series of events, places, and things—from a blueprint of the pyramids of Giza to the area affected by the Battle of Stalingrad to the depth of the Mariana Trench—and type in a zip or postal code; the website then generates a satellite image of the area with the event outlined in yellow. Some dimensions can be printed out as directions for walks, for an even more physical appreciation of the distances involved. History and current events are rendered more tangible and immediate, bridging physical and conceptual distance.

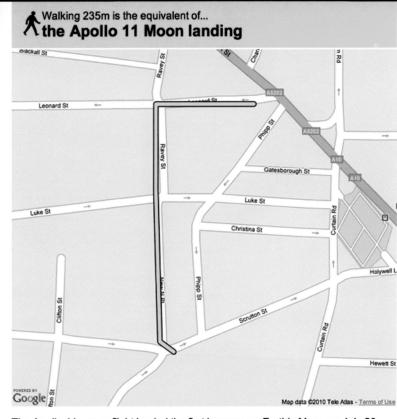

The Apollo 11 space flight landed the first humans on Earth's Moon on July 20, 1969. The mission, carried out by the United States, is considered a major accomplishment in human exploration and represented a victory by the U.S. in the Cold War Space Race with the Soviet Union. Here we've highlighted the route Neil Armstrong and Buzz Aldrin walked on the moon's surface.

Diller Scofidio + Renfro (USA, est. 1979),
Laura Kurgan (American, born South
Africa 1961), Ben Rubin (American, born
1964), and Mark Hansen (American,
born 1964)
in collaboration with Stewart Smith
(American, born 1981) and Robert Gerard
Pietrusko (American, born 1979)

/////////////////////////////

Exit. 2008

/////////////////////////////

Installation using Java, OpenGL, and
Processing software, overall: 12' (370 cm)
high, 29' (8.8 m) diam.

Exit builds on curator and cultural
theorist Paul Virilio's notion that what
most defines humanity today are our
patterns of migration. The installation
visualizes the global movement of
people, both forced and voluntary and
due to various factors (whether political,
economic, and environmental), through
a series of six panoramic narratives
displayed over the course of forty-two
minutes. In the introductory sequence
(opposite, bottom), a globe spins around
the room, leaving trails of population
statistics. In Remittances (opposite, top),
money sent by migrant laborers to their
nations of origin is tracked by country.
Population Weather (top) displays recent
population shifts in a stark white-on-
black graphic that resembles a seismo-
graph, with peaks signaling growth and
trenches locating decline. In Population
Density (center), a matrixlike landscape
of rapidly changing green numbers draws
attention to the fastest growing cities.
In Political Refugees (bottom), waves
of green pixels represent mass exodus
from areas of war. Natural Disasters
(not pictured) presents the relative
magnitude and effects of droughts,
floods, and other catastrophes from
1990 to 2008. And in Rising Seas, Sinking
Cities (not pictured) a projected map of
the world glows brighter in areas with
the highest concentrations of carbon
emissions. Data and geography are thus
fused in multidimensional and dynamic
maps, and the design of the theater and
installation wraps viewers in a universe
of information, transmitting a sense
of global scale and immediacy. Exit was
commissioned by the Fondation Cartier
pour l'art contemporain, Paris, as part
of Terre Natale, an exhibition in 2008.

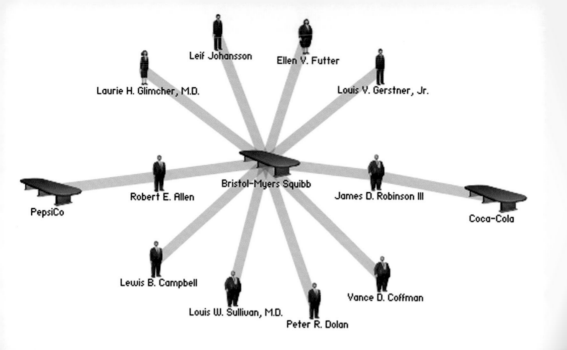

Leif Johansson

Ellen V. Futter

Laurie H. Glimcher, M.D.

Louis V. Gerstner, Jr.

Robert E. Allen

Bristol-Myers Squibb

James D. Robinson III

PepsiCo

Coca-Cola

Lewis B. Campbell

Vance D. Coffman

Louis W. Sullivan, M.D.

Peter R. Dolan

Josh On (New Zealande
of Futurefarmers (USA,

/ / / / / / / / / / / / / / / / / /

They Rule. 2004

/ / / / / / / / / / / / / / / / /

Photoshop, 3ds Max, Fla
Dreamweaver, Notepad
Blender software

They Rule is a website t
the invisible networks o
power. A handful of larg
control and influence mu
economy, and the indivic
on their boards often se
boards and in governme
These connections are t
understanding the exter
of the so-called ruling cl
information is never mac
Rule collected data in 20
directories and SEC filin
visual maps of the links
nies, institutions, and in
select which people or i
would like to research; t
grow into complex, inter
of boardroom tables and
clearly demonstrating th
nature of power in our c
These maps can be sha
by multiple users, buildir
and dialogue around the

Amy Franceschini (American, born 1970),
Josh On (New Zealander, born 1972),
and Amy Balkin (American, born 1969)
of Futurefarmers (USA, est. 1995)

/////////////////////////////

ANTIWARGAME. 2001

/////////////////////////////

Flash, Dreamweaver, Illustrator, and
Photoshop software

ANTIWARGAME is an online video game
that explores the dynamics of the War
on Terror in a simulation of post–9/11
politics. A player's goal as the President
of the United States of America is to
maintain popularity while making decisions about military deployment, social
spending, media spin, and other political
factors. Striking the right balance is
difficult: cutting social spending may
trigger a revolution; shunning the
all-powerful corporate class could lead
to assassination. Although the game's
interface is cartoonish, its constraints
expose the influence of special interests
in policy making and push players to
think through the various implications
of managing the War on Terror.

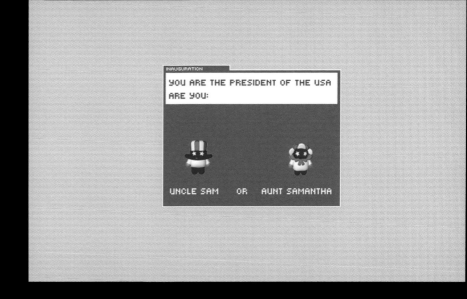

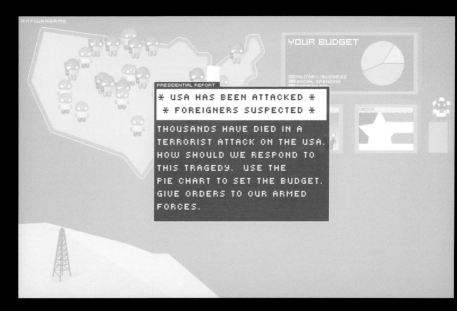

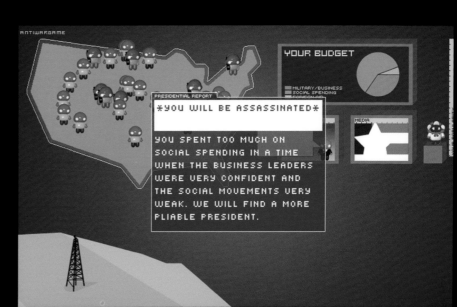

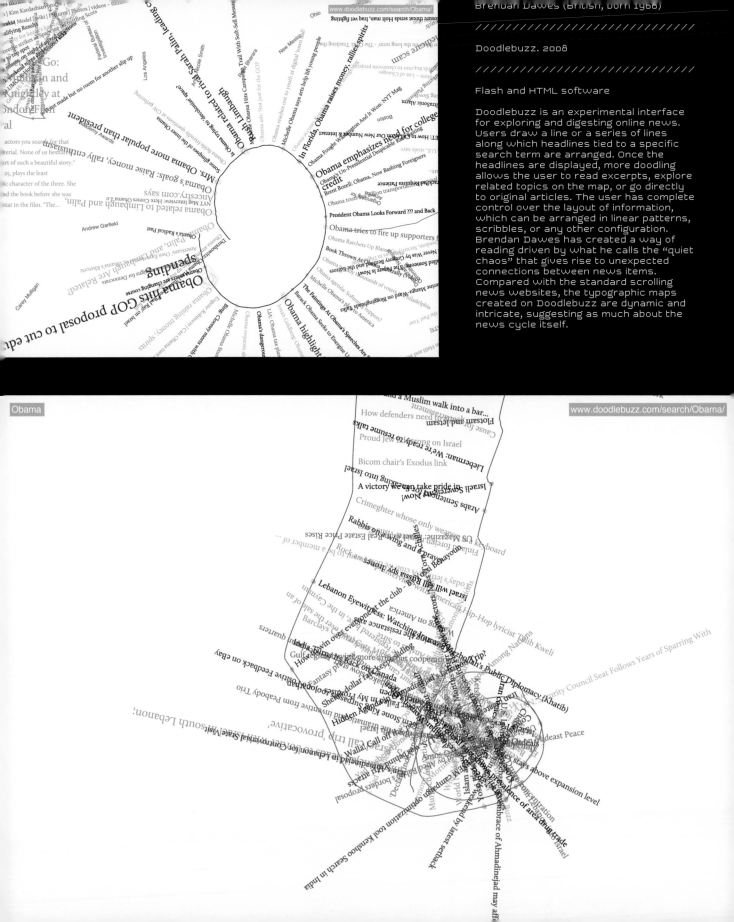

Brendan Dawes (British, born 1966)

/////////////////////////////////

Doodlebuzz. 2008

/////////////////////////////////

Flash and HTML software

Doodlebuzz is an experimental interface for exploring and digesting online news. Users draw a line or a series of lines along which headlines tied to a specific search term are arranged. Once the headlines are displayed, more doodling allows the user to read excerpts, explore related topics on the map, or go directly to original articles. The user has complete control over the layout of information, which can be arranged in linear patterns, scribbles, or any other configuration. Brendan Dawes has created a way of reading driven by what he calls the "quiet chaos" that gives rise to unexpected connections between news items. Compared with the standard scrolling news websites, the typographic maps created on Doodlebuzz are dynamic and intricate, suggesting as much about the news cycle itself.

Marcos Weskamp (Argentine, born 1977)

//////////////////////////////

Newsmap. 2004

//////////////////////////////

PHP, HTML, JavaScript, Flash, and MySQL software

In the age of information saturation and overload, several news-aggregating websites and mobile applications cut through the noise by presenting the news landscape in a visually organized way. Newsmap draws on Google News's constantly updated feeds and is arranged like a treemap (a hierarchical way of representing data that uses nested rectangles as an organizing element). Different stories are contained in rectangular cells whose size is dictated by how much coverage Google News determines that the subject has been given; they are then grouped into easily identified bands and color-coded by topic (such as world affairs, business, entertainment, sports). The news can be filtered by country, by issue, or by whether the subject has been updated in the last ten minutes, the last hour, or more, giving users a more directed way to digest the news while also seeing the larger patterns of the news cycle.

Louise O'Connor (British, born 1982)
Design Interactions Department
(est. 1989)
Royal College of Art
(UK, est. 1837)

//////////////////////////////

Walk the Solar System. 2010

//////////////////////////////

Performance

Visual representations and models of the solar system do not allow us to experience its vastness firsthand, so Louise O'Connor, with Walk the Solar System, re-created it at human scale. Her experiential version took place in a London neighborhood with the help of some of its inhabitants. O'Connor projected the relative distances between planets onto a two-mile route beginning at Kingsland Road, Dalston, and ending in Stamford Hill; at each planet's position she recruited a shopkeeper who, if asked, would produce an object— a ball bearing, an orange, a yoga ball— that proportionally represented the planet, so that visitors could playfully and physically engage with a dimension utterly removed from their own experience. The project was photographed in situ by Mark Henderson.

# WALK THE SOLAR SYSTEM

PSYCHOMYTHIC
NATURE QUEST

1 : 190645161.3

Despite many a primary school drawing or text book illustration, a true scale model of our Solar System is unfeasible on paper. To get a sense of its true vastness, you are invited to walk the Solar System.

A walkable scale model has been installed from Kingsland Road in Dalston, going up to up to Stamford Hill, London; part of one of Britain's most historic and longest Roman roads. Local shopkeepers at the appropriate points on the route are acting as guardians to the planets – hosting models represented by everyday objects, at their correct sizes on this 3.1 km scale.

Those following the trail, or those simply passing by, can pay a visit to the planetary guardians and request to be shown the planet.

Visit www.tiny.cc/solarwalk for full addresses and google map

*Pluto was actually demoted from planet status along in 2006 and is now classified as a dwarf or minor planet along with Eris and Ceres. However, the model just didn't seem right without it...

For further information about the project and to share youre experience of the walk get in touch at www.louiseoconnor.com

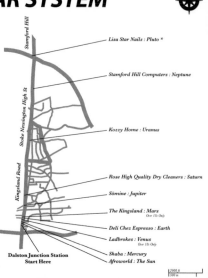

Lisa Star Nails : Pluto *
Stamford Hill Computers : Neptune
Kozzy Home : Uranus
Rose High Quality Dry Cleaners : Saturn
Sömine : Jupiter
The Kingsland : Mars
  Over 11s Only
Deli Chez Espresso : Earth
Ladbrokes : Venus
  Over 11s Only
Shaba : Mercury
Afroworld : The Sun

Dalston Junction Station
Start Here

Will Wright (American, born 1960)
for Maxis (USA, est. 1987),
now part of Electronic Arts, Inc.
(USA, est. 1982)

/////////////////////////////

SimCity 2000 (top). 1994

/////////////////////////////

Will Wright (American, born 1960)
for Electronic Arts, Inc. (USA, est. 1982)

/////////////////////////////

SimCity 3000 (bottom). 1999

/////////////////////////////

Custom software

SimCity, originally released in 1989
with numerous versions and spin-offs
since then, is a classic simulation game,
in which players design, build, and
attempt to run a thriving city. Players
either choose a preset scenario or build
a city from the ground up. The real-life
factors that a player must take into
consideration include zoning laws,
infrastructure, cultural and civic institutions, and tax and crime rates, all of
which affect quality of life and funds
available for further growth. Crucial
decisions require weighing short-term
convenience against long-term sustain-
ability: high-density zoning, for example,
is a cheap way to raise population and
capital but may lead to increased crime;
placing housing near industry seems
convenient, but the effects of pollution
on citizens' health and happiness
are considerable. The game rewards
successful urban strategies with
skyrocketing property values, bustling
malls, and flourishing institutions, and
failure results in urban blight, in the form
of decaying buildings marring the city-
scape. Unexpected disasters—fires,
floods, menacing alien ships—occasionally
sweep through, leaving players to pick up
the pieces. Each major upgrade of SimCity
makes available a broader universe of
information and complexity, both visual
and conceptual. In the latest install-
ments, SimCity 3000 and SimCity4, the
graphics are axonometric, and players
can import architectural landmarks from
anywhere in the world—such as the Eiffel
Tower and the Golden Gate Bridge, among
many others—to add glamour to their
creation. SimCity depicts the city as a
dynamic organism made of interrelated
systems that affect its overall well-being.

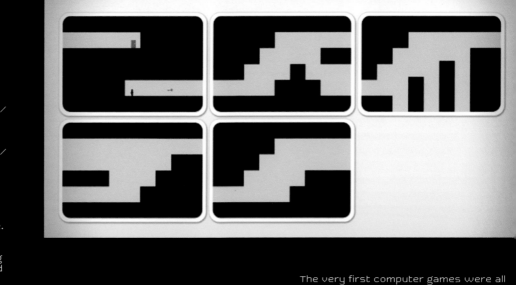

, born 1980),
ovan, born 1985),
an, born 1985),
n (Swedish,

uter Science
2002)
f Technology

////////////////

////////////////

d Steinberg Cubase

ensional
twists our spatial
C. Escher universe.
cter through
hazes, running and
special items along
rs ingeniously fused
es, the tile game
e; the character's
hifting landscape
per Mario Brothers
d there is also
t every level the
d to open a pathway
he challenge is
vell as to solve
zle.

The very first computer games were all made using ASCII (American Standard Code for Information Interchange). Dwarf Fortress, a single-player fantasy game released in 2006, forwent subsequent developments in computer graphics and is also entirely developed in ASCII. Rather than relying on a naturalistic three-dimensional interface, the game generates its own complex world, which the player can modify, out of classic two-dimensional tiled building blocks and text-based graphics. The goal is to build a viable dwarf settlement in a vast user-generated world of continents and seas, shown here (right) in a world map from 2010. Every terrain has multiple levels, on the surface and below it, with more than two hundred rocks and minerals that players can mine and make tools from. In order to succeed, players must consider how a wide range of factors, including natural resources and weather conditions, influence their dwarf colonies, must forge alliances with competing civilizations, and must learn to navigate an abstract world.

Tarn Adams (American, born 1978) and
Zach Adams (American, born 1975)
of Bay 12 Games (USA, est. 2000)

//////////////////////////////

Dwarf Fortress. 2006

//////////////////////////////

FreeType fonts and C/C++, Visual C
compiler, g++, FMOD, and SDL software

an, born 1977)

/////////////

/////////////

GNU Compiler
s, mtPaint, and
re

Sleep Is Death, another video game developed by Jason Rohrer (see page 76), is a two-person storytelling game for a narrator and a player. Each game starts with a basic set of modifiable characters, objects, and environments. The player interacts with and moves around this world using text commands; the narrator reacts to the commands, completing them, writing dialogue, and molding the scene. Narrator and player alternate in thirty-second turns, thus developing an improvised narrative. At the end, the story can be archived in the form of a slide show to be flipped through like a picture book. Rohrer's game turns on its head the dynamic of human interacting with artificial intelligence via scripted patterns; in Sleep Is Death the mind on the other side of the screen can react, feel, and perceive, and the game becomes more of an exchange between partners.

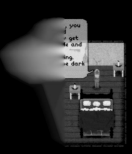

Media Molecule (UK, est. 2006)

////////////////////////////

LittleBigPlanet. 2006

////////////////////////////

3ds Max, Photoshop, and custom
software
Distributed by Sony, Japan

LittleBigPlanet, a game for PlayStation
systems, revolves around control
of a central character, Sackperson,
in a community-generated world.
The game features a set of prebuilt
levels, but it is remarkably customizable:
players can create and alter the world
by building new objects and levels and
sharing them with the LittleBigPlanet
community, and the variety of encounters
and tasks at each level is staggering.
Although the nominal goal is locating and
unlocking prize bubbles, the experience
of the game expands far beyond it,
and virtually no idea or task is repeated.
In one user-generated level, Sackperson
navigates through the human body,
attacking viruses and sweeping brain
cavities, and in another, solving complex
math problems unlocks prizes; other
levels are inspired by the graphics
and stories of classic video games and
movies. Collaboration with other players
is encouraged; the game switches easily
between single- and multiplayer modes,

and some sections require teams in
order to find all the prizes and earn
the maximum number of points. The
emphasis on user design extends to
the Sackperson character, which is
a blank canvas for the player to dress
and accessorize and assign a gender.
In LittleBigPlanet, levels become entire
worlds inside a seemingly endless
universe—one that essentially stretches
as far as its players' imagination and
ingenuity.

Will Wright (American, born 1960)
for Electronic Arts, Inc. (USA, est. 1982)

////////////////////////////////

Spore. 2008

////////////////////////////////

Custom software

Spore is a simulation game about building
and controlling a species from its single-
cell origins through its evolution to master
of the planet and beyond, and victory is
achieved by reaching a black hole at the
galaxy's center and either befriending
or defeating the cyborg species that
guards it. The game is divided into five
increasingly complex phases—cell,
creature, tribal, civilization, and space—
with the outcome of one phase affecting
the conditions that face the player in
the next. In the first two phases the
player engages in a detailed process
of self-fashioning, from number of eyes
and legs to eating habits; the creature
stage, when the player most actively
designs a unique avatar and assigns
the creature its idiosyncrasies, has been
described as particularly intimate, like
getting to know a friend. In the tribal and
civilization stages the game moves away
from the individual creature to strategic
interactions—some poetic, such as
charming allies with song, some brutal,
like the crushing of rival tribes—with
other inhabitants. The space stage is the
game's most expansive, encouraging a
free-flowing, open-ended style of play:
there are stars to explore, colonies to
build, species to abduct or annihilate.
Creation here extends to undiscovered
planetary territories, which can be
terraformed (a hypothetical process
of planetary engineering) to render them
more hospitable. Along the way, players
are given tools to custom-build creatures
and objects, which can be uploaded
for other players in a very connected
and interactive community to use.
Although the game is accessible and
technically uncomplicated, even for
the amateur gamer, the crowdsourced
creations are vivid and expressive and
the epic-scale narrative echoes that
of our own civilization and its individuals.
Spore's broad virtual community also
provides a stage for interactive creation
and communication.

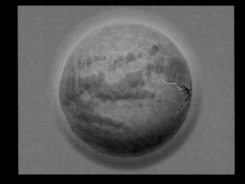

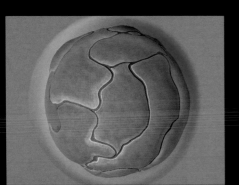

Masa Inakage (Japanese, born 1960),
Yu Uchida (Japanese, born 1984),
Mami Naito (Japanese, born 1986),
Shiho Hirayama (Japanese, born 1986),
and Atsushi Nishio (Japanese, born 1987)
Graduate School of Media Design
(est. 2008)
Keio University (Japan, est. 1858)

////////////////////////////

Kageo. 2007

////////////////////////////

Installation with projector, camera, PC,
acrylic board, wooden table, spotlight,
and Director MX and TTC-Pro Xtra
software, 71" x 6' 7" x 67" (180 x 200
x 170 cm)

Kageo (Japanese for "little shadow")
populates the shadows of everyday
objects—a coffee mug on a table, a pencil
holder on a desk—with mysterious and
delightful animated creatures. A webcam
recognizes darker areas, and a hidden
projector animates the creatures. The
creatures fight, chat, and bounce around,
all the while responding to a shifting
environment: if the coffee mug is moved
to the table's opposite corner, they will
eventually appear there; try to touch
them and they'll run away but tentatively
peek out seconds later. Kageo conjures
a mischievous presence, a kind of invisible
friend, in the most unlikely places.

Marc Owens (British, born 1982)

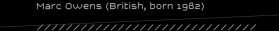

Avatar Machine. 2008

///////////////////////////////

Various materials and electronics, dimensions variable

In the world of gaming and virtual reality, an avatar is a digital representation of a real person, often experienced from a third-person perspective: the player controls the avatar but simultaneously views it as if hovering a few feet behind. The Avatar Machine is a wearable apparatus that simulates the third-person gaming experience in real space. Comprising a full-body suit, a camera mounted behind the head, and virtual-reality goggles, the device replicates the spatial dynamics of gaming as users move in and interact with the real world. It is also designed to look like a virtual warrior, complete with spikes on the helmet, a padded torso, and large armored gloves. In designing the Avatar Machine, Marc Owens wondered whether it might lead users to bring gaming behaviors into real life; during tests in public locations, including London's Hyde Park, he observed that, indeed, some people wearing the Avatar Machine began to move like video-game characters—taking bigger steps and swinging their arms. The sense of estrangement and detachment is reinforced by the responses from onlookers. This mashing of boundaries between virtual and physical worlds suggests a future path for gaming technologies.

Linda Kostowski (German, born 1980) and
Sascha Pohflepp (German, born 1978)

////////////////////////////

Export to World. 2007

////////////////////////////

Inkjet on paper, bubba gum machine:
41 3/8 × 13 13/16 × 13 13/16" (106 ×
35 × 35 cm); old television: 12 3/16 ×
19 5/16 × 7 5/16" (31 × 49 × 18.5 cm)

The hazy separation between the real
and simulated worlds is investigated
by the Export to World project, which
focuses on the nature of digital artifacts
in Second Life, a landmark, if imperfect,
virtual world launched in 2003. In Second
Life every player is able to create virtual
objects that have monetary value,
echoing real-world tenets of commodity
and trade. Linda Kostowski and Sascha
Pohflepp created a temporary shop,
similar to those found in Second Life,
in Linz, Austria. People could purchase
paper kits of replicas of the digital
artifacts, which could then be assembled
into three-dimensional objects, completing their leap into the real world. The
final products are, in the words of the
designers, "paper representations of
digital representations of real objects,
including all the flaws that copying
entails."

Doug Hudson-Powell (British, born 1979)
and Luke Powell (British, born 1976)
of Hudson-Powell (UK, est. 2005)
Joel Gethin Lewis (British, born 1980) and
Jean-Gabriel Becker (French, born 1975)

////////////////////////////////

Hungry Hungry Eat Head. 2009

////////////////////////////////

Installation using openFrameworks
software and various materials

Hungry Hungry Eat Head is an installation
meant to engender interactive play in
a public place. Participants are given
large cardboard QR codes, which are
transformed by video-tracking technology
into three-dimensional animations
broadcast live on a large LED screen,
so that ordinary people turn into strange
animals, grinning monsters, and alien
creatures, all moving and interacting in
real time. In the spirited free play that
has resulted, some participants have
adopted zany attitudes to suit their new
personas, some have danced, some have
just stared, and passersby have become
witnesses to the spectacle. The installation introduces an element of fantasy
and surprise into urban space using
minimal technology, and anyone present
can take advantage of it. Hungry Hungry
Eat Head, which premiered in Edinburgh,
was created for BBC Big Screen, a
collaborative program between the BBC
and eighteen UK cities, as part of the
Abandon Normal Devices (AND) Festival.

Chris O'Shea (British, born 1981)

/////////////////////////////

Hand from Above. 2009

/////////////////////////////

Installation using C++, openFramework, openCV, and custom software

In Hand from Above, passersby are briefly transported to a different reality. The crowds walking near the large-screen LED monitor are broadcast live on the screen, but instead of the expected reflection, they see images of themselves being tickled, assaulted, or flicked away by an enormous hand, as though by some colossal deity. The reactions of the installation's unwitting participants have varied: some run away, others flinch, but many interact with the hand, waving at the screen to attract attention. In every case, people are encouraged to pause in their normal routines and engage with a virtual presence and with each other. Hand from Above was commissioned by the Foundation for Art and Creative Technology and the Liverpool City Council for BBC Big Screen; it premiered during the Abandon Normal Devices (AND) Festival in Liverpool.

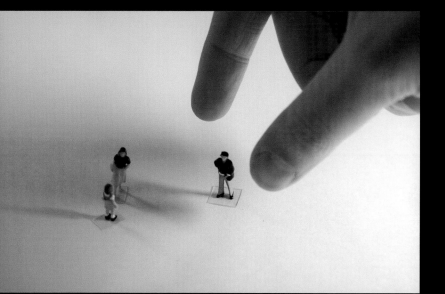

Sander Veenhof (Dutch, born 1973),
Johannes la Poutre (Dutch, born 1963),
and Tobias Domhan (German, born 1988)

/////////////////////////////

Augmented Reality Flash Mob. 2010

/////////////////////////////

Installation using Layar Reality Browser
and AndAR Model Viewer software

Human-statue performers appear in
public places around the world. The
Augmented Reality Flash Mob uses QR
codes and Layar technology, with which
smartphone users can connect to an
augmented-reality platform, to take
the phenomenon one step further. The
designers coordinate, on a specific date
and time and place, a coterie of virtual
three-dimensional characters—including
Darth Vader, zombies, Spider-Man, the
Beatles, and Smurfs—which anyone with
a smartphone can see and walk among.
The characters can only be viewed (and
photographed) through a device; pictures
of the event can then be uploaded
and printed, creating a visual record
of a virtual event.

Mike Clare (American, born 1988)
of Tellart (USA, est. 2000)

/////////////////////////////

Augmented Reality Cookie. 2009

/////////////////////////////

Flour, sugar, eggs, butter, vanilla,
salt, baking powder, chocolate, food
coloring, and Flash, Papervision3D, and
FLARToolKit software, 5/16" (0.8 cm)
high, 2 13/16" (7 cm) diam.

The Augmented Reality Cookie introduces
a virtual dimension to a chocolate-and-
vanilla cookie. Using two colors of dough,
Mike Clare baked a small coding grid into
the cookie, essentially an elementary QR
code, that comes to life when viewed
through a webcam, creating what he
calls "digital icing."

Bernhard Hopfengärtner
(German, born 1982)

/////////////////////////////

Hello World! 2006

/////////////////////////////

Installation in wheat field, 525.2 × 525.2'
(160 × 160 m)

Hello World! is a large-scale Semacode
mowed into a wheat field near Ilmenau,
in Germany's Thuringia region. The
code is formed by dark (mature green
wheat plants) and light (mowed plants
mixed with soil) squares eighteen across
and eighteen down, that when decoded
read "Hello, world!" in keeping with the
tradition of christening any new coding
experiment by programming it to produce
this cheerful declaration. The installation,
now integrated into Google Earth's
database of images, marries a low-tech
method with a decidedly high-tech effect,
while also making reference to and
updating the ancient language of runes
and crop circles. The human need for
expression continues at a global, even
planetary, scale.

computer, projector, IR LED, IR camera, fan, power supply, and C++, OpenGL, openFrameworks, and ARToolKit software, 42 × 42 × 37" (107 × 107 × 96 cm)

The effect of Joon Y. Moon's ghostly ecosystem of shadow creatures and objects is created with blocks on a tabletop that functions as a rear-projection screen and has a computer, infrared camera, and light source installed below it. The shadows exist in both a real and fantasy environment; animations transform the blocks into houses and awaken creatures around them. Moving the blocks around the table sets off programmed reactions: people gravitate toward a light source, trees grow around it, and birds fly away from the dark.

Camille Scherrer (Swiss, born 1984)
École cantonale d'art de Lausanne
(Switzerland, est. 1821)

/////////////////////////////

The Haunted Book. 2007
Le Monde des montagnes. 2008

/////////////////////////////

Installations with book, desk lamp with
hidden camera, screen, computer, black
table, and Ferns custom software,
55 1/8 × 23 5/8 × 63" (140 × 60 × 160 cm)

In The Haunted Book and Le Monde des
montagnes, Camille Scherrer animates
the pages of books with an added
dynamic dimension. The setup appears
low-tech: a book, a laptop, and a familiar
desk lamp on a table. But a camera is
hidden inside the lamp, and when the
book's pages are turned they display
a layer of virtual animation: a flock
of birds suddenly materializes in a stormy
sky, or a skeleton hand creeps across
the page. The Haunted Book is based
on a nineteenth-century gothic poem by
Thomas Hood; Le Monde des montagnes
is based on sayings from the Alpine region
of Switzerland where Scherrer grew
up. Scherrer made sure the reader
could focus on the experience without
being distracted by the technology;
the high-performance custom software
created by Julien Pilet of CVLAB, École
Polytechnique Fédérale de Lausanne,
eliminated the need for visible, often
clunky augmented-reality markers, thus
doing away with a barrier between the
virtual and the real. Neither the book
nor the virtual dominate, reconciling the
traditionally conflicting worlds of paper
and screen and enabling them to enrich
each other.

51

Maarten Baas (Dutch, born Germany
1978)

////////////////////////////

Analog Digital Clock. 2009

////////////////////////////

Digital video (color, silent), 12 hrs.

Maarten Baas's Analog Digital Clock,
available as an iPad or iPhone app as
well as a Blu-ray film, appears, at first
glance, to be a classic digital clock
adapted for mobile devices and screens.
In fact it is a videotaped performance
of an actor painting or erasing sections
of the digital display numbers, minute
by minute, by hand, elegantly combining
the analog and digital worlds. Time is
presented here as a highly physical, even
labor-intensive process, like the clock
machine in Fritz Lang's Metropolis (1927).
Analog Digital Clock was created as part
of Baas's Real Time series, a set of four
works in which people's actions, rather
than traditional clocks, demonstrate
the passage of time: the hands of the
clock are drawn (in Grandfather Clock),
constructed from swept garbage
(Sweepers Clock), and indicated by
people in three different time zones
(World Clock).

Jon Ardern (British, born 1978) and
Anab Jain (Indian, born 1976)
of Superflux (UK and India, est. 2009)

////////////////////////////

The 5th Dimensional Camera. 2010

////////////////////////////

Steel, Perspex, timer display, and LCD
screen, 41 5/16 x 32 5/16 x 15 3/4"
(105 x 82 x 40 cm)

According to the many-worlds theory,
first posited by Hugh Everett in 1957,
although we observe time as linear,
diverging timelines occur in parallel
worlds, with each possible outcome
having a different probability. In the
world of quantum computing, this concept
is reflected in the superposition principle,
the ability of particles to be in two or
more states at once, which is used to
perform massive parallel processing.
The 5th Dimensional Camera explores
how we might see all these different
worlds at the same time, in a metaphori-
cal many-lensed object. All the possible
ramifications of any decision or action
or day would theoretically be visible,
thus visualizing all the worlds that branch
out from our linear timeline; the longer
the period for which the camera's timer
is set, the more time there is for new
worlds to branch out from our own and,
in turn, the more novel some of those
worlds are likely to be. The designers
hope that the camera will make tangible
the wider implications of quantum
computing and its effects on our world.

# Reality Is Plenty, Thanks: Twelve Arguments for Keeping the Naked Eye Naked

Kevin Slavin

Ten or fifteen years ago, the dream on offer was virtual reality.

Virtual reality—VR—would exist somewhere between the holodeck and Second Life (fig. 1): lived experience would be delegated to avatars moving around in synthetic three-dimensional worlds. All we'd need would be a high polygon count and the right glasses, and we could live our lives in worlds free from social or applied physics.

But Second Life no longer has purchase on our imaginations, and holodeck-by-the-hour arcades never materialized. In the same period, however, the multiplayer game World of Warcraft attracted 11 million players and Facebook attracted half a billion users without simulating anything at all, without promising reality. With the largest user base in the world, Facebook doesn't resemble the virtual reality we were promised, because Facebook doesn't look like an Elven castle on the misty horizon. It looks like a website.

In 2011 we're not pining for virtual reality; we've forgotten the texture and detail of the dream. Yet some psychic residue endures. We call this new echo "augmented reality"—AR for short—and it employs much of the vocabulary, technology, and dogma of VR. Augmented reality allows you to look through a magic window and see both what's there and what's not there, all on one pixel plane, all responding in real time to your position, motion, velocity, and heading; thus we can mix what we see locally with what we know globally.

As parlor tricks go, it's a neat one. Reality is built on human perception, entering consciousness through the human eye. If you add to the stack, you have something like reality, only more. But more what?

/////////////////////////////////////

1.      Upside-Down and Backward Town

Twenty years ago I was in art school, studying under a brilliant photography professor named Norman. This was back when studying photography meant messing around with chemicals in the dark. Norman had plenty to teach; he'd been around for a while, including a World War II tour spent on an aircraft carrier.

Norman was one of the ship's radar operators. He monitored a small screen for information—Japanese ships, I suppose—that he would convey to officers by drawing figures on a glass map (fig. 2). He had to be quick; lives depended on his speed and accuracy. What made it difficult was that the map that he had to draw on was, from his orientation, upside down and backward.

This is not easy to do under duress, so Norman was trained by the navy to see the world upside down and backward. The training he described is just crazy enough to be plausible: in some classified location was a town, built by the navy, where radar operators lived before shipping out and where everything was upside down and backward. Newspapers, store signage, posters, everything printed upside down and backward, the whole world constructed through the navy's phony lens. Norman said it took a few weeks to adjust and be able to read the newspapers. It took a few weeks to train his brain to see the world as the navy needed him to see it.

I don't know how much of this story is true. But the training it describes is close enough to some well-known methods of retraining the human eye, and the town, whether it existed or not, is close enough to the desert ghost towns of World War II, simulated European and Japanese environments where American forces could practice the war before fighting it.

When I hear the stories we tell ourselves about our future in augmented reality, I picture

Fig. 1
Linden Lab. Second Life. 2003,
screen shot 2010

Fig. 2
Radar information is charted on
an aircraft carrier stationed in
the Pacific Ocean in early 1945.

this place. Was Upside-Down and Backward Town any more or less real than Midtown Manhattan? The way Norman was trained to see the world: was it more or less real than the ways we see to begin with?

/ / / / / / / / / / / / / / / / / / / / / / / / / / / / / / / /

2.      Emission Theory

In 1929 developmental psychologist Jean Piaget, studying the ways that children see the world, noted that children believed in extramission—that is, that the eye emits images rather than taking them in (fig. 3).[1] This may seem childish, but emission theory was the dominant model for human vision until it was disproved, in 1021, by Ibn al-Haytham. Ptolemy, Plato, and Euclid all formed theories of optical phenomena that involved light beams shooting from the eye to construct imagery in front of the person seeing it. From the stars in the sky to the apple on the ground, all of it, according to emission theory, is painted by the eye.

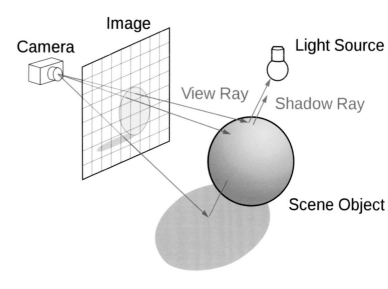

Fig. 3
Diagram illustrating ray
tracing, a computer modeling
process analogous to emission
theory. Diagram by Henrik

Figs. 4 and 5
Boeing workers assemble jet
electrical systems using foam
boards (top) and AR-enhanced
headsets (bottom), c. 1995.

Emission theory might be regarded as a primitive conception of the world, like a flat earth at the center of the universe. But unlike those models, it still has a foothold in mainstream human consciousness. Not just in children (as Piaget noted) but in the United States in general: a disturbing 2002 study revealed that nearly fifty percent of college students understand visual perception as some variation of emission theory.[2]

Intromission theory is a clear, modern alternative: the retina detects photons of light, neural impulses travel to the brain, and the brain produces meaning from that transmission. But if you understand vision as emission theory— as those contemporary college students do— it's only natural to want to augment reality with an additional eye, to project additional meaning onto the empty world that surrounds us.

/////////////////////////////////

3.      High-Definition Sunglasses

A television commercial for HD Vision sunglasses tells us that "just like high definition TV is the ultimate in viewing clarity, HD Vision makes the world come alive!"

As television aspires to high-definition, we aspire to high definition as well. The world would become more real if we could just increase the resolution, the polygon count, the breadth of the transmission.

If we're designing technology that allows us to see beyond the visible spectrum, then we'll also need to design what we'll see there. Emission theory will finally be proven real: the world around us will be what we project upon it, rather than the other way around.

### 4. Augmenting Reality Starts with Building Machines That Fly

The phrase "augmented reality," firmly entrenched in our vernacular in 2011, is only twenty years old. It was coined by Tom Caudell, a researcher at Boeing.

Funded by military grants, Caudell was focused on a specific challenge in commercial airplane manufacturing: developing a better method of assembling the clusters of wire and switches that form an aircraft's neurological system. In 1990 this was done with what were called "foam boards" (fig. 4): large sheets of plywood laid out with life-size diagrams of the airplane's infrastructure. Factory workers wound their way across dozens of boards, pulling and fusing wires according to the markers in front of them; the wires were then embedded, in the correct formation, in the aircraft.

Caudell and his colleagues set out to provide workers with better information about what they were making so that they could work more efficiently in tighter spaces. By 1995 workers were using head-mounted AR (fig. 5), instead of foam boards. The helmet called up different diagrams at the touch of a button, to show them where the wires should go.

Augmented reality began with workers wearing helmets, hooked up to one set of wires terminating at their eyes and a different set terminating at their fingertips, building aeronautic nervous systems with blueprints visible to their eyes alone. Their eyes made the blueprint real, and their hands made the airplane real. Augmented reality started here.

/////////////////////////////////////

### 5. Before a Machine Can Think, It Needs to See

In 1984 James Cameron unleashed The Terminator, a film starring a cyborg assassin sent back through time from a postapocalyptic 2029. The assassin—played by a man who would become governor of a postbankruptcy California—is carefully considered. To all outward appearances it has human traits and appearances; on the inside, like all computing

Fig. 6
James Cameron.
The Terminator. 1984.
35mm print (color, sound),
107 min.

Fig. 7
Lindsay Burroughs of Total
Immersion.Topps 3D Live
Card. 2009

Fig. 8
Diagram by Chin-Chang
Ho and Karl F. MacDorman
illustrating Masahiro Mori's
theory of the uncanny
valley (1970)

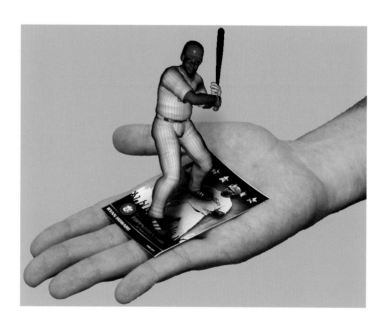

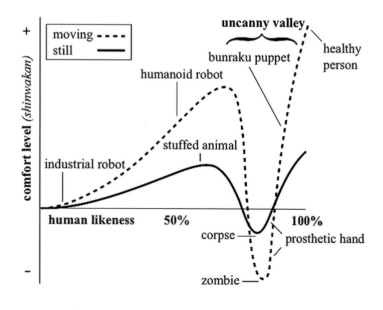

machines, it is metal, wires, and a series of
algorithms. There are sensing apparatuses,
of course, including sophisticated optics that
see just like we do, but they see more.

We periodically see from the point of view
of the Terminator itself. It's one of the earlier
cinematic representations of how machines see
the world, in this case a steady stream of text
superimposed on raw optical input. The machine
sees the world like the worker at Boeing, with
data superimposed on reality to inform, guide,
and evaluate its actions.

What is curious about the Terminator's
vision is the presence of text, as if a computer
would need to read in order to know what to
do (fig. 6). In this model of machine intelligence,
vision is so singularly important that a microproc-
essor needs to take notes and make things
visible for itself, just to know what to do.

This is the fallacy of augmented reality:
it asserts that the eye (not the brain) is the
unified center of perception, thought, reality.

////////////////////////////////////

6.        The Immersive Fallacy and Settlers
          of the Uncanny Valley

In the race to design the landscape for our
new supercharged eyes, we have forgotten that
a lot of reality has little to do with what we see.
Augmented reality proposes that reality is most
effectively transformed through mimetic representation. For example, the AR company Total
Immersion makes baseball cards that "come
alive" (fig. 7), as if the three-dimensional model
of the player had more life than the ten years'
worth of the player's performance stats, printed
on the back of the card.

Game designers Katie Salen and Eric
Zimmerman have defined the immersive fallacy
as "the idea that the pleasure of a media
experience lies in its ability to sensually transport
the participant into an illusory, simulated
reality. According to the immersive fallacy,
this reality is so complete that ideally the frame
falls away so that the player truly believes
that he or she is part of an imaginary world."[3]
But the frame doesn't fall away. In explaining
why, Salen and Zimmerman cite film studies
scholar Elena Gorfinkel, who has written,
"The confusion in this conversation has
emerged because representational strategies
are conflated with the effect of immersion.
Immersion itself is not tied to a replication
or mimesis of reality."[4]

In fact, replication and mimesis often
make things seem less real, a phenomenon

well known to roboticists. Humans are instinc-
tively repulsed by robots whose appearance
and motions register somewhere between
"barely human" and "fully human." The space
in which we are disquieted by what we see
is referred to as the "uncanny valley" (fig. 8).[5]

The valley is not just what we look
at but also how we see; with these new
superhuman eyes, we are always already
at the valley's frontier. On the way to the future
we must navigate the terrain between "barely
real" and "fully real." Equipped with the right
glasses and ambient informatics, this valley
stretches out endlessly across the landscape.

Companies such as Layar and Wikitude
propose augmenting the streets around us
with imports from the region. In New York,
for example, there might be real-time crime
data for the block you're on, there but not there.
With this, the uncanny valley finally has real-
world geography, populated with real-world
citizens who are farther and farther from
home. Cities have secrets, Google has facts;
our cities, which we used to browse, will become
searchable. However, by rendering the city
transparent, we take away its essential qualities

of opacity, mystery, and discovery. Using
the human eye to simultaneously process
information and experience might just make
the city feel farther and farther away.

///////////////////////////////////////

7.      Turning off the Glasses

Dennō Coil (CyberCoil, 2007, fig. 9) is an anime
series set in the faraway city of Daikoku in
2026, eleven years after the general introduction
of Internet-connected AR glasses. A real city
with real residents, Daikoku is also the capital
of the half-virtual world, populated by parallel
pets, friends, objects, and dangers.

The protagonists are children, and the
children's model of emission theory has finally
been realized: the world they see is the world
they construct. When viruses called Illegals,
which are visible only through AR glasses,
threaten the children and trap them in a small
room, a girl named Fumie turns to her sister,
Yuko, and asks, "Why don't we turn our
glasses off?"

Fig. 9
Mitsuo Iso and Takeshi
Honda. Dennō Coil
(CyberCoil). 2007

Fig. 10
Akhiro Yokoi of WiZ Co., Ltd.,
and Aki Mita of Bandai Co., Ltd.
Tamagotchi. 1996. ABS and
LCD screen, 2 1/16 × 1 11/16
× 11/16" (5.3 × 4.3 × 1.8 cm).
Manufactured by Bandai Co.,
Ltd., Japan

But they can't. In 2026 the virtual world continues even when it is not being observed; the threatening entities don't disappear when the children stop seeing them. It is not a layer superimposed but an actual world that takes place parallel to the physical world. In 2026 it may not be visible to the naked eye, but it's no less real.

//////////////////////////////////////////////////////////

8.        What Happens When You Aren't Looking

What makes things real may not be what we see but what we imagine, remember, desire, and fear. Do we use our eyes when we remember? Do we use them when we imagine?

Brilliant designers know that much of human experience lies elsewhere. The digital pet Tamagotchi (fig. 10) built a reality around what you didn't see, couldn't see. Since its 1996 debut, 70 million of them were sold, and the toy's disruptive effects are well known to anyone who has encountered one. They were banned by some schools in Hawaii, because taking care of creatures that could starve to death without care was causing students to prioritize the helpless Tamagotchi over their schoolwork.[6] They were too demanding, in many ways most present precisely when they were inaccessible.

When accessible, they don't look like much: the immersive experience of the Tamagotchi is created with a grid of black-and-white pixels. It doesn't aspire to mimetic visual representation; it becomes real by behaving real, by being demanding, rewarding, hungry, vulnerable.

In 1996 the Tamagotchi was competing for attention with the first wave of three-dimensional video games: Super Mario 64, Duke Nukem 3D, Tomb Raider. The obvious trend in entertainment was to increase the polygon count, taking the slippery slope to the uncanny valley. Tamagotchi outsold every one of those games, suggesting that reality is augmented when it feels different, not when it appears different.

When reality is truly augmented, our senses of obligation, desire, and reward are transformed. By contrast, the collective desire for three-dimensional AR begins to feel like the desire for pornography, a thin veneer of actual experience flattened for the eye, the sense most easily fooled.

//////////////////////////////////////////////////////////

9.        It's Easy to Believe in Ghosts Because They Are
          Invisible

In 2006 we set out to bring a spirit, Papa Bones, to New York City. This was to pay tribute to the spirits that, post-Hurricane Katrina, had no home without New Orleans's second-line Mardi Gras. We designed and built Crossroads (page 119), one of the first mobile games to use GPS. It took place in a small area of the West Village, in homage to Jane Jacobs and with a clear line of sight to geosynchronous satellites.

Crossroads was a two-player game, with each player's location tracked in real time and visible on the phone.

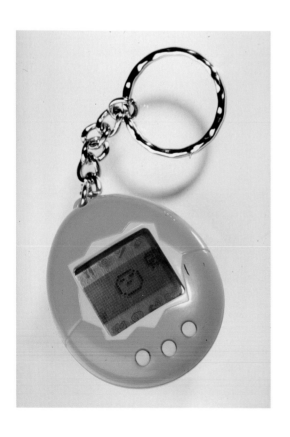

On the same display, Papa Bones's location was also tracked and also visible, but the difference between him and the players was that Papa Bones didn't exist. His entire presence in the game was an eight-by-eight-pixel skull that traveled through the West Village with the players. If his location (his position on the map) coincided with the players' location (on the map and in the world) the player lost a life.

So it was that players were racing down the streets, competing with each other and pursued by something invisible. As we tested the game in Lower Manhattan we would sometimes have ten or fifteen phones running the game, all sitting on one table. Papa Bones was controlled by random movements that corresponded to real-world positions, and when he "swept by" our location, the cluster of phones would vibrate, rattle, and fall off the table.

No experience I've ever had prepared me for how real it would feel, this ghost sweeping through the room. Not because the technology made him visible, but because the technology made him real. Papa Bones would arrive unexpectedly, move things around on the table, and then move on. That is the weight of the invisible, augmented.

///////////////////////////////////////////////////////

10.     Beyond the Eye

The designers of the future know the limits of the human eye and are designing for a reality constrained by them. For example, the designers Che-Wei Wang and Kristin O'Friel describe their project Momo (2007, fig. 11) as "a haptic navigational device that requires only the sense of touch to guide a user. No maps, no text, no arrows, no lights. It sits on the palm of one's hand and leans, vibrates and gravitates toward a preset location. Akin to someone pointing you in the right direction, there is no need to find your map, you simply follow as the device leans toward your destination."[7] In Momo we see an alternative—and optimistic—path to augmented reality. Google Maps shows us our world from above and draws lines for routes, and conventional AR has us look through a lens to see where we are going. By contrast, Momo augments the sense of location not with the eye but with the body.

These design impulses are becoming mainstream thanks in part to the integration of the human body in game systems such as Wii and Kinect. It is notable that the Wii, like Tamagotchi, turned its back on high-resolution polygons just as other game consoles (such as Xbox and PS3) started making more "realistic" worlds.

As with the Wii and Kinect, Momo restores the body's role in interaction and navigation. The user is pulled softly by an object in her hands, nudged toward her destination rather than directed. Her eyes are restored to their original function, taking in the world around her. Not the world in front of her but the world around her.

Fig. 11
Kristin O' Friel and Che-Wei Wang. Momo. 2007. Masonite, motors, GPS, digital compass, microcontroller, and wool, 12 × 6 × 6" (30.5 × 15.2 × 15.2 cm)

Fig. 12
Vision Systems
International for Lockheed
Martin. F-35 Generation II
Helmet with Helmet-Mounted
Display System. 2009. Carbon
graphite and various materials,
dimensions variable

Fig. 13
Johnson Controls for Peugeot,
Inc. Head Up Display for
Peugeot 508. 2009

//////////////////////////////////////////////////

11.      Augmenting Reality Starts with Building Machines
         That Fly

Head-up display (HUD) is a control interface commonly used
by air force pilots. In 1994 researchers Michael Flannagan
and Andrew Harrison published a study called "The Effects
of Automobile Head-Up Display Location for Younger and Older
Drivers."[8] The results of the study show that drivers see the
world in ways that are quite different from the ways that
pilots do.

         In contemporary air combat, the pilot is the slowest
and least responsive component of the aircraft. Thus, the
helmet worn by the pilot of an F-35 Joint Strike Fighter (fig. 12)
is given as much attention as the rest of the plane; inside it,
pilots see—like the Terminator sees—all the necessary telemetry they need in order to navigate and engage a target.
An F-35 pilot essentially becomes a giant eyeball strapped
to a body that is strapped to the plane. This is effective for
pilots, because there's so little time to think when traveling
at speeds faster than Mach 1. In most respects, their reality
is telescoped to what is directly in front of them, and that's
where any new information needs to appear.

         There have been many attempts to transfer the
pilot's augmented reality to the driver of a car, such as the
head-up display installed in the Peugeot 508 in 2009 (fig. 13).
For the most part these experiments have underperformed
or failed. Drivers are different from pilots; their sense of the
world is informed not just by what they are focused on but
by what they are not focused on, what lies in their periphery,
what they hear, what catches their eye.

Thus reality isn't augmented when a driver's focus is drawn to a single point straight ahead. Singular focus—in which the eye looks at rather than around—diminishes reality, closes it down. For the driver and for most of us, reality isn't the road straight ahead, it's the whole world around us.

/////////////////////////////////////////

## 12.    The World Around Us

In World War II the navy gave Norman tools to shift the way he saw the world. These tools didn't change what he saw, as augmented reality sets out to do, but they changed how he saw.

This is the noble purpose facing designers looking at the future. The principles and goals of augmenting reality—of using technology to enhance or alter the perception of reality—may not be best expressed by designing anything to look at.

The artists Chris Woebken and Kenichi Okada have designed Animal Superpowers (2008, page 134), including an ant apparatus that "allows you to feel like an ant by magnifying your vision 50x through microscope antennas in your hand. You can perceive all the tiny cracks and details of a surface through this. It allows you to 'see' through your hands and to dive into a secret and hidden world."[9] Reality is augmented, to be sure, but not by adding a layer, not by making something to look at. It's about making something different to see with, to feel the world—the real world—in ways that we've never known. These are the astronauts on Earth, reexploring the planet none of us will leave.

They are inventing new ways to see rather than new things to look at. Because there's no shortage of things to see: reality is already plenty, thanks.

Notes

1.    Jean Piaget, La Représentation du monde chez l'enfant (Paris: Alcan, 1926); published in English as The Child's Conception of the World, trans. Joan Tomlinson and Andrew Tomlinson (London: Routledge, 1929), pp. 47–49.

2.    Gerald A. Winer, Jane E. Cottrell, Virginia Gregg, et al., "The Persistence of a Misconception about Vision after Educational Interventions," American Psychologist 57, nos. 6–7 (June–July 2002): 417–24.

3.    Katie Salen and Eric Zimmerman, Rules of Play: Game Design Fundamentals (Cambridge, Mass.: MIT Press, 2003), p. 451.

4.    Elena Gorfinkel, quoted in ibid.

5.    On the uncanny valley, see pp. 13 and 17n19 in this volume; on Freud's uncanny, see p. 55.

6.    Debra Barayuga, "Electronic Pets Peep Their Last at Isle Schools," Honolulu Star-Bulletin, June 2, 1997, archives.starbulletin.com/97/06/02/news/story2.html.

7.    Momo: A Haptic Navigation Device, www.momobots.com.

8.    Michael J. Flannagan and Andrew K. Harrison, The Effects of Automobile Head-Up Display Location for Younger and Older Drivers (Ann Arbor: Transportation Research Institute, University of Michigan, 1994), deepblue.lib.umich.edu/bitstream/2027.42/64078/1/85964.pdf.

9.    "Animal Superpowers," Chris Woebken, chriswoebken.com/animalsuper-powers.html.

In this world of constant and ubiquitous communication, ignorance is not considered to be bliss, and misunderstandings are dangerous missed opportunities—except when they are integrated in a script as moments of shock and revelation, as interesting double entendres. Still, mishaps they are, and in common parlance they are conversation, even communication stoppers.

The noble goals of harmony, empathy, and true tolerance are why so many people have devoted their lives to helping us understand others, or at least whomever our local cultural conventions consider "other." History has prepared us for this moment with centuries of war, activism, and progress, however slow, in banishing taboos and embracing diversity. All the important twentieth-century movements of emancipation, equality, and liberation have proceeded in this direction. We also know that we still have a long way to go.

This is why designers, whose focus is always centered on improving conditions for human beings, have become engaged in projects that require not only the classical elements of design education but also basic tenets of cognitive science. In previous chapters we have explored how the Internet and wireless networks have created new layers of complexity and possibility in human communication. Designers are now taking on the communication issues these layers have presented, issues now central to our daily activities: negotiations of privacy and anonymity; the vehemence and violence abetted by the ability to hide behind false identities; the promise of new and unregulated means of expressions, connectivity, and revenue generation, and the responsibilities that go with them.

By focusing on those issues, often with actionable proposals and sometimes with visionary clarity, designers have joined with abandon the ranks of those encouraging cross-cultural understanding. This chapter contains design solutions for curious humans who want to experience what it feels like to be something or somebody else, whether a bat (page 176), a crow (page 177), a menstruating woman (page 182), a person with a disability (pages 190–91), and other kinds of transformers and outliers. The activist efforts of some designers, whose decisive metaphors and statements have the blunt force of manifestos, work toward these simple goals: if not acceptance, at least tolerance; curiosity rather than rejection; a better, more fulfilling, more organic, more just way of living together.

P. A.

The texts in this section were written by Azzurra Cox.

DOUBLE EXPOSURE

5

BATS TAKING OFF FOR INSECT SNACKS

Chris Woebken (German, born 1980)
and Natalie Jeremijenko (Australian,
born 1966)
of Environmental Health Clinic (est. 2007)
Steinhardt School of Culture, Education,
and Human Development (est. 1890)
New York University (USA, est. 1831)

//////////////////////////////

Bat Billboard. 2008

//////////////////////////////

Bats play a key role in many ecosystems, pollinating plants and providing insect control, but in urban habitats they are often misunderstood, thought to be threats or pests. The Bat Billboard, an interactive billboard that doubles as housing for bats, is a way to dispel this misinformation as well as creating a bridge between bats and humans. Inside a standard billboard structure, urban bats find a safe space to live and hibernate, helping to counteract the effects of white-nose syndrome (a mysterious disease that has killed more than a million bats since 2007) and other threats to their populations. Monitoring equipment inside the billboard uses voice-recognition software to map and translate the calls of resident bats, matches them to archives of various call patterns and meanings, currently being compiled by biologists, and displays the resulting messages on a screen. The billboard inventively reclaims urban infrastructure for animal habitat and also functions as a public face for the bats, translating their habits and activities in a way that humans can understand.

Sputniko! (British and Japanese,
born Japan 1985)
Design Interactions Department
(est. 1989)
Royal College of Art (UK, est. 1837)

////////////////////////////

Crowbot Jenny. 2010

////////////////////////////

Installation with video (color, sound),
screens, and printed panels, 3:50 min,
dimensions variable; device: polystyrene,
acrylic, Arduino board, speaker, and
amplifier, 23 5/8 × 11 13/16 × 3 7/8"
(60 × 30 × 10 cm)

The artist known as Sputniko! explores
technology, feminism, and pop culture by
collaborating with scientists on works
that suggest possible intersections
among these fields. Crowbot Jenny,
inspired by Donna Haraway's philosophical memoir When Species Meet (2007),
is a solitary girl who, despite her generation's tendency toward communication
overload, has trouble relating to her
peers. In fact, Crowbot Jenny prefers to
talk with animals and uses the Crowbot,
an instrument that replicates a range of
crow calls, to commune with her army of
birds. Sputniko! collaborated with Nathan
Emery and Nicola Clayton, specialists
in crow intelligence at the University
of London and University of Cambridge,
UK, respectively, who provided her
with sample calls collected in London's
Finsbury and Hyde parks. From that
collaboration she learned that crows
are capable of advanced social communication, even of reading other animals'
minds. Crowbot Jenny contemplates
the potential of cross-species interaction, suggesting a scenario in which
technology lets us, as the artist
says, "re-realize the urban animals
surrounding us."

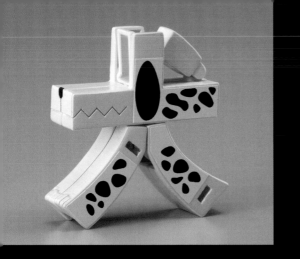

Shigeru Ishitsuka (Japanese, born 1975)
of MegaHouse Corporation (Japan, est.
1962)
Misako Kirigaya (Japanese, born 1985)
of Bandai Co., Ltd. (Japan, est. 1950)

/////////////////////////////

Mojibakeru. 2010

/////////////////////////////

ABS, each: approx. 2 x 2 x 5/16"
(5 x 5 x 1.1 cm)
Manufactured by MegaHouse
Corporation, Japan

Mojibakeru toy figures start as Japanese kanji characters and are transformed into the animals each character represents. For instance, <u>inu</u> (犬), kanji for "dog," goes from black-and-white character to Dalmatian, complete with movable tail. Mojibakeru is both learning tool and unique demonstration of the link between symbol and object. Eighteen different kanji figures are available in various colors.

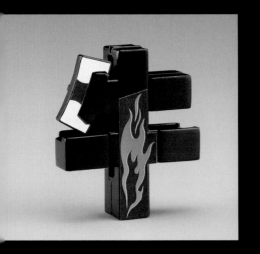

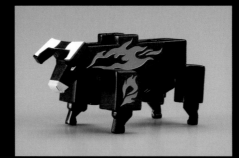

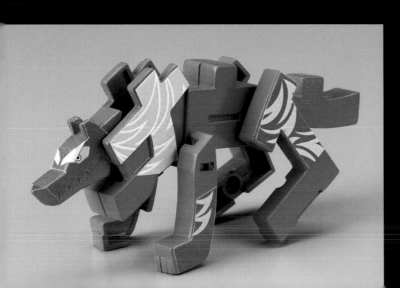

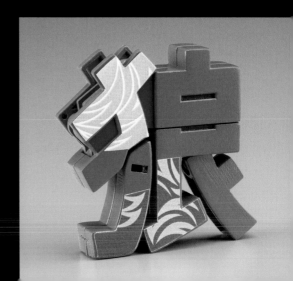

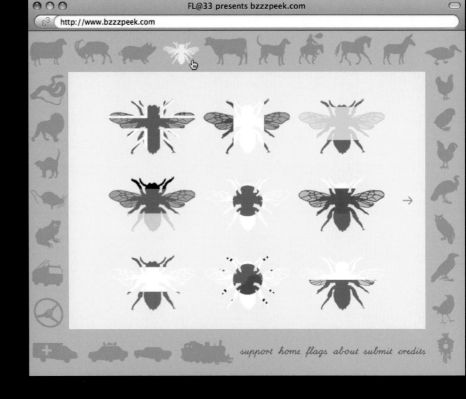

Agathe Jacquillat (French, born 1975)
and Tomi Vollauschek (Austrian,
born 1973)
of FLa33 (UK, est. 2001)

/////////////////////////////

bzzzpeek. 2002

/////////////////////////////

HTML and Flash software

bzzzpeek is a playful online catalogue
of onomatopoeia, composed of audio clips
of native speakers vocalizing animal and
vehicle sounds in their own languages.
Visitors to the site choose an animal
and then click on various flags to hear
renditions of a cat, a lion, a rooster, and
twenty-six other animals in twenty-two
languages. Anyone can submit a recording, and most of the recordings are of
children's voices. The site is entertaining
as well as informative, drawing attention
to both the commonalities and idiosyncrasies of languages and language groups.
A cat's meow sounds the most similar
across languages; South Koreans,
followed closely by Hungarians, most
consistently deviate from the standard
interpretations of sounds.

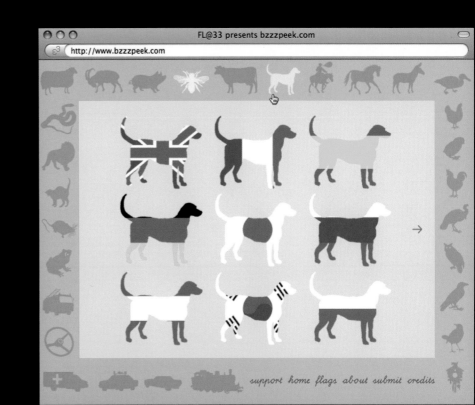

Stephen Spyropoulos (Greek and
American, born USA 1980) and Theodore
Spyropoulos (Greek and American,
born USA 1976)
of Minimaforms (USA and UK, est. 2002)

////////////////////////////

Becoming Animal. 2007

////////////////////////////

Installation with animal masks (Perspex,
neoprene, rubber, wood, and LEDs),
projections, microphones, speakers,
and camera-recognition and custom
software

In Becoming Animal, participants are
invited to interact with Kerberos (or
Cerberus), a digitally generated version
of the mythic three-headed gatekeeper
of the underworld, and with each other.
Participants wear dog masks made
of heavy silkscreened paper and are
guided by three actors wearing special
masks of Perspex and wood. Kerberos
responds with sounds, facial signals,
and gestures to the behavior of others,
based on their movements, displaying
love, hate, anger, and other emotions,
and each of the creature's heads
behaves autonomously. This installation,
which bridges the real and the virtual,
was developed for the Faster Than
Sound Festival in Suffolk,
UK, in 2007.

Sputniko! (British and Japanese, born
Japan 1985)
Design Interactions Department
(est. 1989)
Royal College of Art (UK, est. 1837)

/////////////////////////////

Menstruation Machine–Takashi's
Take. 2010

/////////////////////////////

Installation with video (color, sound),
screens, and printed panels, 3:24 min.,
dimensions variable; device: aluminum,
electronics, and acrylic, 13 3/8 ×
13 13/16 × 13 3/8" (34 × 35 × 34 cm)

With Menstruation Machine, Sputniko!
explores the relationship between
identity, biology, and choice, while also
inquiring into the meaning of gender-
specific rituals. The metal device, which
looks like a chastity belt and is equipped
with a blood-dispensing system and
electrodes that stimulate the lower
abdomen, replicates the pain and bleeding
of the average five-day menstruation
period. It is designed to be worn by
men, children, postmenopausal women,
or whoever else wants to experience
menstruation. A music video that can
be displayed with the device is about
Takashi, who wants to understand what
it feels like to be a girly girl. Takashi builds
the Menstruation Machine and wears
it out on the town with a girlfriend,

strutting around a shopping mall and
occasionally doubling over in pain. Thus
an internal, private process is transformed into a wearable display of identity.
Since the 1960s, advances in hormone-
based contraception have, by suppres-
sing ovulation, made monthly periods no
longer biologically necessary. Sputniko!
notes that the Menstruation Machine
may be particularly desirable in a future
in which menstruation in fact becomes
obsolete.

Jaakko Tuomivaara (Finnish, born 1977)
Communication Art & Design Department
(est. 1999)
Royal College of Art (UK, est. 1837)

////////////////////////////

Hide & See. 2010

////////////////////////////

Framed, mounted LCD screens, and
OmniOutliner, Illustrator, Photoshop,
After Effects, TextMate, BluePhoneElite,
and custom software, face: 18 5/16 ×
15 3/16 × 3" (46.5 × 38.7 × 7.5 cm);
beach: 8 × 6 1/2 × 1 11/16" (20.3 × 16.5
× 4.2 cm)

Hide & See is a device that hides
information in plain sight, with LCD
screens displaying images that communicate coded information. On a close-up
of a woman's face, missed telephone
calls are cleverly announced by the
sudden appearance of dots, like beauty
marks; red dots around the mouth
represent calls from important numbers.
An image of a couple strolling down a
beach communicates someone's where-
abouts; the color of the bag held by the
man in the picture changes for home or
office or other set locations. The information is readily accessible only to the
person who knows the code, allowing,
for example, emergencies to be tracked
during a meeting without the constant
checking of digital devices. Hide & See
also alerts us to the overcommunication
anxiety that pervades everyday life.

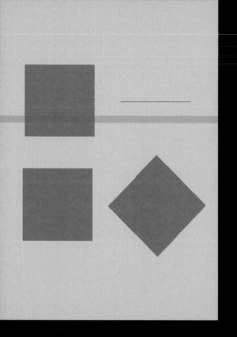

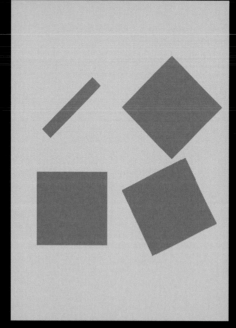

Johan Halin (Finnish, born 1983)
of Ab Parasol Oy (Finland, est. 2007)

////////////////////////////////

Kontrol. 2010

////////////////////////////////

Xcode, cocos2d, Ableton Live, and
Photoshop software

With Kontrol, a music application for
iPhones and iPads, users create techno
compositions by clicking on a simple
interface of four blue squares, each of
which moves and triggers certain sounds
and beats. The sounds and the squares'
movements depend on the order and
manner in which the squares are activated and the structures that result.
While the rules for modifying the soundscape are quite rigid, there is also a
random element to the audio and visuals,
so that trial and error become part of
the game. Complex compositions can be
constructed by layering multiple sounds
and beats, and the lack of precise control
becomes the very mechanism for
creativity.

Toshio Iwai (Japanese, born 1962)

////////////////////////////////

Tenori-on. 2004

////////////////////////////////

ABS, aluminum, LEDs, and electronics,
8 1/8 × 8 1/8 × 1 5/16" (20.5 × 20.5
× 3.4 cm)
Manufactured by Yamaha Corporation,
Japan

Tenori-on means "sound in your palm"
in Japanese; the device named for it is
a handheld step sequencer that creates
synthesized sound and light patterns,
fusing the sequential and layering logic
of electronic music with dynamic visual
display. A sixteen-by-sixteen LED screen
lights up and emits preprogrammed
sounds; each LED pixel is also a switch
that, when pressed, activates a sound.
Two speakers are located at the top of
the screen, and buttons that determine
the type of sound and beats per minute
are arranged along the sides. Users
program a specific sequence of sounds,
which are activated, with bursts of
light, by an illuminated vertical line that
crosses the screen from left to right.
These patterns can be stored in the
device and used during performance.
Artist Toshio Iwai notes that "in days
gone by, a musical instrument had to
have a beauty, of shape as well as of
sound.... Modern electronic instruments
don't have this inevitable relationship
between the shape, the sound, and the
player. What I have done is to try to
bring back these... elements and build
them [into] a true musical instrument
for the digital age." Tenori-on's versatility
and ease make it suitable for both serious
musicians and beginners. The instrument
is in the collection of The Museum
of Modern Art, New York.

Something as simple as playing Tetris or timing the cooking of an egg. The only variables are the three possible grid sizes: the two fifty six (sixteen by sixteen buttons), the one twenty eight (sixteen by eight), and the sixty four (eight by eight). The innovation of designers Brian Crabtree and Kelli Cain lies in foregoing hardwired functionality for versatility. The designers handcraft the units out of high-quality, locally sourced materials and adhere to an efficient open-source softwaredevelopment model that encourages a cycle of continuous improvement and adaptation, including supplying DIY kits to anyone who wants to build the device.

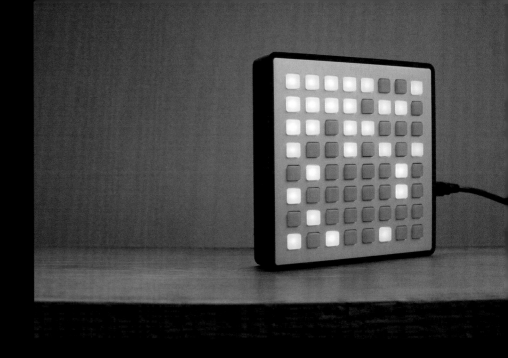

and intention: rhythms at first appear
regular but begin to shift as more balls
activate the space. The application
can be upgraded to increase the variety
of possible sounds through a system
of different-colored lines.

Henry Chu (Chinese, born Hong Kong
1976) of Pill and Pillow (Hong Kong,
est. 2004)

/////////////////////////////

Squiggle. 2010

/////////////////////////////

openFrameworks software

Squiggle transforms the iPad into a
virtual, many-stringed instrument. Users
draw a series of lines in any direction
(horizontal, vertical, diagonal); the note
each line will sound is determined by its
length, and each new line is a different
color. When the composition is ready, the
user simply tilts up the iPad and strums
the lines, which vibrate like rubber bands.

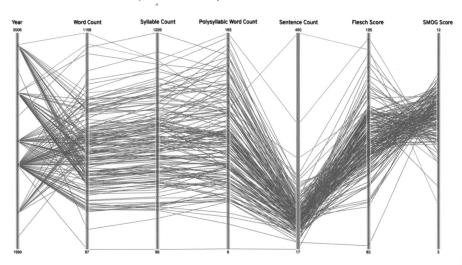

## Rap Almanac Analysis Of 50 Cent's Career

| Year | Word Count | Syllable Count | Polysyllabic Word Count | Sentence Count | Flesch Score | SMOG Score |
|---|---|---|---|---|---|---|
| 2008 | 1158 | 1226 | 163 | 450 | 125 | 12 |
| 1999 | 87 | 96 | 6 | 17 | 83 | 5 |

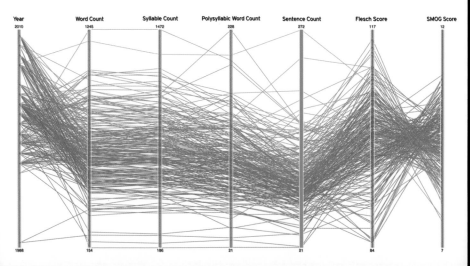

## Rap Almanac Analysis Of Jay-Z's Career

| Year | Word Count | Syllable Count | Polysyllabic Word Count | Sentence Count | Flesch Score | SMOG Score |
|---|---|---|---|---|---|---|
| 2010 | 1245 | 1472 | 228 | 272 | 117 | 12 |
| 1988 | 154 | 196 | 21 | 21 | 84 | 7 |

Tahir Hemphill (American, born 1972)

/////////////////////////////

Rap Almanac Visualization of 50 Cent's
Career from Hip-Hop Word Count. 2010

Rap Almanac Visualization of Jay-Z's
Career from Hip-Hop Word Count. 2010

/////////////////////////////

Protovis software

New York rappers, it so happens, were
the first to mention champagne in songs.
Tahir Hemphill determined this using
his Hip-Hop Word Count, a searchable
database of the lyrics of more than forty
thousand songs from 1979 to the present.
This tool for research and interpretation
illuminates the music's technical details,
such as metaphors, rhyme style, and
frequency of polysyllabic words. Any
term can be searched, and the results
are an exhaustive list of songs in which
that term appears, along with complete
lyrics, artist, location, syllable count,
average syllables per word, and literary
sophistication (determined by Flesch and
SMOG scores, readability rubrics designed
to measure ease of comprehension).
Hip-Hop Word Count also converts
the data into interactive visualizations
that graph and connect on parallel lines.
Users can select ranges in any category
and see how, for example, Jay-Z's
shorter songs fare in terms of syllable
count and sophistication. Hemphill notes
that Hip-Hop Word Count, by assigning
time and place to elements such as
cultural and sociopolitical references,
can be used "to chart the migration of
ideas and map a geography of language."

Jean-Louis Frechin (French, born 1962)
and Uros Petrevski (Serbian, born 1981)
of NoDesign (France, est. 2001)

/////////////////////////////////

Wablog. 2008

/////////////////////////////////

ABS, Lycra, Arduino board, camera,
proximity sensors, and Java and C++
software, 15 11/16 × 2 7/8 × 1 5/16"
(40 × 7.5 × 3.5 cm)

The Wablog is a device made up of
a small speaker between two primitive
screens that is attached to a computer
and functions as a real-time avatar.
Users can communicate with each other
through movements and signs; signal
or perceive physical presence; and be
notified of activity on online networks
such as Twitter. Wablog's communication
system recalls the dynamics of subma-
rine sonar, of machines constantly
signaling their position to each other,
using animations recalling early video
games; in a similar way one Wablog
pings another, and the answer floats
back, like an echo. Wablog arose from
its designers' exploration of what they
call "indirect, blurry and calm low tech"
communication objects; it demonstrates
that the instant connectivity and constant communication we now experience
can be manifested in quiet ways.

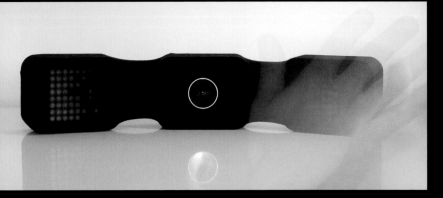

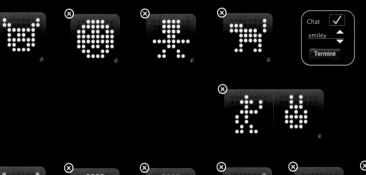

ean Louis Frechin (French, born 1962)
nd Uros Petrevski (Serbian, born 1981)
f NoDesign (France, est. 2001)
rédéric Bevilacqua (Swiss, born 1967)
f IRCAM (France, est. 1977)

/////////////////////////////

MO musical objects from the Interlude
roject. 2010

/////////////////////////////

BS, printed circuit board, and lithium-ion
attery, dimensions variable

lthough recent developments in elec-
ronic music have made ubiquitous the
nalysis, processing, and manipulation
f sound and rhythm, the possibilities
or interaction between physical
novement and sonic elements remain
nostly untapped. The goal of the
nterlude project is to "develop
ollaborative movement interfaces that
nake an expressive exploration of music
either the audio signal or the score) ...
ossible." MO musical objects are a
eries of interface modules that respond
o various physical gestures as aural
ues, creating a platform for "gestural
nteraction with musical content."
he central module (shaped like a bow
ie) contains motion sensors and transmits the data wirelessly; other parts
an be linked to everyday objects or
nusical instruments. Users can configure
an orchestra out of any objects they like.
he Interlude Consortium, coordinated
by Institut de Recherche et Coordination
coustique/Musique (IRCAM) with
support from the French National
Research Agency (ANR) and Cap Digital,
ncludes Grame and DA FACT (both
centers for digital-music research and
creation), Voxler (a company that focuses
on vocal-interaction software), and
Atelier des Feuillantines, Paris (an art
school).

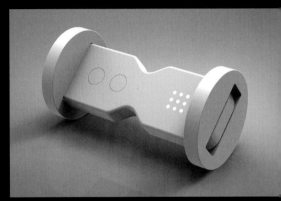

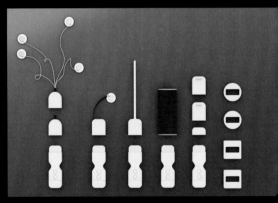

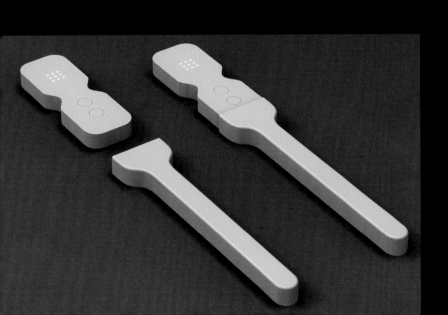

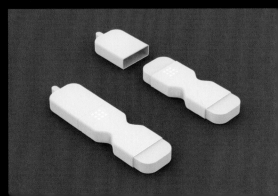

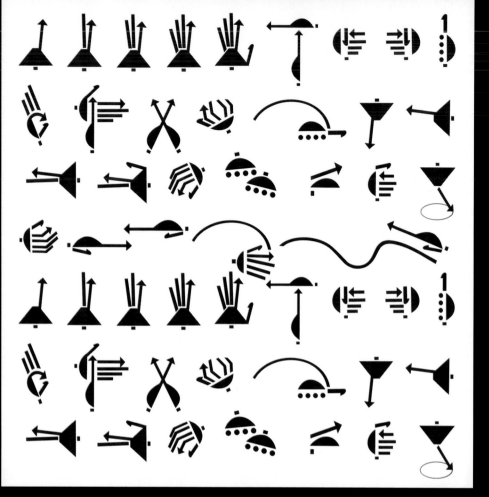

Susan Woolf (South African, born 1949)
Faculty of Humanities (est. 2001)
University of the Witwatersrand
(South Africa, est. 1922)

////////////////////////////

Taxi Hand Sign Shape Lingo for Blind
People. 2010

////////////////////////////

Inkjet print on etching paper, 17 1/2
× 17 1/2" (44.5 × 44.5 cm)

In South Africa, particularly its cities and
townships, commuters use an extensive
system of hand signals to quickly indicate
to taxi drivers where they would like
to be taken. Anthropologist and artist
Susan Woolf documented these signs in
a series of gouache paintings, published
in the guide Taxi Hand Signs (2007), and
then translated them into symbols for
the blind, who tend to rely on taxis for
transportation: basic shapes—triangle,
circle, ellipse, and line—are used in
combination to form each hand sign.
The shapes, currently compiled in a
separate handbook, are slightly raised
on the paper, so they can be perceived
by touch, and are accompanied by Braille
labels. Woolf's guide has been distributed
to blind people throughout South Africa
and is being taught in four schools for
the blind.

Konstantin Datz (German, born 1988)

//////////////////////////////

Rubik's Cube for the Blind. 2010

//////////////////////////////

Rubik's Cube and adhesive plastic pads,
2 3/8 × 2 3/8 × 2 3/8" (6 × 6 × 6 cm)

Konstantin Datz has reimagined the
popular Rubik's Cube for people who
cannot see the toy's original colors. Datz
stuck white panels embossed with the
Braille words for each color over the
squares, transforming the game from
a visual puzzle into a tactile one.

Danielle Pecora (American, born 1979)
Industrial Design Department (est. 1934)
Pratt Institute (USA, est. 1887)

/////////////////////////////

be-B Braille Education Ball. 2010

/////////////////////////////

Gypsum, resin, magnets, chipboard, and
paint, 5–6 1/2" (12.7–16.5 cm) diam.

Designed for both blind and sighted users,
the be-B Braille Education Ball is a game
that teaches the Braille alphabet through
touch and sound. The sphere has
twenty-six holes that fit twenty-six
magnetic pegs representing the complete
alphabet; on one side of each peg is
a Braille letter, and on the other side is
the corresponding letter from the Roman
alphabet. The object of the game is to
match the Braille letter on each peg with
the letter reproduced in each hole; when
the correct peg is inserted, a bell, rings
and the device speaks the name of the
letter. The letters are also spoken when
the indented areas are touched.

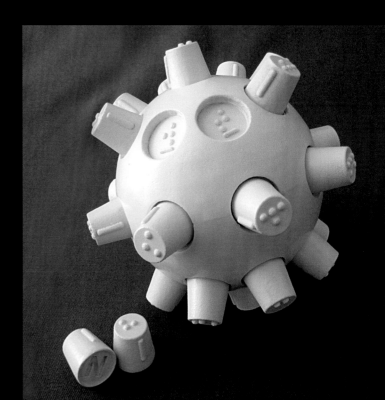

Johan Liden (Swedish, born 1974)
and Olivier Grégoire (French, born 1983)
of aruliden (USA, est. 2006)

/////////////////////////////

Check Mate. 2009

/////////////////////////////

Aluminum, MDF, and walnut veneer,
board: 19 11/16 × 19 11/16 × 2" (50 × 50
× 5 cm)

The design firm aruliden, finding chess
a "very sexy mind game," took the notion
one step further with Check Mate.
Designed for the high-end lingerie and
intimate toy brand Kiki de Montparnasse,
Check Mate is a chess set with thirty-
two pieces that double as dildos,
elegantly renamed "dilettos." The game
pieces retain elements of their traditional
shapes but also resemble sex toys—
the pawns phallic, the knights shaped like
anal beads. A new dimension of play is
thus introduced in a classic game.

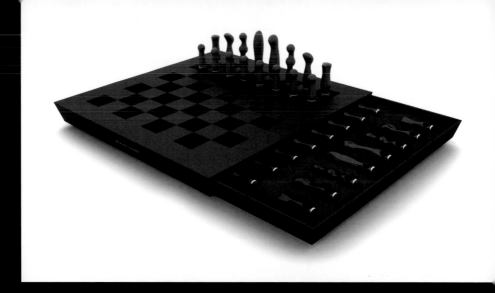

Katrin Baumgarten (German, born 1985)
Innovation Design Engineering
Department (est. 1980)
Royal College of Art (UK, est. 1837) and
Imperial College London (UK, est. 1907)

//////////////////////////////

The Disgusted Object. 2010

//////////////////////////////

Wood, silicone, and electronics,
3/16 × 4 11/16 × 2 3/8" (3 × 12 × 6 cm)

The Disgusted Object series explores
the phenomenon of revulsion. Katrin
Baumgarten's prototypes are abstract
but simulate human reactions: one
replicates the pilomotor reflex, slowly
developing goose bumps when handled;
another squirms when held, as if trying
to escape or move away. Baumgarten
explores interactions with objects that
are not fully under the user's control—
that have what she calls "anthropomor-
phised will" and reactions we only
expect from sentient beings.

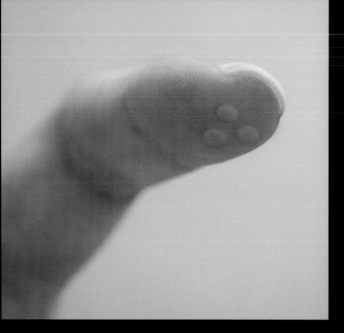

Design Incubation Centre (est. 2006)
National University of Singapore
(Singapore, est. 1980)

/////////////////////////////

Touch Hear. 2008

/////////////////////////////

Finger implant: optical character-
recognition system and network
transmitter, 3/8 × 3/8 × 1/8"
(1 × 1 × 0.2 cm); ear attachment:
text-to-speech system and network
receiver, 3/16 × 5/16 × 1/8"
(0.5 × 0.8 × 0.2 cm)

Looking up unfamiliar words while
reading is disruptive, creating a break,
however momentary, in narrative flow.
The Touch Hear text-recognition
dictionary (unfortunately still a concept)
renders the task built-in and seamless,
requiring only the scanning of a finger
implant over a word or phrase to
bring up related information, such as
meaning and pronunciation, into a small
device attached near the ear. Touch
Hear explores a way for technology to
enhance human capacity in an everyday
activity.

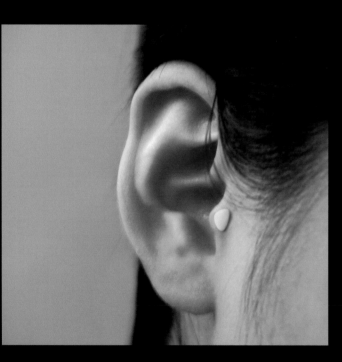

Sebastian Bettencourt (Portuguese, born 1978)
Graduate Media Design Program (est. 2000)
Art Center College of Design, Pasadena (USA, est. 1930)

////////////////////////////

Beyond the Fold. 2007

////////////////////////////

Digital video (color, sound), 3:25 min.

Beyond the Fold imagines the newspaper of the future, as have many speculative projects of the past two decades. But Sebastian Bettencourt's design abandons the now-familiar elements of digital interfaces, such as buttons and icons, to focus on the newspaper's spatial properties, presence, and relationship to a reader's motions, looking beyond the transfer of information to evoke the reading experience. Familiar motions steer the interaction: unfolding the device activates it, turning pages navigates through it, and shaking refreshes content. Cutting-edge technology is maximized while the timeless ritual of reading the newspaper is honored. The concept, presented as Bettencourt's graduate thesis, was illustrated with a video edited by Joel Nathanael Smith.

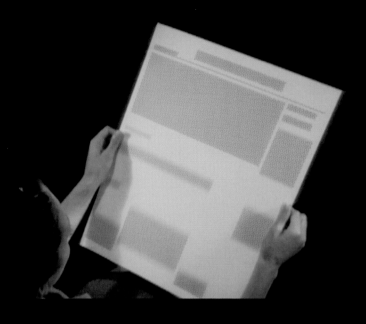

Chie Mitsuyama (Japanese, born 1977)
of Ginghami Co. (Japan, est. 2008)

////////////////////////////////////

Kaoiro. 2009

////////////////////////////////////

Rubber, wood, and steel, 1 5/16 × 1 1/8
× 3 7/8" (3.4 × 2.7 × 10 cm)
Manufactured by Kikuchi Mfg Co.,
Ltd., Japan

Emoticons have become both staples
and clichés of digital communication.
Kaoiro (meaning "facial expression" in
Japanese) is a low-tech emoticon device
in the form of an old-fashioned date
stamp. Seven belts with twenty punctuation symbols each can be used in combination to create more than two thousand
analog emoticons to stamp on letters,
notes, and books. Kaoiro introduces a
uniquely digital mode of expression into
the realm of ink and paper and, made by
hand at a small artisanal stamp factory
in Japan, also unites the disparate worlds
of lightning-quick communication and
time-tested craft.

Matt Kenyon (American, born 1977)
and Douglas Easterly (American,
born 1968)
of SWAMP (USA, est. 1999)

//////////////////////////////

Notepad. 2007

//////////////////////////////

Ink on paper, 8 1/2 × 11 × 3/4" (21.6
× 27.9 × 1.9 cm)

The Notepad is an act of protest and
commemoration disguised as a stack
of ordinary yellow legal pads. Each ruled
line, when magnified, is revealed to be
microprinted text enumerating the full
names, dates, and locations of each
Iraqi civilian death on record over the
first three years of the Iraq War. The
designers imagine each printed edition
of one hundred notepads, meant to be
covertly distributed to US representa-
tives and senators, as a sort of Trojan
horse, injecting transgressive data
straight into the halls of power and
memorializing it in official archives.
SWAMP is now working on a new edition
that takes into account the American
incursion into Afghanistan; with the
disclosure of confidential information

Dan Collier (British, born 1986)

////////////////////////////////

Typographic Links. 2007

////////////////////////////////

Paper and thread, 7 1/2 × 7 1/2 × 5/16"
(19 × 19 × 0.8 cm)

Typographic Links reimagines hyperlinks
as physical, three-dimensional ties in
the pages of a book about typography.
In Dan Collier's hand-sewn publication,
red threads travel through paper to map
interesting connections between typog-
raphers, typefaces, and typographic
terms and phrases. The result is a playful
system of physical tagging, with the
relationships between words tangibly
felt and indicated as the reader flips
through the book.

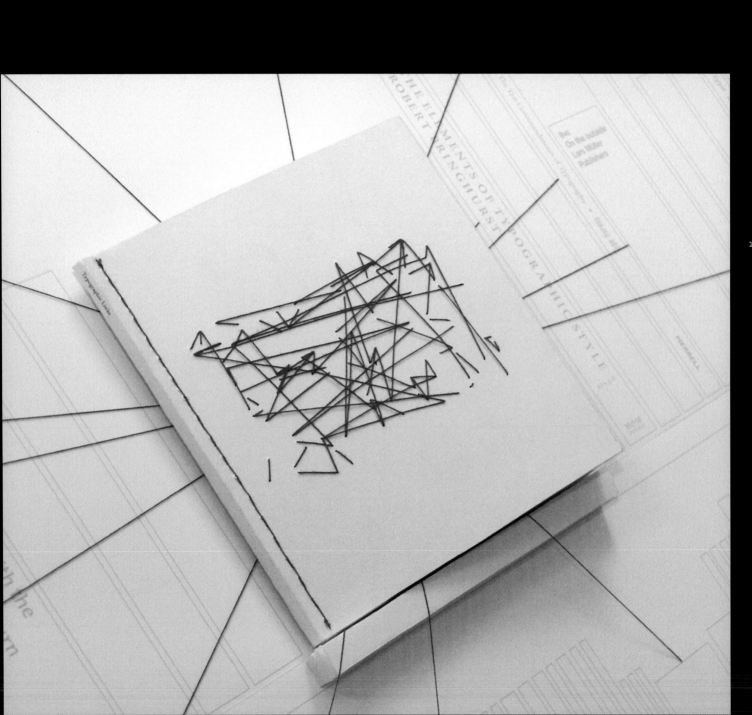

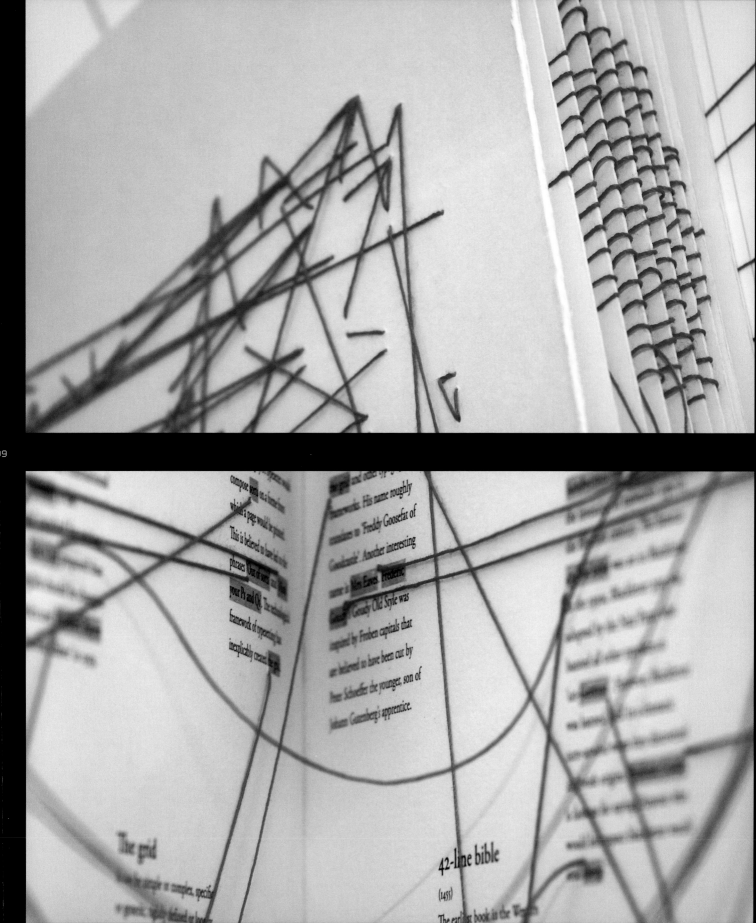

# Index

# Acknowledgments

In planning Talk to Me: Design and the Communication between People and Objects, I relied on a wide network of extraordinarily lively, generous, and talkative people. A diverse team of colleagues, volunteers, friends, and accidental consultants contributed immeasurably to the realization of this exhibition and book, and I will be forever indebted to them.

Personally and on behalf of The Museum of Modern Art, I wish to thank all the designers, engineers, artists, producers, and manufacturers featured here for their cooperation and enthusiasm. I also wish to thank our sponsors, Hyundai Card Company, the Lily Auchincloss Foundation, and The Junior Associates of The Museum of Modern Art, for making this endeavor possible, as well as the lenders, for agreeing to part temporarily with their possessions.

We in the field of design are in the concept business, and concepts need endless discussion and reconsideration. Together with my co-organizer, Kate Carmody, Curatorial Assistant, Department of Architecture and Design, I would like to thank our partners and our closest friends, who so often became sounding boards for our lucubrations and doubts: first and foremost, Larry Carty and Kyle Barron-Cohen, and then Lisa Gabor and Jane Nisselson. Thank you.

Thanks also to the designers, critics, writers, and friends who offered their support, ideas, and recommendations. Throughout the process we have tried to acknowledge everyone who sent us suggestions and ideas; they are all lovingly listed in our online journal at wp.moma.org/talk_to_me/thank-you. A few have also lent us a considerable amount of their valuable time, connections, and expertise, and they deserve a special mention: Rachel Abrams, Sandra Bloodworth, Jennifer Bove, Jeremy Boxer, Jamin Brophy-Warren, Akiko Busch, Allan Chochinov, Liz Danzico, Anthony Dunne and Fiona Raby, Erik Ellner, Avy Eschenasy, Ben Fullerton, Sudhir Horo, Josh Klein, Mike Kuniavsky, Peter Merholz, Kohei Nishiyama, Alice Rawsthorn, Galia Solomonoff, Barbara Tversky, Maholo Uchida, Rob Walker, Robert Wong, and Susan Yelavich.

In MoMA's Department of Publications I wish to thank Christopher Hudson, Publisher; Kara Kirk, Associate Publisher; David Frankel, Editorial Director; Marc Sapir, Production Director; Rebecca Roberts, Senior Assistant Editor; Tiffany Hu, Production Manager; and Bairbre O'Brien and Emily Schlemowitz, Interns, for their efforts in bringing the book to light. Singled out for special effort and glowing recognition is Emily Hall, Editor, the real force behind this volume. For the book's design, so uniquely attuned to the show, we are grateful to Henrik Kubel and Scott Williams of A2/SW/HK.

The Museum's Board of Trustees deserves special acknowledgment, and in particular, I wish to thank Ronald S. Lauder, Honorary Chairman, and Agnes Gund, President Emerita, both knowledgeable and enthusiastic fans of design, as well as David Rockefeller, Honorary Chairman; Robert B. Menschel, Chairman Emeritus; Donald B. Marron, President Emeritus; Jerry I. Speyer, Chairman; and Marie-Josée Kravis, President, for their passionate support of the Museum's curators. Glenn D. Lowry, Director, provided early and unwavering support that was crucial to the realization of the exhibition. Ramona Bannayan, Deputy Director, Exhibitions and Collections; Peter Reed, Senior Deputy Director, Curatorial Affairs; Nancy Adelson, Deputy General Counsel; and Henry Lanman, Associate General Counsel, were integral in successfully bringing this huge ship to port.

I wish to thank Maria DeMarco Beardsley, Coordinator of Exhibitions, and Carlos Yepes, Associate Coordinator of Exhibitions, for working out the complicated administrative details, and Stefanii Ruta-Atkins, Head Registrar; Susan Palamara, Registrar; Corey Wyckoff, Assistant Registrar; and Steven Wheeler, Assistant Registrar, for keeping track of the diverse loan items, and, in Collection and Exhibition Technologies, Jeri Moxley, Manager; Kathryn Ryan, Coordinator; and Ian Eckert, Assistant, for helping us keep all our information in order. I would also like to thank Rob Jung, Manager of Art Handling and Preparation; Sarah Wood, Assistant Manager of Art Handling and Preparation; and Steve Burkart, Lead Preparator, as well as Peter Perez and his team in the Frame Shop. My deepest gratitude furthermore goes to Roger Griffith, Associate Sculpture Conservator, for caring for all the blinking, moving, crying, and sneezing objects, as well as to Lynda Zycherman, Sculpture Conservator; Karl Buchberg, Senior Conservator; and Erika Mosier, Conservator.

The installation was a challenge even for our heroic Department of Exhibition Design and Production. With careful and sensitive guidance by Jerry Neuner, Director, Betty Fisher, Production Manager, designed the installation; their incomparable crew built it, as usual, to perfection. My gratitude goes to them and to those who took care of the virtual part of the installation: Steven Peltzman, Chief Information Officer and K Mita, Director, Audio/Visual Services, as well as to the whole fantastic IT crowd: Howard Deitch, Ben Fishner, James Heck, Charlie Kalinowski, Bill Moore, Matias Pacheco, Bjorn Quenemoen, and, especially, Mike Gibbons, who together with Lucas Gonzalez performed miracles in order to ensure that the technology worked smoothly and effectively.

The exhibition lives on the web thanks to the magic touch of the Department of Digital Media: Allegra Burnette, Creative Director; Shannon Darrough, Media Developer; David Hart, Associate Media Producer; Spencer Kiser, Media Technology Developer; Dan Phiffer, Media Technology Developer; and John Halderman, Application Developer, for his expertise in QR tagging. We would also like to thank the wizards at Stamen Design for their dynamic, elegant, and thoughtful exhibition website.

In the Department of Development and Membership I thank Todd Bishop, Director, and Lauren Stakias, Assistant Director, who secured funding for the show, not a negligible feat. I thank Kim Mitchell, Chief Communications Officer, and Daniela Stigh, Assistant Director of Communications, for brilliantly condensing the whole show to get the press irresistibly interested, and Julia Hoffman, Creative Director of Advertising and Graphic Design, for promoting it. I also wish to thank Samuel Sherman, Senior Graphic Designer; August Heffner, Design Manager; and Claire Corey, Production Manager, for their untiring devotion to this project.

I thank the whole Department of Education for their suggestions on how to communicate the show to the public, in particular Wendy Woon, Deputy Director for Education; Pablo Helguera, Director, Adult and Academic Education; Laura Beiles, Assistant Director, Adult Programs; Sara Bodinson, Director of Interpretation and Research; Sheetal Prajapati, Temporary Assistant Director, Adult and Academic Programs; Beth Harris, Director, Digital Learning and Associate Educator; Stephanie Pau, Associate Educator; Kirsten Schroeder, Coordinator, Community and Access Programs; and Lisa Mazzola, Assistant Director, School and Teacher Programs, and I also thank Jennifer Tobias, Librarian, and David Senior, Bibliographer, for their enthusiastic assistance with our research.

In the Department of Architecture and Design I am deeply grateful to Barry Bergdoll, The Philip Johnson Chief Curator of Architecture and Design, who believed in the exhibition and offered his support throughout the project. The entire department was helpful and encouraging and I thank each of its members. A special mention to Emma Presler, Department Manager, and Shayna Gentiluomo, Administrative Assistant, for their generous help. Several brilliant interns worked on this project; I wish to thank Caroline James, Alma Zevi, and Laurene Gitton. Without them this catalogue and exhibition would not have been possible. Special thanks go to Helga Schmid, who tirelessly scoured the web for apps and video games; to Azzurra Cox, who participated actively in the writing and production of the catalogue and the website; and to Hideki Yamamoto, who helped us secure many loans in Asia and contributed ideas, texts, and invaluable criticism.

Lastly, I would like to thank the person with whom I shared this adventure, Kate Carmody. It is only our second curatorial undertaking, but it feels like we are well-worn, comfortable partners and she is invaluable. I am very lucky to be working with her.

Paola Antonelli
Senior Curator, Department of Architecture and Design

# Photograph Credits

Tarn Adams: 149 (bottom).
Ah&Oh Studio: 34 (bottom).
David Allison/Whitney Museum of American Art: 49.
Courtesy of Antenna Design: 46.
Area/Code: 118, 119 (top), 136.
Timo Arnall: 21.
aruliden: 192.
Ross Atkin: 47 (bottom).
James Auger: 84.
© BANDAI: 178.
Jacek Barcikowski: 81 (bottom).
Antoine Bardou-Jacquet and Ludovic Houplain of H5: 12 (bottom).
Toby Barnes/Mudlark: 120-21.
John Batspad: 188.
Katrin Baumgarten: 193.
© Benrik: 12 (top).
BERG: 127, 139.
Sebastian Bettencourt: 195.
© Bettmann/CORBIS: 165 (bottom).
© Boeing: 166 (center, bottom).
Brandon Boyer: 75, 76.
Richard Brain: 135 (top).
Bug Labs: 39 (bottom).
Kimberly Butler/TIME & LIFE Images by Getty Images: 170.
Ray Carson, University of Florida: 63 (top left).
James Chambers: 25 (top), 26.
Henry Chu: 186 (top right, bottom).
Revital Cohen: 27 (top), 54, 72 (top).
Dan Collier: 198-99.
Brian Crabtree and Kelli Cain: 185.
Pedro Miguel Cruz: 122.
Thomas Xaver Dachs: 159.
Ricardo sà da Costa: 162.
Konstantin Datz: 191 (top).
Brendan Dawes: 144.
Sylvain Deleu: 94 (top).
Benjamin Dennel: 79.
Dentsu London: 7.
Electronic Arts, Inc. © 1994: 148 (top); © 1999: 148 (bottom); © 2008: 152.
Electronic Ink: 103.
Grégoire Eloy: 140 (top, bottom).
EyeWriter Team: 57-59.
Nicholas Felton: 77.
© Malcolm Finnie: 29 (top, bottom right).
Eric Fischer, base map data © OpenStreetMap, CC-BY-SA: 126.
Futurefarmers: 110 (top); Josh On, Amy Balkin, Amy Franceschini: 143.
General Electric: 42.
Alexandra Daisy Ginsberg and James King: 61 (center, bottom).
Cody Goddard: 197.
Golfstromen and Coen Rens: 112.
Gunnar Green: 68.
Wesley Grubbs and Mladen Balog of Pitch Interactive with Wired magazine: 14.
© Steven Guarnaccia 2000. All rights reserved to Maurizio Corraini srl: 93 (top).
Dorit Guenter, www.doritguenter.com: 13.
Johan Halin: 184 (top left and right).
Gary Hamill: 73.
Katsutoshi Hanada/Katachi Co., Ltd.: 32.
Usman Haque: 41 (bottom).
Simon Heijdens: 27 (center, bottom).
Hans Hemmert, courtesy Kavi Gupta Gallery, Chicago: 70.
Tahir Hemphill: 187.
Mark Hendersen: 146 (center, bottom), 147.
Alfonso Herranz: 69 (top).
Chin-Chang Ho and Karl F. MacDorman: 168 (bottom).
Richard Hogg: 45.
Tim Holley: 43.

Robert Hösl: 117.
Hudson-Powell: 156 (top).
Jody Hudson-Powell: 156 (bottom left).
Véronique Huyghe: 62.
© IDEO: 44 (top).
Interaction Research Studio, Goldsmiths University of London, UK: 87.
© Mitsuo Iso/Tokuma Shoten, CyberCoil Production Committee. Animation production: Madhouse (Tokyo), Producers: Sanae Mitsugi (Tokuma Shoten), Shigeru Watanabe (Bandai Visual), Hisako Matsumoto (NHK Enterprise): 169.
Agathe Jacquillat, Tomi Vollauschek, FL@33: 179.
Ösa Johannesson: 61 (top).
© Stuart Johnstone: 28 (top), 29 (bottom left).
Crispin Jones: 30 (top).
Jae Kim: 88 (top).
Rob King, Michael Longford, Geoffrey Shea: 71.
Kacie Kinzer: 23.
© Paul Kirps: 24.
Tomo Kitano: 196.
Ron Klinken: 41 (top right).
Andrew Kuo: 80.
Dmitri Kurteanu: 149 (top).
© Chris Labrooy: 28 (bottom).
Yann Le Coroller: 31.
Golan Levin: 36.
Armin Linke, Kolsterfelde, Berlin: 108.
Andy and Carolyn London: 99-100.
Make Magazine: 41 (top left).
David McCandless: 78, 137.
Greg McInerny and Stefanie Posavec: 90.
Media Molecule/Sony Computer Entertainment: 151.
Christien Meindertsma: 82-83.
Alex Metcalf: 135 (bottom).
Courtesy MGM Media Licensing: 167 (bottom).
Mobilistar: 158 (center).
Modular Robotics: 38 (bottom).
Joon Y. Moon: 160.
Trey Moore and Kory Brown: 60.
Bernd Müller, © Fraunhofer EMFT: 63 (bottom).
The Museum of Modern Art, New York: 94 (bottom); John Wronn: 184 (bottom).
Nicolas Myers: 37.
Nadra Bank: 10.
© National University of Singapore: 194.
J. Paul Neely: 25 (bottom left and right).
Mayo Nissen: 81 (top), 102.
Michiko Nitta: 34 (top), 85 (top).
NoDesign-Simon Bouisson © Interlude: 189.
Sascha Nordmeyer: 64.
Louise O'Connor: 146 (top).
Yuki Omori: 115.
Josh On: 142.
Chris O'Shea: 157.
Paul Ott: 116 (bottom).
Rhiân Owens: 154.
Soner Ozenc: 89.
Courtesy Palm, Inc.: 50.
Park: 153.
Danielle Pecora: 191 (bottom).
Dennis Pedersen: 33 (bottom).
© Automobiles Peugeot: 172 (bottom).
Sascha Pohflepp: 155.
Poke: 101 (top, bottom left).
PostSecret: 86.
Gerard Ralló: 66-67.
Emily Read: 111.
Rethink: 104.
Damaris Rodriguez: 22, 40 (bottom).
Jason Rohrer: 76, 150.

Colin Ross: 183.
Evan Roth: 114.
Rai Royal: 177 (top), 182.
© Camille Scherrer 2007 ECAL: 161 (bottom and bottom center); © 2008 Camille Scherrer ECAL diploma-support: EPFL+ECAL lab: 161 (top and top center).
Harry Schiffer: 116 (top).
SENSEable City Laboratory: 109.
Mark Serr: 38 (top left and right).
Akem Singh: 35.
Kevin Slavin: 91.
Southwark Circle CIC: 110 (center, bottom).
© Sprint 2001: 51.
Stephen Spyropoulos: 180-81.
Square, Inc.: 44 (bottom).
Stamen Design, base map data © OpenStreetMap, CC-BY-SA: 123-25.
Sun Haipeng: 8 (top, bottom).
Superflux: 163.
Swype, Inc.: 47 (top).
Tellart: 158 (bottom).
Mike Thompson: 19-20.
Per Tingleff: 53, 93 (bottom).
Sissel Tolaas: 106-7.
Courtesy the Topps Company, Inc.: 168 (top).
Noam Toran: 96 (bottom).
Trinity Mirror Archive: 85 (center, bottom).
© Troika, 2007: 30 (bottom).
Diego Trujillo (lighting): 15.
Ted Ullrich: 39 (top, center left and right).
Ushahidi: 138 (top left and right).
2004 UT-Austin/UCSF iGEM team: 6.
Kevin Van Aelst: 88 (bottom).
Tuur Van Balen: 72 (bottom).
Sander Veenhof: 158 (top).
© 2007 Philip Vile/Applied Information Group: 105.
Vitality: 63 (top right).
Vitamins: 33 (top).
VR/Urban: 113.
Bradley Walker: 119 (bottom).
Charlie Wan: 69 (bottom left and right).
Che-Wei Wang: 171.
Max Weisel: 186 (top left, center).
Marcos Weskamp: 145.
@WhiteAfrican (Erik Hersman): 138 (center).
John Wilson, Lockheed Martin: 172 (top).
Chris Woebken: 133-34, 175-76.
Susan Woolf: 190.
Hitomi Yoda: 177 (bottom).
Ludwig Zeller: 65.
Andrew Zolty: 101 (bottom right).

# Trustees of The Museum of Modern Art